A Voice from the Chorus

RELATED TITLES

1920 Diary
Isaac Babel

The Lower Depths and Other Plays
Maxim Gorky

Untimely Thoughts
Maxim Gorky

Stalin's Letters to Molotov
Josef Stalin

A History of Russian Literature
Victor Terras

Strolls with Pushkin
Abram Tertz (Andrei Sinyavsky)

A Voice from the Chorus

Abram Tertz
(Andrei Sinyavsky)

With a new preface by the author

Translated from the Russian by
Kyril Fitzlyon and
Max Hayward

With an introduction by
Max Hayward

Yale University Press
New Haven and London

To my wife, Maria,
I dedicate this book based
almost entirely on my letters to her
during my years of imprisonment
1966–1971

First edition, 1976
Portions of this book first appeared in *American Review*
A Russian-language edition is available from Octagon Books, New York

Paperbound edition published 1995 by Yale University Press

Printed in the United States of America by
Book Crafters, Inc., Chelsea, Michigan.
Library of Congress Card Catalogue Number: 94–61487
International standard book number: 0–300–06119–6 (pbk.)

A catalogue record for this book is available from the British Library.

The paper in this book meets the guidelines for permanence and durability of the Committee on Production Guidelines for Book Longevity of the Council on Library Resources.

10 9 8 7 6 5 4 3 2 1

On the History of This Book

I neither wrote nor conceived of *A Voice from the Chorus* as a book with a clearly defined plot, heroes, or level of language. The book took shape of itself, almost without my knowledge, out of the short passages I wrote while in the labor camp. When I returned from camp, overflowing with the experience of it, I extracted, selected, and arranged those entries, which I had sent in letters to my wife over the course of six years (knowing this was the only means of giving them form). Naturally, these passages were not arranged in the same sequence as they appear here, nor were they in "edited form", but were submerged in the epistolary context, at times camouflaged, like disassembled "spare parts"—observations and allegories—which I later assembled from memory.

Writing in a labor camp is a complicated and artful science. Yet in rearranging the "blocks" to put together *A Voice from the Chorus,* I changed neither their substance nor their style. The book contains the documentary story of how I lived and thought, impelled solely by the instinct for artistic self-preservation. Of course, I did not know at the time that these passages would be published. What was important to me was to remain, despite everything, in my own eyes and in the eyes of Maria, my first and sole reader, the writer Abram Tertz. And only thus—to survive.

That's probably why the theme of art and literature occupies so much of *A Voice from the Chorus*. It may seem improbable that rather than describe the reality of the hard labor camp that surrounded me, I concerned myself with art. "What are there in your camps—museums and libraries?" I have sometimes been asked regarding *A Voice from the Chorus*. "You picked a fine time and place to discuss things that are so far removed and irrelevant to the camps! Nevertheless, in my prison experience, art and literature were matters of life and death.

When someone lands in prison—especially in its Total, most annihilating form—he or she experiences something like dying dragged out for years. Prison puts an end to the captive's entire preceding life and future (not necessarily in the form of physical death—although it is also sometimes difficult to survive physically). It is the death of human dignity, purpose, vocation—of your higher calling in life. For me, writing was that calling, and it was also the crime for which I was indicted, the "especially dangerous" crime of which I was convicted. Accordingly, my name was blackened, my access to literature was cut off, and brief instructions from Moscow were written on my camp "dossier": "use only for hard physical labor". My every word, every step was watched, searches were periodically conducted, all of my records were taken away and carefully examined, so that I would never again write anything criminal. In the eyes of the state I was not a writer but an enemy, worse than a bandit or a murderer. It was time to write my "last will and testament", time to sum up what I had done on earth up to that point and what was most important to me, what I loved more than anything else. . . . Thus, *A Voice from the Chorus* came into being, and the theme of art, indispensable to me as a means of salvation, as my final prattle. . . .

The other aspect of my life at that time was the camp per se. After all, I was one of many Soviet prisoners, and my writer's voice, for all its individual coloring, was nothing more than one of the millions of voices of the enormous, newly discovered camp world. Close and intimate acquaintance with that world aroused in me, particularly in the early years, a sensation of profound, bitter happiness. It was the most difficult time of my life, both physically and psychologically (the end, the loss of books, of my wife, of my son, who was eight months old when I was arrested), and at the same time, it was aesthetically the happiest. I was honored to be a zek (prisoner)—something which, contrary to common sense, I had dreamed of for a long time. I met there my "reality", my "medium", my "nature"—what every artist dreams of. After all, I am an author with a bent for the fantastic, for fairy tales, for all sorts of "strangenesses" in nature. It's simply not interesting to me to describe how people usually live. If I were asked to be a realist writer, I would give up writing for good. But there, in the camps, to my amazement, reality itself turned out to be fantastic—confirming my conjectures about it. I landed in a fairy tale. A horrible fairy tale, of course, but a beneficial one for a writer. There I found myself, my style, my manner in the surrounding world. Simply to see this "adequate" reality afforded me the greatest artistic enjoyment, verging on despair that I could not (and never would be able to) transfer this "miracle" onto paper. But I began, a little at a time, in fits and starts, in little pieces, concealing myself, to transfer it all the same. That is how *A Voice from the Chorus* came into being.

In the camps, people's fates and psychologies are revealed in a more concentrated form—as more good or more evil. Also, political prisoners were often unusual; some were remarkable—intellectually, morally, and biographically. The majority of people convicted of political offenses, like myself, had never been engaged in politics. Nonetheless, they were all interesting characters who represented a deviation from the boring norm and who embodied the quintessence of life in the camp and of life at large. A "political" could be a poet-graphomaniac (or, perhaps, a genius); a peasant truth seeker who had written a letter to the Kremlin with good advice about how to save ourselves from a new world war; a thief who, out of despair, had posted a leaflet reading "Down with the CPSU"; a passing bandit who had accidentally and heedlessly, while being captured, shot a kolkhoz brigade foreman; or a religious preacher stubborn in his faith. They were all people of exceptional fates, of extraordinary acts, of great historical and personal experience. . . .

The history of my native land opened up to me in the camps: the war, people's attempts to flee abroad and travel to different countries, Stalin's camps, the partisan struggle in the Ukraine and in the Baltic states, the underground religious life of churches and religious sects, some of which could be traced back to pre-Petrine times. I was particularly drawn to the two extremes of the Russian national nature—thieves and saints from the many persecuted churches. You would never meet such people outside in freedom, and if you were to meet them, they would not tell you of their fates and their souls. . . .

I was lucky in my contacts with other prisoners. I was the "writer" among them (Russians generally respect writers as literate people of superior intellect), imprisoned for writing books that displeased the powers that be (which, of course, no one had read, but if I had been arrested for those books, then it was assumed they must be good and truthful); I was called names in Soviet newspapers (that meant I was a worthy and honest man). Moreover, Yuly Daniel and I had not pleaded guilty: that meant we were almost "heroes". As a result, zeks of different stripes and characters confided in me and brought me words of consolation, precepts, stories, and reminiscences so necessary to a tormented man who had lost all hope for life and justice.

The very geography of Russia stretched out before me in greater breadth in the camps than I could have imagined it in freedom, although I had traveled through the country a great deal. There I didn't have to travel. The whole Soviet Union surrounded me in a miniature, condensed form. Isn't that rare luck for a writer? I finally met my people—in such scope and at such close quarters as had never happened to me and could never have happened in normal conditions. It was this people I wanted to reproduce in the chorus of voices in *A Voice from the Chorus*: let them speak for themselves, objectively, and I wouldn't interfere.

As a rule, I did not include the voices of intellectuals (or dissidents), although there were more than enough of them in the camps. It is enough that I, with my "lyrical part", am too much of an intellectual. By the same token I did not devote much attention to everyday life in the camps: the working conditions, food, and so on. There is an enormous documentary literature about that. "Camp books", like books of any other genre, should not repeat one another. The camp is just as big as our entire world, even bigger—because it's more capacious. A writer has the right to take from the surrounding world what interests and concerns him. I took my aspect: the sounds of the camp. And camp life was interesting to me either as it diverged from the norm or as it renewed the ontological value of such simple things as bread, water, air. . . . In prison, living conditions (once taken for granted) have their value, their essence, restored. My intensified interest in metaphysics, in the myths of different times and peoples, probably came from that.

This is also linked with the unheard-of spiritual and artistic resources of the common people that opened up before me there. These resources manifested themselves on the most diverse and at times "commonplace" levels. I discovered them in their everyday language, for instance, or in the intricate design of their fates and personalities. I became convinced in the camps of how talented the common people are, regardless of their individual talents. I brought away from the camp a sense of great and completely undeserved riches that had rained down on me there. In that sense, my writer's voice (from the chorus) is only a detail, a thread, *by* and *on* which the creative work of the artist-people hangs.

So we met: the writer and the people. And in a broader context, all existence granted to us by God presented itself to me in the camps as a work of art, grains of which we can only try to glean in our books.

TRANSLATED BY CATHARINE THEIMER NEPOMNYASHCHY

Introduction

For spring, my child, you'll wait —
You'll find it lies.
You'll call out for the sun to rise —
It will not rise.
When you begin to cry, your cries
will sink like lead . . . .

Then be content with life today,
Stiller than water, lower than grass.
Oh children, if you only knew
The cold and gloom of days ahead!

(From Alexander Blok's "A Voice from the Chorus", February 1914)

Few writers, in this or any other age, can have had such a bizarre literary career as Andrey Sinyavsky, otherwise known as Abram Tertz, the author of the present book. A decade has now gone by since the trial in Moscow at which he and his fellow-defendant, Yuli Daniel (Nikolai Arzhak), attracted world-wide attention; it may, therefore, be helpful to give here some account of the events, and of the background to them.

Until his arrest in the autumn of 1965, Andrey Donatovich Sinyavsky was known only as a teacher and writer who, though still young, had already established a modest reputation in Moscow literary and academic circles. As a member of the Gorky Institute of World Literature (a dependency of the Academy of Sciences of the Soviet Union) he had published a number of scholarly essays and studies on modern Russian writers and poets – contributing, for instance, signed chapters on Maxim Gorky and Edward Bagritsky to a three-volume history of Soviet Russian Literature published by the Academy in 1958. The range and depth of his learning was demonstrated in *The Poetry of the Revolutionary Era* (1964; written together with A. Menshutin), the first work in the field after Stalin's death to revive many forgotten or suppressed names of the early years of the new epoch. Even more significant was Sinyavsky's lengthy introduction to a selection of Pasternak's poetry that came out in 1965 – it was passed by the censors for publication only three months or so before Sinyavsky and Daniel were arrested. Nothing better has ever been written on the nature and sense of Pasternak's work: it is illuminating in the precise meaning of the word. The achievement was all the more impressive in that Sinyavsky was unable even to mention, let alone discuss, many of the poems included in *Doctor Zhivago*, particularly the religious ones, which – together with the novel itself – are still under a ban in the Soviet Union. Although the mere fact of the publication of this new and somewhat fuller selection marked a further stage in the gingerly process of "rehabilitation" that had been going on since his death in 1960, Pasternak's unprecedented act of defiance in having deliberately published *Doctor Zhivago* abroad, and the consequent award of the Nobel prize to him in 1957, had still not been forgotten or forgiven by the Soviet authorities, least of all by the rancorous, backward-looking literary "establishment" associated with them. Sinyavsky had already given public proof of his allegiance to Pasternak at a time when it was decidedly even less healthy to do so. At Pasternak's funeral in May 1960, which was attended – despite the best efforts of the authorities to head them off – by many members of Moscow's liberal intelligentsia, he and Yuli Daniel had played a conspicuous part as pallbearers – there is a photograph which shows them leaving Pasternak's house with the coffin. The policemen later involved in the investigation of their "crime" must have been struck at how the pair thus boldly associated themselves, at his death, with the great poet who had shown them the way. In the light of the revelations to come, it was indeed a breathtaking gesture . . .

Side by side with his scholarly publications Sinyavsky wrote articles and reviews for a much wider audience in *Novy Mir*, the monthly literary journal which, under the editorship of Alexander Tvardovsky, became the chief forum and rallying point for the liberal intelligentsia during the Khrushchev years. Sinyavsky made his first appearance in this journal in 1962 with a strongly critical review of an unrepresentative and biased volume of Pasternak's verse (some of it actually tampered with!) that had come out a couple of years after the poet's death and could only be seen as a preliminary step, now that he was out of harm's way, in a familiar process of falsely making him out to have been, despite everything, a loyal son of the age. This attempt to protect Pasternak's memory from a posthumous affront naturally did nothing to endear Sinyavsky to the more retrograde section of the literary community – which in those years, thanks in part to Khrushchev's erratic policies, was somewhat on the defensive. Even worse from this point of view were other subsequent articles in *Novy Mir* where Sinyavsky wrote with a gentle but none the less devastating irony about some of the shoddy literary products of several "conservative" or neo-Stalinist writers. In other articles written at this time Sinyavsky left no doubt where his sympathies lay by his very choice of subject: Anna Akhmatova, Isaac Babel and other such authentic representatives of Russian literature who had been silenced or persecuted, and could be partially restored to their rightful place only in the post-Stalin years.

In the first half of the sixties – indeed until the time when Sinyavsky's and Daniel's arrest and trial precipitated an abrupt change in the climate – there was nothing very unusual in such a display of liberal sentiment. The process set off by Stalin's death and the revelations about him at the Twentieth Party Congress in 1956 had affected most intellectuals of Sinyavsky's generation in much the same way: disillusionment, not to say disaffection, was all but universal. In this respect Sinyavsky could scarcely be said in those years to have stood out particularly among the many other young scholars and writers who hastened to express themselves in cautiously worded (and often heavily censored) articles written for learned periodicals, for *Novy Mir*, and for certain other journals where liberal influence predominated. But in Sinyavsky's case there were some special features . . .

First of all, there was the circumstance – later to prove

fateful – that in 1947, as a student at Moscow University, he had become acquainted with Hélène Pelletier, the daughter of an attaché at the French embassy, who by way of a diplomatic courtesy had been given permission to attend courses in Russian literature. In the late Stalin years, when truly fantastic measures were taken to isolate the Soviet population from corrupting outside influences, and when the few Westerners resident in Moscow as diplomats or newspapermen were treated as pariahs (even though materially privileged ones), this was a very rare concession, granted to only one or two other foreigners; it would certainly have been unthinkable a year or so later, when the last of the token goodwill generated by the wartime alliance had vanished. In her account of her meetings with Sinyavsky in those days[1], Hélène Pelletier (later, by marriage, Zamoyska) recalls that he seemed to share the basic articles of faith to be expected at that time in one of his age and background: "The son of an active revolutionary, he shared his family's cult of the Revolution . . . he belonged to the Communist League of Youth (Komsomol) and was, needless to say, an atheist". Although curious about the outside world and relatively open-minded, he was not impressed (nor is he still!) by any claims on behalf of Western humanism and its institutions. He believed in a kind of ideal Communism (whose remoteness from Stalinist practice, however, was certainly dawning on him already then), and felt that Christianity had nothing to offer: "Christianity has been going downhill ever since the Renaissance, ever since it made personal salvation the only thing that mattered. Modern Christianity is individualist; Communism is concerned with the good of mankind, so its moral meaning is higher". With all this, he was already delving into virtually forbidden areas of the Soviet past, particularly the literature of the twenties, which would inevitably raise fundamental doubts in his mind. But, as in the case of many younger Russian intellectuals, it was a sudden personal confrontation with an act of arbitrary injustice that first really jolted him: in 1951 his father – whom he several times fondly

1 "Sinyavsky, the Man and the Writer", by Hélène Zamoyska in *On Trial. The Case of Sinyavsky (Tertz) and Daniel (Arzhak). Documents edited by Leopold Labedz and Max Hayward*, London, 1967.

recalls in *A Voice from the Chorus* – was arrested on a trumped-up charge; though released after the end of the Stalin terror in 1953, he died shortly afterwards.

Khrushchev's "secret speech" on Stalin at the Twentieth Congress demolished the very foundations of the beliefs on which Sinyavsky and his contemporaries had been reared. Many of them, however, had become emotionally and intellectually dependent on faith in an all-embracing system of values of the kind that Communism claimed to be. The only alternative to despair or cynicism was to set about immediately on the search for a substitute. But what? And where to begin looking? The collapse of the old had been as total as its continuing pretension to undivided predominance; only a small minority felt able to try and salvage something from the débris – it was easier to return to "pure" Marxism in the West, far away from the inescapable evidence of what an impure form had wrought in practice. There was no question at that moment of fruitful contacts with the external world. Russia was still effectively sealed off and the "half-men" – as Osip Mandelstam once called them – who inherited Stalin's power were determined to keep it so. Any hope of spiritual renewal could only come from an internal source, from somewhere close at hand.

It may seem barely credible, but it is a literal fact that in the period after Stalin's death – and as a consequence of his vast depredations – there was only a single figure alive in the whole of the Soviet Union who enjoyed any wide measure of genuine authority and to whom at least some section of the educated or thinking community could look for guidance in their sudden perplexity, and who could serve, if only in silence, as a moral exemplar – and hence as a potential source of alternative values. This solitary figure was Pasternak. The reason for Pasternak's lonely eminence was that he was the only indisputably great poet of his generation who had lived through and survived the whole of the Soviet era on his own terms: he had made no concessions of principle, and had never yielded to the blandishments, intimidation or direct coercion that had led almost everybody else to various degrees of compromise – of which the least was to lie low in the usually vain hope of being spared. But Pasternak made no effort to bargain for his life, even on these minimal conditions. Already during the war, as he confided to friends, he had determined to speak out if the Stalin régime continued unchanged after victory over the Germans. It was at this time that *Doctor Zhivago* was conceived at least partly as something which would place his own age in the perspective of the whole Christian era, and beyond that, of eternity. In this light the Soviet epoch, with its Great Leader ruling over the anonymous masses, was seen in effect as a reversal to Imperial Rome where "you had blood and beastliness and cruelty, and *pockmarked* Caligulas untouched by the suspicion that any man who enslaves others is inevitably seond-rate . . .". In the late forties, at the height of the post-war terror, Pasternak gave draft chapters of the novel to friends and acquaintances – an act of unimaginable courage, not to say foolhardiness, in those years. When copies inevitably found their way into the hands of the secret police, Pasternak was subjected to unspeakable tribulations, the full story of which is still to be told. It was a strange, largely silent duel between the "pockmarked Caligula" and the poet – who even perpetrated unheard-of acts of public defiance: on one occasion in 1948, for instance, at a poetry reading in Moscow's largest auditorium (to which he had only been invited in the expectation or on the understanding that he would demonstrate his "loyalty"), he explicitly dissociated himself from the other poets present and the propaganda topic ("Down with the Warmongers!") to which, according to the advertised programme, they were all supposed to address themselves. It was this – his last public appearance in the Stalin years – that showed the packed audience of Moscow intellectuals in the hall that he had not surrendered. If Stalin's hand was stayed in this unique instance it was partly because he undoubtedly planned a sweeter revenge than mere physical removal of the rebellious poet would have afforded, calculating that by a combination of unbearable pressures he could still force him to sing his praises in verse – as he had forced Akhmatova to, by using her son as a hostage.

When Zamoyska returned to Russia after Stalin's death and renewed her contact with Sinyavsky, she learned that, like other leading Russian dissidents of the future, he had found his way to Pasternak's house in the writer's colony at Peredelkino near Moscow. He read *Doctor Zhivago* in manuscript and was particularly struck by the religious poems, though at that time he did not agree with all of Pasternak's ideas. As Zamoyska writes, Sinyavsky "was even more impressed by him as a person than as a writer" . . . this was not surprising, for if freedom from convention and affectation is unusual in the West, it was more rare in the Soviet Union so soon after Stalin's death. There was no prudence in Pasternak, not the slightest attempt at evasion or concession to political expediency and conventional jargon. The fear of what others might think, the distrust, the terror fostered by Stalinism seemed to have passed him by, leaving him as full as ever of enjoyment of life and of confidence in his fellow-men . . . Pasternak's courage in sending his manuscript abroad, his deep conviction that he had a perfect right to do so, as well as a positive duty to "bear witness to his time" . . . none of this did anything but enhance his reputation and stimulate others to follow his example. Certainly Sinyavsky was influenced by the example of a man he admired as "a great patriot and a great poet".

Thus inspired by the way Pasternak had acted in defiance of all the taboos, Sinyavsky now asked Zamoyska to arrange for the appearance of his own work abroad. Not being protected by the fame that Pasternak enjoyed both in Russia and the outside world, Sinyavsky knew of course that his attempt to publish free of censorship would immediately be cut short if he did so under his own name. He therefore chose the pen-name "Abram Tertz", the hero of an underworld ballad in the tradition of the romantic Jewish freebooters of the Moldavanka, the thieves' quarter of Odessa immortalized in the early stories of Isaac Babel. Ballads like the one about Abram Tertz became popular in Moscow after Stalin's death, partly, perhaps, because the criminal underworld had achieved a certain autonomy unique in Soviet society, and also because of the extraordinary fact that under Stalin there was honour *only* among thieves: their peculiar "law" emphasized loyalty to each other as the supreme virtue. As Sinyavsky shows in his account of them in *A Voice from the Chorus*, they constituted a kind of order of chivalry which contrasted very favourably in some respects with the rest of society. The choice of this pseudonym was also appropriate, needless to say, in its implied allusion to the way in which the untrammelled exercise of the writer's craft is regarded in official Soviet circles.

The first "Abram Tertz" manuscript, an essay entitled "On Socialist Realism", was printed in the French literary journal *Esprit* in February, 1959, and was followed shortly afterwards, in 1960, by a short novel, *The Trial Begins*, published in the original Russian in the Paris emigré Polish journal *Kultura* (and a little later in English translation in *Encounter*). A collection of five stories under the general title "Fantastic Tales" (*The Icicle and Other Stories* in English translation) came out in Paris the next year and was soon translated into the major Western languages. Another short novel, *Lyubimov*, appeared in 1964 (*The Makepeace Experiment* in English translation, 1965). *Unguarded Thoughts*, a small book of notes and reflections – a kind of inner monologue almost in diary form – was published in America a few months before the arrest of the author, and a final story, "Pkhentz", in *Encounter*, in 1966, a month after his trial.

The stylistic accomplishment of Sinyavsky's writings, and the unusual literary culture patently lying behind them led one or two Western specialists in Russian literature to surmise that "Abram Tertz" must surely be an emigré pretending to write from inside the country. In its very few references to the matter before the truth came out, the Soviet press did what it could to foster this view of the shadowy Tertz as a "White emigré bandit of the pen", and it seems possible that the Soviet authorities may actually have believed this themselves for a time. It did indeed seem wellnigh incredible not only that any living Soviet author should possess this degree of literary sophistication, but that – even more unaccountably – he should also have the ingenuity to evade detection for so long (nearly five years by the end of his clandestine career) in a country where police informers are as numerous and inconspicuously ever-present as sparrows.

In "On Socialist Realism", after showing up official literary doctrine for the poor, hollow thing it is, Tertz-Sinyavsky concluded that "realism" of any stripe, whether genuine or pretended, was inadequate as a means of representing the improbable present, and he invoked Hoffmann, Dostoyevsky, Goya and Chagall as necessary teachers in the creation of a "phantasmagoric art" to replace it. What he meant is illustrated by some of the stories he composed during the following years in the precarious secrecy of his Moscow apartment, ever mindful of the Draconian penalties he would incur if found out. In the "Fantastic Tales" the familiar surface of everyday life is often suddenly shattered and then reassembled in the manner of surrealist painting. In one of them ("The Icicle"), for example, the tramcars racing along a Moscow street are transformed by the fantasy of a bystander into mammoths charging through a pre-historic canyon. Time and place are no longer stable categories to be taken for granted: in *The Makepeace Experiment* a small Russian provincial town suddenly slips into a different dimension and becomes the scene of occult happenings. Sinyavsky's "phantasmagorias" are disciplined, tightly constructed narratives which never descend to mere whimsicality and are always geared to the serious purpose of conveying, by unexpected "dislocations" and shifts of focus, the otherwise unimaginable quality of life in the Soviet era, at the same time commenting, with a profundity lightly disguised by humour, on its ideological assumptions. The only modern Russian writing to compare in this use of comic inventiveness as a means of bringing home the deadly earnest, is that of Mikhail Bulgakov whose *Master and Margarita* (published in Moscow in 1967, twenty-seven years after the author's death) also depicts Soviet "reality" as something surely conjured up by a magician with the power and genius of Satan himself. This is as much as to say that Sinyavsky belongs in the Gogolian tradition of Russian literature – a debt of affinity handsomely acknowledged by him in a brilliant study of Gogol written in the forced-labour camp and recently published in London. As in Gogol's tales of the Ukraine and St Petersburg, nightmare constantly obtrudes; in Sinyavsky's stories, however, it takes the form not of the phantom emanations of the subconscious (these, like other Gogolian devices, are sometimes wittily parodied – the strange bird, for example, in *The Makepeace Experiment*), but of the hallucinatory mental disorders endemic in a populace ruled for decades by fear and mutual distrust: there can be no more telling study in modern literature of what by understatement must be called paranoia than "You and I", one of the "Fantastic Tales". The special conditions that made such obsessive terrors so all-pervasive are given the sharp immediacy of a bad dream in *The Trial Begins*, where the leaden oppressiveness of Stalin's last years receives its literary deserts in a fashion unlikely ever to be rivalled – unless, as may be hoped, by Abram Tertz himself in his new incarnation. Perhaps the most affecting of the stories is "Pkhentz", the last of them. To some extent inspired by the author's own situation, it is about a being from another planet, the sole survivor of a spaceship that had crash-landed on Earth some years previously in the wilds of Siberia, who now lives in a Moscow communal apartment – that is, sharing a kitchen and bathroom with other tenants. Since his biology and metabolism are non-human, this involves elaborate disguise and constant vigilance, and hope is sustained only by the dream of one day meeting another creature similar to himself, or of an eventual return to the nostalgically remembered culture from which he has been separated with such finality.

Unguarded Thoughts is in a very different vein from the stories – so much so that it was at first believed by some people to have surely come from another pen than "Abram Tertz's". In form – and to a lesser extent in substance – it is the precursor of *A Voice from the Chorus*, consisting of the author's ideas and musings on a variety of topics, and written down just as they came to him; the mode of expression thus tends to the aphoristic, and the book has no preconceived structure except the loose one imposed by the recurrence of certain dominant themes. If *The Trial Begins* and "Fantastic Tales" often show preoccupation with the consequences of loss of faith in Soviet Marxism as a debased product of Western humanism (itself transplanted to Russia, it should always be borne in mind, in a predigested form, and in such an imperious way as to provoke enduring social, cultural and psychological distress), *Unguarded Thoughts* is largely the record of how Sinyavsky came to find himself under the spell of the God so rudely ousted in the few years before he was born to make way for the new idols which he and his generation were brought up to worship. Perhaps the key to his new sense of the world (it is a sense rather than a view) is to be found in the following passage: "I never know what liberal philosophers mean by the 'freedom of choice' they are always talking about. Do we really choose whom to love, what to believe in, what illness to suffer? Love (like any other strong feeling) is a monarch, a despot, who dominates us from within, capturing us to the last remnant and forbidding us to glance back. How can we think of freedom when we are *swallowed whole*, when we see nothing, are aware of nothing except the One who chose us and, having chosen, torments us or bestows favours on us? The moment we wish to free ourselves (whether from sin or from God), we are already swayed by a new ruler who whispers about liberation only until the day we have totally surrendered to him." The words about being "swallowed whole" are perhaps especially significant: they suggest that Sinyavsky's theology is intimately related to his artistic perception of things, indeed as his aesthetics already summed up in "On Socialist Realism", where he wrote of the rapture we may feel at "the metamorphoses of God taking place before our eyes, at the giant peristalsis of His viscera, at the convolutions of His brain".

Sinyavsky's dual existence came to an end in September 1965 when he was arrested by the KGB – they had possibly picked up the scent because of an indiscretion in the West and were soon able through a little detective work, aided by the installation of listening devices which monitored conversations in Sinyavsky's apartment, to gather all the evidence they needed. At the same time they arrested Yuli Daniel, whose manuscripts had also been smuggled out of the country by the same channels. For several months the two were held in almost solitary confinement, seeing no one except their interrogators, stool pigeons put in the same cells with them, and material witnesses occasionally brought in for a "confrontation". In these post-Stalin times, no physical brutality was used, but the usual array of sometimes even more effective torments was deployed in full – playing on the prisoner's anxiety about his family, hints at supposed betrayal by friends, and so forth. Each of them could have made things easier for himself – and received a shorter sentence when the case came to trial – by admitting that what he had done was "wrong", and by indicating willingness to express public repentance. But neither yielded. The three-day trial which eventually took place in February, 1966, was unique in Russian history: neither under the Tsars, nor even under Stalin had there ever been proceedings in which the main corpus delicti consisted of the actual contents of works of imaginative literature. The trial was hopelessly prejudiced by vituperative and grossly misleading articles in the press, and reports from the courtroom (to which access was severely restricted) were meagre and flagrantly biased[1]. The verdicts – seven years for Sinyavsky and five for Daniel – provoked a storm of protest in the outside world which, for a case of this kind, was unprecedented in its intensity and in the degree of unanimity between Communists and non-Communists alike. The result of the trial also gave rise to the first widespread and organized protests in Russia itself: this was the beginning of large-scale dissidence and *samizdat*. But it did not help. Sinyavsky and Daniel were sent off to forced-labour camps, and both served their sentences almost to the end.

The area to which they were sent is about 300 miles due east of Moscow, near a small town called Potma, at a junction of the main railway line from Moscow to Kuibyshev. On both sides of a branch line (not marked on the maps) running off north from Potma for about thirty miles are the numerous camps and other installations of the extensive "corrective labour colony" – to use the official term – which is still called by the code-name *Dubrovlag* ("oak-forest camp") assigned to it in 1947, the year when Stalin personally ordered the establishment of "special camps" with bucolic and geographically anonymous designations such as *Ozerlag* ("lake camp") and *Rechlag* ("river camp"). All "political" prisoners were to be concentrated in these camps with a view to their speedy liquidation in the event of a new war. After the winding-down in the post-Stalin years of many of the much larger and

[1] A proper record was made by Sinyavsky's wife and several friends who afterwards collated their notes – no one person was allowed to attend all the sessions of the court. The transcript was smuggled out to the West and may be found in English translation in *On Trial*.

remoter camp complexes of Gulag in the far North and East, Dubrovlag remained as one of the major camp areas for all categories of prisoners, including "political" ones.[1] It has certain advantages: it is conveniently situated for the "feeding" of convicted prisoners from the big Moscow jails (where people are held only during their interrogation and trial); it is an old-established, practised mechanism with about fifteen camps of the familiar kind: barracks surrounded by compounds with searchlights, watchtowers and "forbidden zones" round the perimeter – all administered by experienced personnel and located in a region where the population has long been schooled in mistrust towards the occasional escapee; last but not least, Dubrovlag has an industry in which the prisoners can be productively employed: a furniture factory, served by its own sawmill, foundry, etc. (The exploitation of prison labour in the economy thus continues, though it is now a question of consumer goods rather than of such primary industries as mining and lumbering; the railway brings fuel and other materials – together with prisoners – to the stations along the Potma branch line, and back to Moscow go the products of the factory, such as cabinets for television sets, to be sold in the capital's shops at a profit to the state, even after it has covered the upkeep of the camps and paid a pittance to the prisoners from which they can supplement their meagre rations by purchasing extras in the camp store.) Sinyavsky and Daniel – kept apart from each other in different camps because they had been "accomplices" – were put to work at the various kinds of manual jobs mentioned in *A Voice from the Chorus*. Estimates of how many prisoners there were in Dubrovlag in the sixties vary, but the lowest puts the total at about 15,000. The majority were common criminals and persons convicted of "white-collar" offences, but there were also many prisoners sentenced for alleged "anti-Soviet" activities, including "nationalists" from non-Russian minorities (such as Ukrainians – a large and growing category), and members of religious sects – including one thought to be extinct until Sinyavsky en-

[1]. There are still many other camps throughout the country and those of Dubrovlag are simply the ones about which most is known; as in the past, there is no official information about the scope of the Soviet penal system.

countered representatives of it among his fellow-prisoners. Although common criminals no longer virtually run the camps, as they did at times in the Stalin years, the "politicals" are by no means segregated from the others, so that a Jewish intellectual, for example, may well find himself rubbing shoulders with anti-Semitic Russians who were sentenced many years ago for collaborating with the Nazis during the war. As we see from his book, Sinyavsky came to know a very motley range of humanity, and the contact is reflected in numerous ways – though he attempts no systematic account of his fellow-inmates, nor indeed of any other aspect of the camp and his life there.[1]

As already indicated, *A Voice from the Chorus* is not a descriptive narrative in the ordinary sense and is based almost entirely on the lengthy letters written by the author to his wife Maria twice a month – all that was allowed under the regulations. The contents of all letters were examined by the camp authorities, and any detail or comment thought to be too outspoken could result in a letter not being passed, and in the writer being put in the punishment cells into the bargain. This is, therefore, not just another book about the camps, written after the prisoner's release, but a record of the author's own inner preoccupations as he actually noted them down during his long sojourn in the "house of the dead". The title is borrowed from the poem by Alexander Blok quoted at the beginning of this Introduction. Written not long before the outbreak of the First World War, these are some of Blok's most cheerless lines, full of characteristic foreboding of the horrors to come – "the cold and gloom of days ahead". Blok put "A Voice from the Chorus" as the first item in an anthology of his work which he published the year before his death[2] – when he had already understood that his own cries would indeed "sink like lead", and that his poet's voice would be drowned out by the rising din of the post-Revolutionary "chorus". As a child of the Revolution and a Russian intellectual Sinyavsky was fated to endure in actual fact what Blok and some of his

[1] Important descriptions of Dubrovlag written by prisoners who were there in the middle sixties are: Anatoly Marchenko's *My Testimony* (London, 1969), and Mykhaylo Osadchy's *Cataract* (New York, 1976).

[2]. I am indebted for this detail, as well as for the translation of the poem, to Sergei Hackel's *The Poet and the Revolution* (Oxford, 1975).

contemporaries had only foreseen and summoned forth in apocalyptic premonitions, not, for the most part, living to see them come to pass in full. In choosing his title, Sinyavsky may also have had in mind the reference to a similar poem of Blok's by a surviving friend of Yuri Zhivago in the epilogue to Pasternak's novel: "A thing which has been conceived in a lofty, ideal manner becomes coarse and material. Thus Rome came out of Greece, and the Russian revolution came out of the Russian enlightenment. Take that line of Blok's: 'We, the children of Russia's terrible years' – you can see the difference of period at once. In his time, when he said it, he meant it figuratively, metaphorically . . . now the figurative has become literal, the children are children, and the terrors are terrible . . ."

The "chorus" which Sinyavsky himself supplies at certain points in his book as a background to his own voice is picked out of the general hubbub around him in the bleak, overcrowded barracks, the camp compound, or the factory to which the prisoners were taken out under escort for the daily grind of "corrective" labour. The "chorus" serves at most times as a confused demotic counterpoint to the author's silent thoughts on art, literature, the human condition, and many other topics. Since most of the "chorus" sentences (given in italics in the present translation) are devoid of specific context, representing isolated snatches of talk which invaded the author's ears from the surrounding Babel, their individual import is frequently left to the imagination – though it can generally be inferred from its connection with neighbouring phrases, or from the reflections sometimes set in train by them. The meaning of what the "chorus" says is, however, of less concern than its tone or flavour; in vocabulary and phonetic colouring, it vividly echoes the submerged vernacular of the Russian "lower depths" into which the author was cast; it is a speech abounding in Malapropisms, non-sequiturs, grotesquely garbled forms, pathetically inadequate attempts at "educated" parlance, slang words from the criminal underworld, camp jargon, etc. To a Russian ear (and, alas, in all the nuances *only* to a Russian ear) this verbal flotsam and jetsam evokes – not with condescension, always with compassion and wonderment – a whole world in which language mirrors a desolation of the spirit such as is everywhere closer, perhaps, to the essence of society at large than may be readily avowed.

With the difference, then, that his voice is no longer unaccompanied, Sinyavsky now continues in much the same manner as in *Unguarded Thoughts*. But we see a distinct shift of emphasis in the burden of his meditations: there the main themes were God and Christianity. By the time he arrived in Dubrovlag, this matter had been settled. As a believing Russian Orthodox Christian, he could now pass on to other subjects, secure in a faith which embraced all else (including art, the other redeeming link that besides his religion means most to him) and made him in the core of his being invulnerable to the ordeal ahead. As he had written before his arrest, in *Unguarded Thoughts*: "Truly Christian feelings are against human nature, they are abnormal, paradoxical. You are beaten, and you rejoice. Misfortunes shower on you, and you are happy. Instead of running away from death, you are attracted to it and assume its likeness in advance. To any normal, healthy person it seems mad . . . but here everything is in reverse – unnatural, say the humanists; supernatural, say the Christians . . . we don't overcome our nature – it is replaced by some other, unfamiliar nature which teaches us how to be ill, suffer and die, and relieves us of the obligation to fear and hate."

The predominant theme in *A Voice from the Chorus*, the theme from which nothing distracts the author for long, is art in all its forms. It was the subject of many of the books he ordered from home (two packages a year under the regulations), or borrowed from fellow-prisoners. Apart from miniature essays on the general nature of art, literature, myths and folklore, we find vignettes devoted to an astonishingly wide range of individual writers, artists, works and styles: Swift and Defoe, Akhmatova, Rembrandt's "Prodigal Son", Hamlet, Hogarth, Stevenson's "Dr Jekyll and Mr Hyde", Matisse, Kipling, the Javanese shadow theatre, Mandelstam, the Irish legend of Cuchulainn (inspired by the perusal of a rare work by Alexander Smirnov, the only Russian Celtic scholar), Yoshida Kenko and early Japanese painting, the myths of Oceania, Russian church architecture, and many others which the reader may browse among at will – as the author himself emphasizes, his book is not the usual purposeful affair that progresses in one direction to a final destination. There is no lack of topics of a different kind: the code of the Russian criminal underworld, the theory of evolution, the importance of the Holy Ghost for the Russian national character, the reason for the ten years' war over Helen of Troy (what an illumination to come from Dubrovlag!), and – particularly dear to the heart of Abram Tertz – a great deal on magic and fairy-tale transformations, which are assigned no less credibility, and certainly not held in lower esteem than all the monkey tricks of the prideful technology they anticipated.

There is an element of what can almost be called drama in the contrast between the scholarly, contemplative nature of these notes, and the circumstances in which they were written. But the truth is that Sinyavsky – at one point he says as much – did not really think of himself as being under the constraint normally implied by such circumstances. In a word, he remained beyond the reach of his judges and jailors, and in a vital sense it is perhaps they, rather than he, who were and are in the captive state. During his time in the camp, he managed to write a superbly original essay on Pushkin, now published in Russian in the West.[1] Here he quotes what Pushkin remarked in 1836 about Silvio Pellico's account of his prison life: "Silvio Pellico spent ten years in various dungeons and, when he was released, he published his notes. There was general astonishment: people were expecting bitter complaints, but instead they read touching reflections full of serenity, love and benevolence." The same could be said of Sinyavsky's letters *de profundis*.

MAX HAYWARD

Oxford,
February, 1976.

[1] *Progulki s Pushkinym*, London, 1975.

Translators' Note

For the reasons mentioned in the Introduction, there seemed to be no satisfactory way of doing full justice to the peculiar quality of the language of the "chorus". Attempts at the systematic employment of roughly equivalent English usage might have produced misleading and even disconcerting associations with a very different kind of cultural and social environment. On the whole, therefore, the translation of the italicized passages attempts little more than to suggest a generally uneducated, or muddled type of speech, avoiding excessive use of British or American slang. In some cases there appeared to be no alternative but to omit lines or words where the whole point resides in a phonetic eccentricity or an unconveyable double-entendre. A few other passages which defied translation, or seemed to lose their point in it, have been left out, but liberties of such a kind have been kept to a minimum – even in the one or two places (as on p. 217) where the author resorts to seemingly inconsequential speech in order to suggest a process of free association, or the breakdown of ordinary structure in language and consciousness.

The book is divided into seven parts – one for each of the six years the author spent in Dubrovlag, and a seventh recording first impressions and thoughts when he returned to his home in Moscow.

All footnotes, unless otherwise specified, are by the translators.

Part One

. . . a book which goes backwards and forwards, advances and retreats, sometimes moves close to the reader and at other times runs away from him and flows like a river through new countries, so that as we sail along, the head starts to whirl from the sheer abundance of impressions, even though everything passes slowly enough before our eyes, allowing us to view it at leisure and then watch it till it drops out of sight; a book which has a number of themes but only one trunk, and grows like a tree, embracing space with the totality of its leaves and air, and – in the manner of the lungs which have the shape of an inverted tree – breathes by expanding almost infinitely, only to contract again down to a small point; a book whose meaning is as inscrutable as the soul in its innermost kernel.

5

I shall speak straight out because life is brief.

*

. . . In general it is interesting the way a man looks for an excuse to survive, saying to himself: why not just be contrary and go on living when it's no longer possible, when thought itself is almost extinguished by fatigue and apathy? Here, at rock bottom, is where you get to your feet and begin!

*

Everything here is a little fantastic – both faces and things. It is rather a "storybook world". The air is thick with expectations (of the end of one's sentence, of the end of life, or of the world) and this lends an unusually frenetic quality to the slightest thing. When the sun is low on the horizon the shadows are longer.

*

I have suddenly realized how important it is for an artist to paint "from life" – provided it is approached not simply as an object to be depicted, but as a metaphor, as something that breathes his own inner world. It is certainly a great thing for an artist to find subjects within himself (reality is never adequate and he is forced to fall back on his imagination), but whenever fate or chance wills him to stumble upon something in real life that corresponds to his own thoughts, he is very happy indeed. He looks at what he sees and says "it is mine", as if it were intended solely for his contemplation. The joyful recognition of signs familiar and congenial to his eagerly receptive soul affords exactly the same kind of perfect pleasure as the painting of a picture conceived entirely in his own mind. He encounters himself in the outside world and at such moments life attains the power and richness of art. And whether or not he is able to give actual expression to his discovery is of no importance. It is his to possess and this is enough. In this way Pushkin first encountered Bessarabia and found the gypsies awaiting their portrayal in a work still to be written.[1] And Lermontov remains transfixed for all eternity before the mountains of the Caucasus.[2]

*

. . . Your own life comes and goes. You are merely form. The contents are not you, are not yours. Remember, you are merely form!

*

They do not live – they exist. (Prisoners in a camp)

*

"*Look: the moon in the window – how life-like it is!*"

*

When life is bleak and empty and clothes are drab, the human face acquires the right to greater expressiveness by contrast: its allotted role is to make up for all that is missing and answer for the man as a whole. And so it takes on a frankly hyperbolic quality. Why do the faces of city folk – faces that are nice and decent enough on the whole – all look so much of a muchness? Personality, clothes and status make no difference: the features of the well-fed lose their distinctiveness and character under a layer of fat. But in prison and in old age, when not much is left to a man, the face is etched by suffering and stands out sharply: the nose is as pointed as a spear, the eyes are beady and the teeth, ungraced by any semblance of a polite smile, are bared like the fangs of a wild animal – the craving to live is

[1] Reference to Pushkin's poem "The Gypsies" (1824).

[2] Mikhail Lermontov (1814–41): Pushkin's younger contemporary who became fascinated by the Caucasus after boyhood visits there. Some of his best longer poems are on Caucasian themes. He was killed in a duel in Pyatigorsk in the Caucasian foothills, and there is a monument to him there.

unconcealed. It is the face that has the honour of representing us at the last.

*

An old man is reading a text-book on elementary mathematics sent to the man in the next bunk by his son. He doesn't understand a word of it – all this business about sines and cosines. But all the same he reads right through, from cover to cover: it was sent by somebody's son!

(So much for the question as to whether things have souls. If you sent someone here a text-book on geometry I could probably not resist borrowing it and having a look in the same way. The sense of personal contact you get from this is more important than the book's contents.)

*

"*Every fellow in our mob came through just by sheer luck and never forgot it or stopped talking about it for the rest of his born days.*"

*

"*There's those that likes to eat and those that likes to sleep – each according to his ability.*"

*

"*Six whole cells of us there were – all murderers.*"

*

"*If the Lord wants to know what the worst and the best things were in my life, I'll tell him: the worst was four episodes that happened to me, and the best was* anasha[1].

*

"*What always ruins us is thinking we'll get away with it.*" (About crime)

*

[1] A kind of drug, like hashish.

"*Time was approaching to go to the latrines . . .*"[1] (Epic style)
"*The way they laugh at a Russian!*"[2]
"*My organism is atrophied.*"
"*Have a sweet, so your mouth will feel sweet.*"

*

. . . When anything of interest happens within or around me I make a mental note to tell you about it, and it is this habit of thinking of things in connection with you that gives them their meaning.

*

When people ask me what art is, I start laughing to myself out of sheer amazement at the immeasurable vastness of it and at my own inability to say in what it actually consists, to define something that changes so continually and fascinates like light. I have spent all my life, for heaven's sake, trying to grasp its meaning and am still none the wiser or any more able to explain it. I hedge everything around with vague qualifying words ("perhaps", "it could be that . . .") and am soon out of my depth, unable even to hazard a guess. It really takes your breath away to listen to all those pundits who know precisely what it is (as if anyone has ever succeeded in finding the answer, or as if it were possible to know!). Art is always a more or less impromptu act of prayer. Try to catch hold of smoke.

*

I always imagine there is some book which absolutely must be read, only I can never find out which one it is . . .

*

[1] i.e. it was getting towards evening. The lavatories could be visited only in early morning and in the evening. The evening visit is a long-awaited moment and a very important landmark in the daily life of prisoners. Besides, it marks the end of the long prison day. (*Author's note*)

[2] The Russian original is spelt to indicate a strong Ukrainian accent. 'They' refers to the Soviet authorities who treat even Russians with contempt. The charm of the expression resides in the fact that the man feeling sorry for Russians himself speaks a faulty kind of Russian. (*Author's note*)

9

It is curious to see what sort of things give pleasure to a man:

"Covered all over in roadside dust,
I shall come back quite unlike myself."[1]

The passion with which this is sung! It is as though we wanted to become unlike ourselves and to understand – if only in this way – the miracle of the Transfiguration. This is the origin of our theatre, of dressing up in fine clothes: I am not really I.

We also like to be unhappy:

"We have no relatives or friends
Or anyone to send a present to."

or take the well-known popular ballad: "A poor orphan now am I". It is not riding along in a *troika* that the hero revels in, but the fact that he is an orphan.

The horrific is fun as well:

"And I shall die a terrible death by fire, I shall . . ."

This was said by someone with pathos, with a catch in his voice: he was quite overawed by his own solemn tone and the portentous fate in store for him . . .

I have but a short time to live –
Just fourteen hours, no more.
I walk around my solitary cell,
Back and forth across the floor.

Then suddenly out of the darkness
My true love appears to me.
All covered in blood is her blouse,
And a smell of blood is in the air.
Tell me, my darling child, she says,
Tell me what has happened to you.

Quick, not a moment more to lose,
I have come to take you from this place,
Horses await you outside the walls,
And the dark, dark blue of the night.

[1] From a convict song.

This is the kind of thing you find in Zhukovsky's[1] ballads. For some reason I thought of "Lenore."

*

Don't be too sad, my dear. By the will of fate we have been transported back to that pale-green, romantic time of life when young people declare their feelings in passionate letters, swear eternal love, plan their future life in common and sigh over photographs of each other. We had no such overture at the beginning and now it is being played somewhere in the middle, a little out of place, rather late in life – to make up for what we missed. This means we can go back and make our first steps in very deliberate fashion, thinking about what we are doing, instead of rushing through them harum scarum, as most people do. And, having so much to look back on, we can now add to past memories all the trembling hope and bashfulness that go into the first word, spoken shamelessly, with a sob: my love!

6th May, 1966.

*

My memory of the whale's belly: ladders, rigging, masts, a ship's deck (but *inside* the ship for some reason), an iron hold, iron innards, a half-light that seemed at first to be pitch-darkness, a feeling of having seen it in a film, someone on deck with legs wide apart and neck craned vigilantly, waving you along with his hand – an alphabet of gestures instead of speech; silence and the solemn calm of a clinic or hospital: the medical section. A ward. A reception room. Undress! In the hush the unnatural twitter of birds. Rigging, girders. A floating sanatorium. The Lubyanka Prison.[2]

*

[1] Vasili Zhukovsky (1783–1852): wrote a number of original ballads as well as adaptations from English and German (such as Burger's 'Lenore').
[2] The main political prison of the Soviet Union, on Dzerzhinsky Square in Moscow, where the author was taken for interrogation on his arrest.

II

A man enters into art in rather the same way as he comes into the world at his birth. Thereafter everything is art for him, and like the cricket in Krylov's fable, he finds his home "under every little leaf". People say of someone: "He has a good eye" (because he is an artist). But what does he see with his "good eye"? Only this: that the world is filled with art.

*

"In the world I'm all alone
Ain't got no roots and no support
Ain't got no sisters and no brothers,
No fathers and no mothers."

The striking thing here is the use of the plural in the last line. Illiterate and ungrammatical language, a sudden lapse into slang or dialect, shift attention from the actual words to their sound, so that even a tale told by a *besprizornik*[1] sounds real in spite of the hackneyed theme of the wicked step-parent.

An eight-year-old child hears his step-father saying to his mother:

"It's either him or me!"

"Don't worry, Stevie, we'll bury him in a week's time."

He then runs away from home and life begins. "We observe the presence of social neglect and a pathological development of the personality." (From a psychiatrist's report)

*

When there is nothing else at hand art begins to talk about itself and can be quite carried away by the subject.

There have been poets who have written of one thing only – the fact that they are poets. Art preens itself in front of a mirror like a woman waiting for a lover. It sometimes remains an old maid all the same, but no matter.

[1] An abandoned or runaway child, of the kind who roamed the country in vast numbers at various periods (e.g. after collectivization and the last war). They formed criminal gangs and had their own slang and songs.

It is good when every word in a song seems to follow almost automatically from the preceding one, and when the story unfolds with all the inevitability of a conditioned reflex:

A judge and his wife, the fortunate pair,
had a peach of a daughter with golden hair,
blue-eyed she was (her name was Rita),
stuck-up like her pa – tho' a darn sight sweeter –

At eighteen years old so cold and severe
none of the boys dare come anywhere near,
never a smile would she give or a kiss
and looked down on them all – a prim little miss.

But once at a dance a neatly-dressed pro
Came sidling along, bowed down to her low –
a real fancy fellow from the criminal class –
and carried her off in the boston – what brass!

And the beautiful Rita, whose pa was so grand,
fell for that fellow and promised her hand,
with his canny thief's eye he looked in her face
and saw at a glance that he'd turned up an ace.

O the passion and fire in that love of theirs –
A thief's love is short, but sweet while he cares –
He had no desire and now never did pine
Except for his Rita – and a glass of good wine!

But life for a thief is uncertain at best
– when he's not on the run, he's under arrest –
And once on a Tuesday, doing a job at the *ban*,
They were nabbed by the cops and hauled off in a van.

In a gloomy dark courtroom he sat and swigged water
– her father the judge – as he tried his own daughter:
before him she stood in the black dock of shame
with this unknown *zhigan* who bore all the blame.

No word did she utter – not on your life! –
But the thief begged leave to speak with his wife,
and she kissed him so fondly as he said goodbye
that a tear welled up in that hard judge's eye.

(The whole song was composed for the sake of this tear shed by the judge at the end! In real life such an encounter in the courtroom between a judge and his daughter would be quite improbable, but from the artistic point of view it is both crucial and convincing. I believe that Victor Hugo's *Quatre-vingt-treize* concludes with a similar twist of fate. "Tango" might have been more natural than "boston" but was evidently thought to be not quite as chic. The two lines "with his canny thief's eye," etc., get top marks!)[1]

*

Getting up to every imaginable trick, writing about everything on earth, art is in fact concerned solely with its own appearance, with admiring its self-portrait. Solely? Yes, in the final analysis it goes on and on only about its own inexplicable presence, the way it comes into being and blossoms forth. It is always ready at the slightest provocation, bewildered by a reality which has nothing to do with it, to point to the silliest things as confirmation of its own existence in the world.

Potentially every word is artistic. Pronounce a word with a certain stress or intonation and it will ignite and take off into poetry where rhythm and rhyme are merely the means and outer signs by which speech is inflected in some way or other.

Any utterance can be melodic or euphonious: it only has to rise very slightly above the level of the ordinary rhythmical cadence of everyday speech to call attention to itself and turn

[1] The songs of the Russian criminal underworld, for which there is a tradition going back into the last century, have no equivalent in modern Western culture. They are distinguished by a certain attempt at literary flavour, mixing "elegant" words and turns of phrase with professional argot, as in this song where *ban* (from the German *Bahn*, via Yiddish) means "railway station" – an important centre of activity for Russian criminals, and *zhigan* is one of the many words for thief or bandit.

into poetry. It is rather like the "white horses" on the sea – they are totally unnecessary and absurd, but they give it its particular accent, transforming it into an object of wonder and plunging us into the contemplation not just of an expanse of water but of the *sea* in the full sense of the word, of the sea which roars and heaves, which is very visibly present before us. And so we see that art is no mere trifle, but the very seal and token of existence, the means by which being is made manifest...

*

"*But don't expect a picnic! What have I got apart from my soul and a prick?*"

(I think the last word came in here because it rhymes with "picnic". In general, people use rhyme or assonance in their speech far more than they suspect.)

*

"*But why are you swearing?*"
"*Just because it sounds good.*"

*

A conversation about a fist fight:

"*He's got shoulders like Stenka Razin.*"[1]

"*He's a pint-size fellow, but the way he uses his fists is nobody's business – a couple of lightning jabs and he knocks the other fellow out cold. This other one can land you a wallop enough to send you flying through the air for half-a-dozen yards, but then you pick yourself up and run off as right as rain – that's because he's got a fist like a cushion: plenty of punch alright, but no real cutting edge to it.*"

"*Only twenty-three years old he is – and as headstrong as they come.*"

"*The other fellow has more strength. But this one has more guts.*"

"*He got a bullet through one arm when he was trying to escape,*

[1] Stenka Razin (executed in 1671): leader of a peasant revolt, and subject of a well-known popular song.

and all his strength has gone into the other arm."

"*I don't care if they slap ten or twenty times as much again on me – if I have to fight I'll damn well fight.*"

*

The queue at dinner-time is like a bookshelf: suddenly, among the uniformly well-thumbed tomes, you find some wretched little novel . . .

*

I have no time to read books, but think of them constantly, with wonder and gratitude. And never cease marvelling at a book's capacity to absorb and then conjure up on demand a whole world for you to see.

In childhood a book resembled a folding screen. A heap of animals and plants would suddenly pop out at you from behind dreary grey covers and when you shut it, everything vanished again. A book has something of the "magic cap", or the "magic table-cloth".[1] This peculiar property of books was well understood by the old calligraphic scribes, who were sensitive to the need of words to flower into pictures or transform themselves into leafy trees hung with toys. Letters leapt out at you with a roar from the beautiful pathways of the ornamented initial, quite distinct from the undergrowth of the text, and the book was read slowly, with delicious pauses. The art of the calligraphic scribe cannot be brought back. But we can help the book's age-old longing to be arcane and impenetrable by making its verbal texture so dense that it fairly dances before the reader's eyes, and, catching his breath, he sees little green leaves and the pretty muzzles of red fox cubs running out on to the page from under the black, charred tree stumps of the printer's words.

*

[1] The reference is to Russian fairy-tales in which he who dons a magic cap becomes invisible and where a magic table-cloth becomes instantly laid with plates, cutlery and food.

In prison Chekhov's letters depressed me and A. K. Tolstoy's[1] gave me real pleasure. Chekhov distressed me because for all his intelligence, perceptiveness and charm he is on the whole rather graceless in his letters and gives the impression that his life was boring and he had to fill the vacuum with small practical matters and forced schoolboy humour. Even Western Europe comes out in his letters from abroad as utterly devoid of interest. Perhaps this could be explained by the fact that like most of his contemporaries, Chekhov was indifferent to the visual arts and understood culture mainly as education. He was a "literary man" from head to foot and yawned when looking at cathedrals and museums. Like a schoolboy he longed to go to Africa and America, although as an artist he could make no use of such exotica: one need only take his trip to Ceylon, for instance, which was quite as absurd in its way as the tomfooleries of Charlotte and Epikhodov,[2] or as the name Chimsha-Himalayski[3] borne by one of his characters! If only he had at least been amused by it all. But one could weep with the pity and sadness of it when one discovers that even writing bored him to death: 'I now loathe writing and don't know what to do. I would gladly take up medicine, or get a job of some kind, but I no longer have the physical adaptability. Nowadays when I write or even just think about it, I have the same feeling of disgust as if I were eating soup out of which a cockroach had just been taken – excuse the comparison." (25th July, 1898)

It is not, of course, incumbent on a writer to be interesting in his letters. But, still, he should have an interesting life. And yet Chekhov regarded literature mainly as intellectual drudgery – he dreamed of idleness as if it were a holiday, and saw nothing magical in his wretched profession. A terrifying thought . . .

*

[1] A. K. Tolstoy (1817–75): poet, playwright and novelist; a distant cousin of Leo Tolstoy.

[2] Charlotte & Epikhodov: characters in *The Cherry Orchard.*

[3] Chimsha-Himalayski: character in *The Man in a Shell.*

17

Books resemble windows when the lights come on in the evening and begin to glow in the surrounding darkness, forming little golden pictures from the window panes, the curtains, the wall-paper, and creating the impression of a cosy existence known only to those who dwell within, a secret life invisible to the outside world. This happens particularly when it is cold or snowing (most of all when it is snowing) and looking up from the street at the light cast by patterned lamp shades you imagine that sweet music must be playing and glamorous, cultivated people walking about there inside. In my childhood this kind of gazing at strangers' windows remote in the night was accompanied by fantasies of a private apartment with three rooms, about which mother talked so passionately during our games of make-believe – when I grew up, I was to buy it (or win it on a lottery ticket) and we could picture it vividly, hanging in the sky like the gardens of Semiramis. We would even say: "Let's go and have a look at our apartment", as we walked before bed-time in the snow-covered streets where we had our eye on three or four windows that were our first choice. They changed according to my age and the way they were lit.

The whole object of illustration (I almost said illumination) is to intensify the light shed by a book even before it is read. Powerless to compete with the text, playing no role in the elucidation of the words as such, illustration is called upon to proclaim the festival which a book brings into our life. It is closer to the work of a jeweller than to drawing or painting.

This was well understood by the old binders and miniaturists and by the publishers themselves who gave books the sort of appearance that makes your heart miss a beat at the very sight of them. It is the art of creating pleasurable anticipation, of enticing the reader to delve deeper, of launching him on an expedition into a wonderland of letters – for we look at the pictures before we read the book, accustoming our eyes to its glimmering light.

Even if the writer's work is the most thankless of occupations, exhausting and desiccating, the product of it is still – in principle – an entertainment, a way of pleasantly passing the time by the light of a lamp, akin to the theatre or a carnival. Flaubert and Chekhov, agonizing over their literary work, forgot this and ever since it has been customary to talk about the "toil" or "labour" of writing. Well, what if it is labour? Hard work it may be, but no less sweet for that. Writing *Salambo* or *Kashtanka*[1] was not the same as loading timber. And they forgot that a book should always have pretty pictures . . .

*

From a letter:[2]

"*Mother, as you well know, is suffering on your account. Whenever she gets a letter she starts crying, she cries all the time anyway. And Dad cries too, because of you. Whenever he sits down to eat he cries and says: here we are, eating – but our Slavka isn't with us*".

*

Verse:

"*Oh comrades, life is like vodka drunk neat –*
To some it tastes bitter, but for me it's a potion
When a glorious beauty sits at my feet
Showing me all her dog-like devotion!"

Vulgarity knows no bounds.

*

"*And the vicissitudes of fortune resulted in my having to live abroad for a while.*"

*

Jackdaws over the wood are like flakes of soot.
Art and life? But perhaps there is no life – just art?

*

[1] Story by Chekhov.
[2] This, like many similar items throughout the book, is something told or shown to the author by a fellow-prisoner.

. . . At times I feel in terribly good spirits, and for no particular reason. With the radio blaring away, I could be watching a film and seeing my own life unfolding hilariously on the screen.

The feeling of having been transferred in time as well as space does give a peculiar quality to life – something indescribable, a new dimension, so to speak, in which one is able to look at everything from a great height, with an almost otherworldly eye. One is no longer certain, in this state of curiously detached wonderment, whether time passes slowly or quickly, whether something is large or small, good or bad.

How could so much be crowded into the archpriest Avvakum's dungeon?[1] Because it was a pit, a hole? The smaller and more confined a place is, the more is liable to be crammed into it. There is no other way of explaining the appearance of this self-portrait of a panoramic scope hitherto unknown to the iconography of Ancient Russia.

*

Man is engaged in a constant process of dying, yet does nothing but dream of reaching a point where he will really begin to live.

*

It is always interesting to speculate as to how a man will behave after his life has collapsed in ruins.

Let us assume, for instance, that he has been sent to a labour camp and while he is there, his wife marries another man, his friends forget him and his whole way of life, so familiar and apparently stable, suddenly disappears into a yawning abyss that has opened up in place of reality. The question is, how will he live and what will he do after all this has been borne in upon him? Will he take to drink, go out of his mind or

[1] Avvakum (c. 1610–1681): wrote an account of his persecution for disobedience to the ecclesiastical authorities at the time of the Schism in the Russian church. He was put in an underground dungeon made of earth and timber. His "Life" of himself is the first Russian autobiography and is written in a vivid style that makes it one of the few pre-Petrine works to possess a certain literary quality.

simply turn into an old man with a grudge against the whole world? An old man marooned on the island of the room where he lives alone begins to gather together all the little souvenirs of the past that have accidentally escaped destruction and are important chiefly as a reminder of the misfortunes he has borne through the years, and he smiles at the recollection of the voyage undertaken such a long time ago, without thought for all the winds and currents which have cast him up with this pathetic wreckage at a latitude and longitude he had never imagined he would reach . . .

*

What makes us what we are? It probably all depends on our relationship to surrounding space. A man unconfined in space constantly aspires to go forward into the distance. He is sociable and aggressive, and needs ever new pleasures, impressions and interests. But if he is constricted, cut down to size, reduced to the minimum, then his mind, deprived of forests and fields, creates an inner landscape out of its own immeasurable resources. This is something that monks well knew how to take advantage of. To give away all your worldly goods – is not this to throw out ballast?

We are not outcasts or prisoners, but reservoirs. Not men, but wells, deep pools of meaning.

In our sleep we are confined to a minimal cell precisely conterminous with the body, but where does the spirit escape to in this restricted space? It wanders not somewhere outside us, but retreats deeper into ourselves. We melt away in sleep and, free of all burdens, easily swim over to the other shore.

Driven into a cage, the mind is forced to break out into the wider open spaces of the universe through the back door. But for this to happen it must first be hunted down and brought to bay.

*

In the *Book of the Dove*[1] clouds are said to derive from thoughts.

[1] An early Russian mediaeval collection of questions and answers purporting to give an explanation of natural phenomena, the origin of social and political institutions, and originally known as the Book of Wisdom.

"Stormy winds are the breath of God. Thunder clouds are the thoughts of God." In the same way, according to the Icelandic "Eddas", when the Gods were creating the world out of the body of the giant Hymir, they fashioned the sky from his skull, and the clouds from his brains. And I've read similar things elsewhere. Clouds, clouds, flying islands. Thoughts are like a procession of clouds, like aerial balloons sailing past, full of moisture . . .

*

In the Lefortovo[1] prison I tried to recall the significance of several books I had read in childhood. Thinking back to various travel stories I was bound to conclude that it was Swift who subjected man to what was on all counts the severest test of all.

. . . Swift, it should be noted, describes the contents of our pockets as if they were something quite extraordinary, a very rum collection of items which need to be explained. Gulliver's watch is not a watch, his comb – a comb, or his handkerchief – a handkerchief, but in the eyes of the Lilliputians something unimaginable, beyond comprehension and therefore described at great length in page after page of entertaining narrative. Swift's discovery, fundamental for art, is that there are no uninteresting objects in the world so long as there exists an artist to stare at everything with the incomprehension of a nincompoop. "We know! We know!", people shout at him, "these are simply scissors, that's all they are! Why go on about them?" But an artist cannot and must not understand anything. The word "scissors" is unknown to him. Taking a couple of steps back, and still gaping open-mouthed, he describes them in the language of riddles: "Two ends, two rings and a screw in the middle." Instead of comprehension, instead of answers he offers a word-picture – one that keeps you guessing.

As he sets his riddle, Swift puts on the straightest of faces,

[1] Prison in Moscow to which the author was transferred after first being held in the Lubyanka.

waiting for the scissors to snap to, like a trap. Altered out of all recognition are not just watches and combs, but man as such with all his primeval attributes. Everything was exposed to these variable dimensions, to the fatal rays of a relativity theory which inspired the good Dean to a vivisection so daring that nothing was left of his guinea-pig (already then, at the very dawn of modern civilization . . .). Rabelais elevated man, built him up to reach the skies; Swift, following in his footsteps, destroyed man.

He revealed himself a born natural scientist, dissecting a frog or a rat, a king's ganglia or a hanged man's scrotum with academic impartiality. Not for nothing did Swiftian insight anticipate Darwin's man-from-ape theory, artificial satellites and the whole of our cybernetic stupor. The haughty disdain of a professional for quacks and ignoramuses is clearly discernible in his jibes at scientists (as in the episode of inflating the dog).

Few if any writers can be compared to him in his power of scientific analysis, and the care with which he sets up an experiment is pharmaceutical in its precision: mixing the ingredients for his long-legged Lilliputians he measures and weighs down to the last inch or ounce – he could have bred homunculi, or probed into the bio-chemical nucleus . . .

Compared to the other characters in the book Gulliver lacks personality, and is thus better fitted to represent man in general. What can one say of him except that he is Homo Sapiens – but a specimen subjected to entirely different criteria according to the changes in his environment? These variations in the conditions of the experiment mean that Gulliver has no fixed or permanent characteristics: he is short or tall, clean or unclean only by comparison; he is a man by comparison and a non-man by comparison. He is a giant among Lilliputians, a Lilliputian among giants, an animal among the houyhnhnms, a horse among men.

What is left after these operations on the immense Procrustean bed of the Universe? What beliefs, laws, customs or statues? Even the dream of immortality turns into a mockery.

Even nostalgia for one's native country and the longing to return to one's own kind dissolve in the face of unconcealed disgust. Having become Gulliver, what had man left to lose or forget, where could he flee to, what could he hope for under Swift's scrutiny? From Gulliver Swift drew one conclusion: man is a fiction, a sham . . .

Defoe rescued Gulliver from the dismaying uncertainties of freedom and put him on a desert island. Man was now given back his normal height and the qualities of an ordinary human being: his reason, a sense of family and property, a healthy desire to make his way in the world – all lost in the course of adventures with other authors. Defoe forced man to revert to form by drastically restricting him, by making it impossible for him to jump out of himself or escape from the need of living "like everyone else". He banished him to his own society.

Defoe makes shipwreck play the role of the Flood (and of Creation too): man remains naked and alone on the naked earth. And what happens? After shedding a few tears, the castaway Robinson Crusoe starts building up his capital. The primeval wilderness turns into prosperous farmland, and the Bible into a manual for future Henry Fords – who also, like Robinson, began not by owning skyscrapers, but by finding a grain of wheat in the lining of their pockets.

If, instead of domesticating Friday in deference to the new colonial attitude of his times, Robinson had run across an obliging cannibal girl to settle down with, he would have founded a little England on his island and there would have been no reason to return home. In fact, however, there is nothing in the whole book to indicate that our Adam has ever really left his civilized motherland, where each man is a microcosm of society as a whole, and every shopkeeper, clerk, milkman, miner or factory-owner may justly consider himself a Robinson. To think thus of himself is open to anyone marooned on a desert island of work, family, hunger, sickness or wealth – in short, to anyone having no choice but to seek refuge in a saving self-centredness, in the instinct of self-preservation which forces us to go on struggling to raise ourselves up within the confines of a prison cell or of the entire universe, as the case may be.

Defoe's hero is saved from triteness and the novel from tedium by the poles of life and death, of fertility and barrenness between which Robinson's existence is suspended. Approaching them from a different angle than Swift, Defoe focuses attention on ordinary, everyday objects and skills, arousing our interest by inviting us to consider the unusual technical difficulties involved in making or performing them. He shows that such things as planting vegetables, sewing clothes or making a table can be remarkably demanding and crucial jobs, fraught with hazards and pitfalls, and calling for the employment of all kinds of cunning stratagems whose detailed description adds tension to an otherwise exiguous plot. When life itself hangs by a grain of wheat, the account of how it actually germinates and sprouts out of the soil has all the suspense of a detective novel . . .

Some books beckon us on to freedom, to embark on a voyage. But how we may survive without sailing anywhere, without moving from the spot, simply staying in our cage – this we can learn only from *Robinson Crusoe*, the most useful, exhilarating and benign novel in the world.

*

"*In a camp you can get by on dog's meat.*"

*

"*A bit of tobacco is as good as a feast.*" (Proverb)

*

"*A man can lose his strength even if he's free.*"

*

"*All I have left is the bones in my body and the skin stretched over them.*"

*

"*I'm clothed to all intents and purposes.*"

*

"I may be an animal, I said, or an insect, but I know what's what."

*

"They'll live to regret they didn't kill me."

*

"Everyone has his favourite thing in life – what I used to fancy most of all was jellied pig's feet with a bit of horse radish."

*

"I look at the door and just don't believe it: on the other side of it there is freedom!"

*

"I ask him about Samara: 'What's new there? What cell did they put you in?' I've only ever been there myself in prison."

*

"Today I had a dream and saw the place where I was born."

*

"So my letters won't do you any harm." (From someone's letter to his brother)

*

"I wrote one letter after another – like applications for a new pair of boots."

*

The usual joke when something heavy is up-ended for loading: *"Stands right up like a young man's!"*

*

"First you live to be seventy-five – and then you can talk!"

*

In the labour camps people are literally preserved. Having come here as a boy you can live to be an old man, yet still remain something of an adolescent in your physical appearance and habits. I was surprised when I arrived here at how youthful many of the long-termers look. The usual explanation is that they have fewer worries, or that it is the effect of sexual continence. But this is doubtful. Rather it is the influence of the psycho-physical climate – one's isolation from the general flow of human life. Earth's time no more applies here than it does on Mars, and the whole system of co-ordinates is to some extent different.

We don't "grow old". But whether this is for better or for worse is hard to say. Probably it is nature's way of providing compensation. Nature knows best.

*

"*Thirteen years have slipped by, as in a fairy-tale . . .*"
(A standard turn of phrase I first heard on waking up in the morning in my upper bunk in the camp, and I thought: how right, how good – "as in a fairy-tale!")

*

"*If anyone tells you he was not able to hold out because it was beyond his strength – don't believe him. A man is given precisely as much as he is able to bear.*"

*

"*Everything depends on force!*", *he said to me in a whisper.* "*On the force of passion!*", *I added and nearly choked . . .*

*

. . . Could the violin have originated as an imitation of the singing voice? May it not have started off, in other words, as an illegitimate attempt to extract from strings sounds that actually violate their nature, to introduce a human element into them by faking and distorting their natural properties (strings are made to be strummed and twanged, for which purpose there have always been harps and guitars)?

A train of thought such as this can be set off just by listening to a Beethoven record – the sort of modest thing we do on Sundays as earnestly as free people going to concerts. Not out of boredom or snobbishness, but because here things in short supply or hard to get are all the more appreciated and valued as a result. Not to go and "listen to music" would be like refusing breakfast or a cup of coffee. It is no longer a question of satisfying the flesh (or the spirit), but of responding to things which from being commonplace and insignificant have suddenly become precious: Robinson Crusoe's Law.

*

. . . I note a strange new feeling of fascination – almost romantic I'd say – about a spoonful of butter or a small slice of cheese. It flows down into you and becomes instantly and wholly absorbed before it even has time to reach the stomach, it would seem. Digestion and absorption into the blood stream begin somewhere under the tongue or in the esophagus, and one small morsel is enough to revitalize you beyond measure, almost going to your head. The reason for this is the purity and refinement of the product. One old man expressed himself very aptly on this score when he assured us quite seriously that people occupying high government posts eat such fine fare that they have to obey the call of nature no more than once a week. I did not try to disillusion him: poverty has the advantage of knowing the value of riches and of being able to convey it in an amazingly telling way.

*

"*In Kiev the grub is good.*"
"*In Moscow the grub is cheap.*" (Conversation)

*

He is in for 25 years and year in year out reads the magazine "*Health*".

*

A terrific thing – boots. The time it takes to earn enough for a pair!

*

Art is insolent because it is so clear. Or rather, it is insolent in order to make itself clear. First it sticks a knife into the table and then says: there you are – that's what I'm like. (While listening to Haydn)

*

"What a fright he looks!" said a free employee[1] when someone pointed me out to him in the work zone. Whereupon another prisoner went up close to him and said: "If they dressed you (swear word) that way (swear word) you'd look even more of a fright."

But actually I don't at all mind creating such a fearful impression. On the contrary, it rather amuses me – like a masquerade. We are still not sure, furthermore, exactly what kind of external appearance best corresponds to our function in life.

Now as regards hair: its true significance has yet to be appreciated – not just as a personal adornment, but in its primary role both as protection for the head and an instrument of perception. "It's easier to think if you have hair," said an old man and I was very struck by this revelation. It really is easier. Perhaps our hair, like antennae, serves to pick up useful currents in the air, rather as a forest attracts clouds and helps to increase rainfall. At the same time hair may afford protection against certain electrical discharges – at least I always have a splitting headache whenever my head is shaven.

*

Finding the right word in modern poetry is a residual form of

[1] The camps employ some personnel who are not prisoners – as overseers, technicians, clerks, etc. The author's notoriety, created by newspaper accounts of his trial, would be enough to make him look a "fright" to this particularly "loyal" category of citizens.

magic: a name only has to be discovered and the reader put under its spell for something to be conjured up before his very eyes. A precise epithet can spark off a whole train of thought, or cause an image to appear in a flash of light, summon it forth out of dust and ashes into quivering life, so that it rivals nature itself in vividness – that is, in its ability to take root and live in the mind for as long as real individuals and events, and perhaps even longer . . .

I always have the feeling that nature – the air, leaves, rain – sees and understands everything, and wants to help – wants to help very much indeed, but cannot.

9th September, 1966

*

Psychologically, life in a labour camp is like travelling in a long-distance train: the automatic forward movement of time creates the illusion that an otherwise empty existence is being filled and made meaningful. Whatever you may be doing, your sentence is "going forward", so that the days do not follow each other needlessly, but have a purpose, working as it were, for you and the future, and thereby acquiring significance. Again as in a train, the passengers do not feel particularly called on to occupy themselves with useful work since their journey is anyway justified by the steady if slow progress towards their destination. They can permit themselves to live in whatever ways are open to them – playing dominoes, wandering around and gossiping – without any qualms of conscience about wasting time: the very fact of being engaged in serving out your sentence injects a dose of splendid utility into everything. But I am still made frantic by the constant cries of: "What are you hurrying for?", "We have all the time in the world!", "Why don't you find some way of enjoying yourself?"

I find it hard to get used to the idea of living at the expense of the future. However, the point is not what I feel about it, but the peculiarity of a situation in which you make up for the lack of a purpose in life by finding meaning only in the process of living out your days. It sometimes seems to me that in these conditions of simply waiting for their sentence to end, men may well be happier than they are living in freedom – only they have not quite grasped the fact.

*

"He served only one year for every two."

"?!"

"In his imagination: every year that went by he counted as two. To make it easier to bear."

*

"To disentangle a vicious circle."

*

"In the dark smells are stronger, I've noticed."

*

"The good thing about this place is that a man feels he is nothing but a naked soul."

*

Reading Pushkin you sometimes come across quite unexpected lines which for him were nothing more than trial runs or momentary lapses of the pen, but which put in a nutshell some idea found much later on in some other writer. Last winter in Lefortovo I chanced, for instance, on the following lines from a fragment written in 1821 (there is no indication who is speaking, probably a witch):

Silent! You are young, a silly pup,
And scarcely the one to trip me up!
Remember, 'tis not for money that we play,
But to while eternity away!

It struck me how similar this is in intonation to something by Khlebnikov.[1] It could easily have served as a very suitable epigraph to his long poem "A Game in Hell". But the most

[1] Velimir Khlebnikov (1885–1922): one of the Russian Futurist poets.

remarkable thing is the idea of aimlessly spending a whole eternity (as always with Pushkin, just one change of word in some set expression – here "to while away time" – can make an entire stanza sparkle), the notion of eternity as an inescapable, empty continuum of ever-lasting duration, yet passed within restricted spatial limits: this is the eternity where there is no time, only infinite confinement to a narrow space, which many years later Svidrigaylov[1] was to picture to himself as "a bath-house full of spiders". Or, as Dostoyevsky said in another, but similar connection: "There was a foreboding of eternity in a yard of space."

*

. . . How diminished people seem, once they are freed – only in our eyes, of course, not in their own; in their own eyes they are taking on a new lease of life; in ours they blur and fade away. It is not that they become strangers, but rather that they are no longer of our world, as though they were dead, and if this is the effect of such a minor transposition in space, how much more must it be true of those who depart for other lands or planets . . .?

This is probably why we do not envy those who leave. They are too remote, and appear unreal.

One is engulfed by the environment. I do not mean by a particular set of local interests, nor through becoming accustomed to a specific way of life, but because of something not subject to a normal explanation, to logic: a feeling of growing isolation and detachment.

Perhaps the monasteries were founded on this simple geometry of drawing a circle round people – all that was needed to create a place of retreat.

*

Tattoo markings on a shoulder:
"*Keep well and happy, Vasya my son!*"

*

[1] Svidrigaylov: character in Dostoyevsky's *Crime and Punishment.*

From letters sent to prisoners:
"*Besides, your guilt is apparently so great that there is nothing you can hope for.*"
"*And I am a young and vigorous woman.*" (Wife to husband)
"*Mother and uncle Sasha have had a capital set-to.*"
"*Uncle Kostya beat her so much she's lost the sight of her eyes.*"
"*Since your exact location has now been located.*"
"*He is big now, almost six years old.*"

*

Sometimes one gets the impression that time has stopped and we are flying inside a missile or an ark: it is a combination of immobility with the sensation of flight – not a bird's, but the earth's. This feeling is heightened by the wind. It flows round the hull and whistles in the ears as we plough on through time. It is very tiring to live in a constant wind.

*

When a wind like this is blowing, it somehow comes home to you that man has been *flung* into the world.

*

It is impossible to say anything about Avvakum;[1] he has told everything there was to tell about himself; he tumbled like a bear into his pit and left no room for anyone else.

*

In the old days people probably read much more slowly and put much greater meaning into words. Compared to the very close print of a later age, there were fewer letters to a page. A story which we would now consider short filled a whole volume, and this affected the reader's visual perception of the text and his understanding of it: it seemed much more considerable to him . . .

*

[1] see note on page 17.

A little square of lined paper is the barred window from behind which I peep out.

*

The large letters in children's books make for much more attentive reading. I remember how much – after growing old enough to read small print – I missed the large letters which had enabled me to read my earliest books with such intensity. I had a sense of loss, of deprivation – of going over to grown-up language.

*

A gem of a sentence from something written here:

"Far away, vaguely colouring the horizon, stood an orange-tinted tree." An entirely literary landscape as seen from behind the barbed wire through the eyes of a prisoner!

From the same piece of writing:

"Each man is born in only one copy and when he dies no one can take his place."

*

It could be that particles of art are strewn like grains of salt throughout our existence, and that the artist's job is to discover them, refine them and gather them together in their pure state. At any particularly unexpected turn of events we say: "as in a novel". This seems to admit the existence of a distinct lack of resemblance between our insipid everyday existence and everything that by its very nature is rare, extraordinary, "as beautiful as a picture". What survives from past ages – if they have deserved it – is mainly works of art. Is this not why the past so often seems to us more colourful than the present? In actual fact it was perhaps no more colourful at all. It is simply that it left some colour behind – the pure unadulterated salt of art.

Art is an attribute of individuals, of nations, of epochs and of humanity as a whole, like the instinct of self-preservation. It is inherent, too, in life generally, in existence as such. The colours of a flower, a peacock's tail, the rays of the setting sun – anything that singles out the species or the individual in defiance of the levelling action of death belongs to the realm of art. Is this perhaps what links art to sex and the continuation of the race? If so, is it possible that art is the bright mating plumage in which life decks itself out with a view to its self-propagation?

In ancient times art centred round the two extreme poles of human life: its prelude (weddings, spring games and dances) and its aftermath in death (wakes, traditions, burial chambers and other means of preserving human remains). In both cases the predominant idea is the overcoming of death. At the same time, festivities celebrating conception and memorials to the dead, while striking deep roots in a people's whole way of life, somehow stand above and beyond it. It is this sense of its being a thing apart from humdrum human affairs that makes art literally out of the ordinary and hence not an obligatory part of them – it is indeed easily dispensed with, as something extra given to us over and above our basic needs, a kind of luxury, ornament, plaything or keepsake, a mere bauble. But it is only this "surplus" that gives any permanency to our existence. Without it, vast hordes would have vanished without trace, like the Avars.[1]

The hardiest of all man's creations, art turns even death, its enemy, into an ally. Feeling responsible for the continuation of the race, art exists by creating itself because of, and under the threat of impending extinction. In his urge to record his surroundings before he vanishes, the artist casts a last, all-embracing look at the world. As though death were already close at hand, he is eager to remember for ever what he sees and the representation therefore becomes richer than the original. Art is created in order to overcome death, but in a state of intense expectation of it, in the lingering moments of farewell.

*

To all intents and purposes space no longer exists here and since time is constricted by the obstacle in its path it endeavours to expand by allowing the mind to race ahead to distant years,

[1] An ancient tribe akin to the Huns.

so that on waking up in the morning you always find that things are either nearer or further away than you expected; they simultaneously lag behind and outstrip themselves, attaining dimensions at once bigger and smaller than usual.

*

"*And so you grow like a weed.*"
"*Nothing grows out there except scorpions the colour of soap, and their sting is fatal to both man and beast.*"
"*If I could just get these weak hands of mine on him . . .*"
"*What I'd give to* listen to *the television and* watch *the radio.*"[1]

Life everywhere fuses into one single lamentation.

*

In Georgian 17th-century miniatures illustrating *The Knight in a Tiger Skin*[2] every scene shows the Sun and Moon in the guise of two faces looking down watchfully at what is going on. Ephemeral earthly events are thus placed in the perspective of a landscape which represents the whole world, and the action unfolds before us (in the very generous space allotted to it) in such a way that, as it slips out of sight, it does not swallow up the universe with it. Each picture is like the sea, where a storm on the surface co-exists with calm in the depths.

The past was aware that beyond time there is eternity and knew how to reveal its presence in every fleeting moment. It is not that time then went more slowly, but simply that any rapidly moving process, even in the subjective eye of the beholder, was seen to be submerged in something else of everlasting duration. Probably this has only now come home to me in a more than purely intellectual sense.

*

Recently I overheard someone say:

"My wife is angry at my long sentence."

The misery in these words, and what a long past they must

[1] Sic – an indication of how long the speaker has been in prison.
[2] An epic poem by Shota Rustaveli (12th cent).

have! The soul weeps: "My wife is angry at my long sentence."

*

What's wrong with having a bald head? People think there's something funny about it. But look at the little hairs still growing at the temples: come now, gentlemen, this is like the Alps, like the mountains of the Caucasus, whose covering of scrub gradually becomes thinner with each passing century! . . .

*

My cares are simple, my pleasures unsophisticated: yesterday, for instance, I cut my toe-nails.

10th October, 1966.

*

When information about yourself comes to you from outside you no longer recognize yourself.

*

Don't hurry, let us listen to the epic flow of time.

*

Sometimes you feel that you must be reading a book, and that once you have finished it and look around – life will be over.

It seems likely that time is perceived here in the same way as space. This is what makes it so mysterious: you seem to be walking through it, which is all the more peculiar in that you have no sense of motion but seem to be stuck in one spot, or even feel you are being carried backwards – and then all of a sudden you realize with a start that another year has passed and it is autumn again.

The Russian proverb which says that to go through life is not as simple as crossing a field does not apply here. A field is just what it is and we have to cross it.

*

The striking effect of a personal likeness to individuals in the Fayum portraits and those of a much earlier date in Egypt was dictated by the need to assure a future place of residence for the departing soul. These portraits give the co-ordinates of the soul's departure and resurrection, and serve as a guide so that it should not lose its way. Furthermore, apart from their resemblance to the faces of living individuals, they manifest the aloofness of the soul in flight as it hovers uncertainly, wondering where to alight, and how to establish its identity.

The physical exterior of the face, including all the biographical and psychological information imprinted on it, does not itself retain the attention, but lets you straight through to those depths of contemplation in which all are sunk after death. You do not here have that feeling of confronting a blank wall, a final unsought and unchallengeable judgement, as in portraits of the realist school, where the living face is trained on you like a gun, forcing you into an unwanted acquaintance with itself. Here likeness to a real person does not give you pause or stand in your way; instead of disturbing you, it serves as a window, an arrow pointing the way through an open passage, into which you happily run: the face draws you on, unlike the self-satisfied gaze of a 19th-century portrait which keeps you at arm's length with a cry of: "Go away, this is I!", or: "Look – here I am", in one way or another holding you back and barring your passage.

. . . And so, for the first time in the art of portraiture, realism was used not for self-display or self-admiration, but as a means of subsequently locating oneself in time and space; and the seriousness of this purpose sustained and justified it, gladdening one's heart at the sight of a man preoccupied by the imperative need to find his proper place in the hereafter.

But then the problem arises: what is a face, not in a portrait, but in real life? What is its purpose, and why do we run up to each other and peer into the other person's face like a mirror when we talk with him, cavorting in front of it and sizing it up, as if we wanted to enter? . . .

*

He licked his spoon like a dog and stuck it in his pocket. I licked mine too and also stuck it in my pocket.

*

"He pointed a gun at me and shouted 'Hands up', and I put my hands up, but I could see that his face was twitching with fear."

*

"That's what sort of eyes I have! And how do I know? Whenever I gave him this look of mine, it showed on his face as well: I could see it written all over him . . ."

*

"He opened his mouth as wide as it would go. His eyes were popping out of his head and for the first time in my life I saw a man turn white in front of my very eyes. His hair stood on end with such force that his cap fell off. It looked just as if somebody was pouring milk over his head and face."

*

Laughter from below and tears from above – two different ways of convulsing reality and never allowing it to settle down.

*

When we cry our lips are drawn downwards; when we laugh they are drawn upwards, but in both cases the whole face is contorted and twitches convulsively. Is this not a way of regaining our balance, of going back to a state of equilibrium we have momentarily lost and can recover only as a tight-rope walker recovers his: by swaying jerkily back and forth for a little while? And do not both the grimaces of weeping and the paroxysms of laughter, so similar to each other, serve as a defence mechanism, a pantomime enacted by our organism, which prefers to imitate the spasms of death rather than experience them in actual fact? These gymnastics of the facial muscles and the accompanying prophylactic tremors that shake the body are followed by relief. We calm the trembling of the soul by allowing free play to its physical integument – thus preventing an inner explosion by means of an outward disturbance . . .

*

Nature itself has adorned the head with a face.

*

"*Pity – messed my features up a bit!*" (After a fight – looking at a torn-out tuft of beard)

*

"*He has a moustache on his lip – transplanted from his pubic hair.*"

*

"*My life is written on my face!*"

His whole face was covered with scars and lumps. And his long nose ended in a forked tip divided into two bulbs.

*

A warder:
"*I can see what you are by your face.*"
– "*And if you take my clothes off, you'll see even more.*"

*

Tattoo marks:
On the chest (or shoulders) a stock phrase – "*There is no happiness in life*"
On the belly – "*Still hungry*"
On the legs – "*Tired*"
On the penis – "*Naughty*"

The complete paradigm of man!

And sometimes – as an extra touch – flowers are tattooed on the knee-caps.

*

Good nicknames:
Kolya the Bird and
Vitya the Wise

*

I find I can stand the bitter cold better than could have been expected. When I was free I used to suffer a lot from the cold in the early evening, when the sun is almost gone and there is a feeling of death in the heart. Here it is not so – the fact that there is no discrepancy between mood and environment is a great help. Somehow you put yourself in the right frame of mind from early morning to get through the whole day.

The view outside is quite majestic, and there is a broad glittering halo round the moon. The stars shatter into little splinters of ice, impossible to catch hold of. For some reason the spectacle cheers me up. You don't believe me? I really mean it!

19th December, 1966.

*

I often sit down to a letter not because I intend writing anything of importance to you, but just to touch a piece of paper which you will be holding in your hand . . .

*

All our troubles come from being for ever caught in a divided state: we want to do something, but cannot – or vice versa. We constantly hover between life and death; feelings and actions are only half-realized. With fear and bated breath we wait: will something happen or not? Expectations or dreams fail to materialize. But once you are over the dividing line, plunged into a situation in which, however hopeless it may be, there is no turning back, no chance of escaping or trimming your sails, then the wholeness of an existence that neither threatens further loss nor holds out hope of gain envelops you in a feeling of serene and trusting calm.

*

. . . And because of the bitter cold the dogs howled with almost human voices.

*

Part Two

The first day of the year has meanwhile changed to night, and now it is the morning of another very cold day.

2nd January, 1967.

"*Outside the cold is like in 1942.*"

*

Yesterday the frost reached 37° C and today pillars of smoke, supernatural as in a child's drawing, rise vertically into crimson skies and stay there for hours without dispersing. It looks like the eruptions of a volcano or a geyser, and our stoves could aptly be called furnaces.

*

He lies on his bunk studying outer space:
"*And the whole of our system is rushing into the constellation of the Capricorn! . . .*"

*

The little trucks that run about the factory have their names written on them in large letters, like ships: *Lolita, Gertrude, Suzanna,* and that sort of thing.

*

A Yoga walked barefoot on the snow and said mysteriously that everyone imagined he had boots on:

"You see, I have reached the third degree of initiation."

But everybody saw that he really had no boots on and laughed.

*

"God has given us time – to collect our thoughts . . ."

What extremes of cold for a soul that has escaped, naked, from the body. How icy it is. Imagine it: mouth wide open, swallowing the air, tons of air.

*

"Even dying is useful to a writer."

*

I am always distressed by the unproductivity of a life which goes up the chimney in smoke, leaving nothing but a tiny residue of sympathy for something that can be called "unprofessionalism", the inability to make thinking and working into a vocation fit only for seasoned veterans, the preservation of one's gifts at the level of a personal foible or youthful self-indulgence which has never raised its eyes from the ground or overcome the diffidence of childhood, so that life ends where it began, at the lowest rung, without titles or honours – like an artist who becomes a cobbler but never learns to make a pair of boots and smiles guiltily at his own fecklessness – sympathy, in a word, for an unformed quality which to the question: Who and what are you? can only answer: You see, I never . . .

*

Mercifully the snow distracts one a little. Ordinary winter weather has returned and the snow falls day and night. Somehow it makes you calmer to see it go on and on in spite of everything. What could it care? It just gets on with its job and comes down like manna from heaven.

*

Another pleasant thing about snow is that it falls quite soundlessly – like light.

*

"What does it matter what stake you're burned at when you've got to go and the door's open for you?"

*

A writer's word (the more one thinks of it) can be of any kind he likes. It does not have to be figurative, precise, concrete, grammatically correct or even literary. "What an apt epithet!" is the cry of the gushing amateur. Absoluteness is the only criterion. Once uttered, a word should be absolute.

*

You must live in such a way as not to eat anyone out of his ration.

*

The wood blocks are light and pleasant to handle, like loaves hot from the oven: they have a somewhat baked appearance and smell a little of kerosene – in fact it is the resin in them. What makes us sweat is mainly the vast quantity and the incredible speed at which we are expected to unload and stack them, catching them as they are tossed to us. It's rather like playing with a child's building blocks. I think Yegor[1] would find it interesting.

The factory as a whole gives the feeling of something real and useful, producing not the kind of metal parts we were making in the other camp, or the sort of thing associated in my mind with the abstract word "output", but honest-to-God chairs and cupboards, etc. It is quite intriguing to watch, like a conjuring trick: with masterly sleight of hand, ordinary logs are fed in at one end and emerge at the other as furniture, having passed through many stages of cutting and polishing along a conveyor formed by tubes with compressed air whishing through them . . .

It is worth considering what a factory like this represents. Such a large and complex undertaking can hardly have no kind of lesson for us, or be without its analogy in human and physical nature. What is the need for this process designed to ensure what is here called "chair production"?

A comparison with a living organism inevitably suggests itself: the circulation of the blood, digestion, the metamorphoses

[1] The author's son.

of things and substances passing through various embryonic stages. But the similarity ends once you see that all the changes are imposed from without and have nothing mysterious about them.

The process of furniture production is rather more similar to one of the well-known models of biological evolution – whether the Lamarckian one with its emphasis on the influence of the external environment (the drying shop[1] will do for a desert, and the power-saw with its water-cooler for the amphibious period), or Darwin's natural selection, by virtue of which the primitive plank is stripped of everything superfluous and non-viable in the species "chair". Viewed in this light, the theory of evolution has a hint of parody about it and arouses the suspicion that it originated under the influence of the factory, which inspired the basic analogies and suggested the idea of progress as a worldwide conveyor-belt . . .

12th January, 1967.

*

"*It's work fit for a king – you don't have to think.*"

*

"*It's all a load of bullshit – I'll never have any fun as long as I live.*"

*

A sudden question:

"*Andrey, what do you think of dragons?*"

"*?!*"

"*I mean: where did they all go to?*"

*

"*What did they mean by monkeying around with matter like that?*"

*

[1] i.e. in the furniture factory where the author worked.

"*I smoked it* (opium) *for two years and was well-nigh at the very gates.*"

*

"*Oh yes, God exists alright. If anyone says there's no God I'll poke his eyes out.*"

*

"*If there's any life after death, then a fellow like that should be hanged twenty times over when he gets to the next world.*"

*

About a shirt crawling with lice:
"*I have to live in it too!*"

*

About the Earth when they drop a hydrogen bomb on it:
"*It won't leave its orbit, of course, but it'll shake like the very devil.*"

*

How people go mad:
"*He was sitting with the rest of us, and talking, and all of a sudden he says in a whisper:*

'*Someone's come in through the door.*'

We look, but there's no one there – the door is shut. Again he says:

'*Someone's come in.*'

And then he jumped out of the window. Later they looked for him in the forbidden zone."[1]

*

. . . They described how they slaughtered a young pig, how it came out of the shed with a knife sticking in its heart, looked

[1] The forbidden zone in a camp is a system of wooden fences and barbed wire entanglements with strips of land between them ploughed up and raked (to show up footprints). Every camp is surrounded by a fairly wide forbidden zone. One of the ways to commit suicide in camp is to rush into the forbidden zone. A man who has entered it is shot at without warning . . . (*Author's note*)

round and went back to die, entirely in silence. Not a sound was heard throughout. Only the woman of the house standing at the window whispered to the butcher's wife:

'My legs are trembling. Let's swear and curse as loud as we can! . . ."

At this point in the story I could almost hear the flight of the Valkyries.

*

"*What are you in for, boy?*" (By way of striking up acquaintance)

*

Art, I think, does nothing but convert matter into spirit and vice versa – just like the plants which, in breathing and feeding themselves, create our soil and atmosphere by a continual process of transference up and down their stalks, making this labour into a mode of existence.

*

What do I see on someone's bedside table but a woman's fashion magazine! It was like an electric shock! And in dumb admiration I could only think: there's resourcefulness for you! . . .

*

"*All the same, women enjoy great popularity in this world!*"

*

Far, far away in distant Northern regions
I loved a girl – indeed I love her still –
It was a love so wild, so cruel,
I can't forget her and I never will.

Where are you now, my pretty darling girl?
Oh where, oh where, in what far distant camp?
I think of you; I dream of legs so shapely
That through the snow in natty *lapars*[1] tramp.

[1] Criminals' slang for "boots", evidently from the word *lapa* ("paw"). (*Author's note*)

The years go by, the hours and minutes vanish,
Your love for me will also vanish soon;
You will forget my kisses, and another
Will call you his beneath the silver moon.

You'll give yourself, not thinking what you're doing.
You are a woman, yes, but still a child.
Oh darling, dearest, oh my sweetest girl,
My grown-up child, even now you drive me wild!

Where are you now, my pretty darling girl?
Oh where, oh where, in what far distant camp?
I think of you; I dream of legs so shapely
That through the snow in natty *lapars* tramp.

Where are you now and who is now your lover?
The commandant or just a common thief?
Maybe by now they've killed you on the quiet,
Or shot you down 'while trying to escape'?

The years will pass, and happiness as well
– like your youth and beauty. To many men
You'll give your body with no thought of love –
And you'll forget how much I loved you then . . .

*

"*If you want to understand women read the* Decameron, *and then you'll know what kind of birds they are!*"

*

"*I don't know yet what a woman is. And my life is over. You may laugh, but it's a fact.*"

*

"*With women I used to be merciless!*"

*

"*I'm interested only in women and cars.*"

*

"I've knocked women out of myself."

*

During a visit (they had not seen each other for twenty years) a sister asks her brother, with the interest of a woman by now grown up and married:

"Is it true what they say: that they do it here with horses? . . ."

*

"That's the sort she was . . ."

*

"You can talk her into it in no time at all."

*

"Any little tart can make you feel like a schoolboy – it's not fear, but reverence . . ."

*

"We found a woman's voice as sweet as an apple, even coming out of a wireless set."

*

"Our cashier girl has pink knickers. I saw them in a dream!"

*

"Women of the Madame Bovary type are more to my taste."

*

"He cohabited with the cook."

*

"He dressed her in real style: to make everything show – the same as with mermaids."

*

"She was lying on top of me, rubbing against me. And would you believe it: a general's daughter she was!"

*

"They were all sorry later that I didn't fall in love with them."

*

"The girls really love me: I always let them have a puff on my cigarette afterwards."

*

"Only whores like a man who smokes in bed."

*

"Every woman has her idea of what she wants in life."

*

"She was more than I could have expected for the likes of myself. And in any case, I'd never have got mixed up with her if I hadn't been pushed into it by a friend. Pretty free and easy she was with everybody, as it turned out."

*

"And there she was, coming straight at me dolled up in those seductive clothes, smiling and showing all of her 32 teeth."

*

"I'll take someone with an officer's pips," she says, *"but you're no good to me."*

*

"I was intimate with a city woman."

*

"I met a beautiful lady of the night." (From a song)

*

"One of these dames was real beautiful, I'm telling you quite seriously . . ." (If you talk "seriously" about a "dame" – a beautiful one at that – it has to be specially pointed out!)

*

"I looked at the dame and saw she was a real doll! But right then I had no time for dames or the flicks because I was on the run . . ."

*

"In fact it was all over a dame, if you ask me: he was done in because of his doll of a wife." (About Pushkin)

*

"Nothing but beautiful words should be coming out of her mouth, but she swears like a trooper!"

*

After swallowing some coffee:
"Just as if one of these little Mordvin[1] *girls was tiptoeing over my chest in slippers!"*

*

"She's a girl with an all-round education."

*

"A real honey, she is – you can screw her any time."

*

"If there'd been a girl there who could talk about serious matters, I would soon have found a common language with her."

*

"I don't want to lead her up the garden path: how do I know what will happen to me tomorrow?"

*

"It just comes over you sometimes – with one of those women-engineers, or a virgin, or some little whore . . . you go down on your bended knees and say: 'Will you marry me . . .?'"

*

[1] A small people related to the Finns. The camp where the author was held is in the region inhabited by them.

"I have never in all my life used bad language in front of a woman."

*

"And some fascinating woman will be kissing me on the lips! . . ."

*

"Any woman will give in if you threaten her with a knife. But whether she'll play along as well is another matter."[1]

*

"I added her to my collection." (About a widow)

*

"I had sexual intercourse with her."

*

"They cracked her hairy safe." (A group rape)

*

Nobody here believes in overstraining himself while unloading heavy objects, and the common saying is:
"It'll lie down itself – like a woman."

*

There was a woman, they say, who had "Welcome" tattooed on her belly.

*

"I can turn really nasty. I get sort of attached to dames. I know she sleeps around, but I'll go back to her all the same and stay around for a couple of weeks or so. I tattooed an airplane on her belly so she could never get married. But now I'll tattoo something even more peculiar on her . . ."

*

[1] There is a veiled reference here to the questionable loyalty of the nation to the Soviet government, which commands loyalty only by force. (*Author's explanation*)

The erotic is in fact exotic: a man with no trousers on just looks so much more out of the ordinary than one decently dressed. This is the point of the whole style ("astride the governor's daughter", "Africa in a bath-house") for which I was accused of "pornography": it opens the door to fantasy and excites only wonderment – like a conjuring trick.[1]

A tattoo mark: in front – an eagle tearing Prometheus's breast with his beak; behind – a dog screwing a lady in some bestial way. The two sides of a medal. The façade and the back. Light and darkness. Tragedy and comedy. Also a skit on one's own feats. And the closeness of sex to laughter – and death.

*

A naked lady in a grand-looking hat sits mounted on a skull, as on a globe – at the sight of this drawing tattooed on someone's back I felt that it must have been intended as a metaphorical representation of the man's mind.

*

Conversation with someone about to leave:

"Why the . . . should I go to the Tretyakov Gallery?"[2]

"To see the dames without any clothes on – look alive, they do."

Museums have now achieved the same status for sightseers as shops or the zoo: they are places to go and have a look, successors to the old fairground peep-shows in the best sense, and as regards their educational value.

*

Well, now, how, at the present moment – I ask myself – would you describe a woman's nakedness? I mean, can you seriously imagine and see a nude?

[1] The reference is to phrases and scenes out of the author's works: *Lyubimov* ("astride the governor's daughter") and *At the Circus* ("Africa in a bath-house"), which the Soviet press called "pornographic". The sense of the whole passage is that such scenes interested the author for their exotic, imaginative quality and not for their eroticism. This exotic quality the author later (in camp) perceived in the tattoo marks with which many criminals adorn themselves.

[2] Main art gallery in Moscow.

. . . It was like a rush of blood to the head, when you just see a black wall in front of your eyes, but then the blackness, the stunning darkness dissolves, leaving a beautiful girl cast up on a beach, and she is dazzlingly white, white to the point of taking your breath away.

*

Someone musing aloud:
'*I just don't understand why* it *should have been given such a rude name . . .*"

*

May not all the scurrility, the crudeness in our sexual terminology be a desperate revolt, an attempt to break loose – because we are all so submissive to it, incapable of escaping or forgetting it, and so try to exorcize it and frighten it away (Out of my sight! Away! I'm not afraid of you!), while in fact we remain all too dependent on it?

A quotation from somewhere, it came to me in a dream:

"Zander turned pale at the thought of his duty to copulate with almost every girl who had just happened to remain alone with him.

'They all want something from me' – he said, blinking nervously."

Question: What if sex is a diabolical way of reaching the gates of paradise? A poisoned ersatz for what we have lost? In that case may not the substitute enable us to imagine the forgotten source, to reconstitute the sublime original from the debased imitation? And is not the whole realm of sex beautiful only in so far as it is a distortion of that lost image (a distortion it may be, but of *that* image all the same!). If this is so, recognizing it for the parody it is, let us try to recapture the approximate style and mystery of the original – if the substitute throws us into such rapture and terror, what effect must *that* have had?! Let us use every cunning to seek out the truth, shuddering as we sense to what low depths we are confined, and what the spirit must be like if mere flesh has such power . . .

*

One of my latest acquisitions is that I feel you more and more tangibly, like my own body – I feel that you are spun out of me, cell by cell, almost like Yegor, and even more closely perhaps, because it is not a question of heredity, but of something simpler and more direct – as with a plant.

Someone has recently been telling me – apropos of a theory of genetic purity – that a wife becomes similar to her husband not just figuratively, but quite literally, and not merely because of his spiritual influence on her, but because the very tissue of her physical being is gradually replaced by his molecules. In this sense carnal love is considerably deeper and more complex than one imagines – the husband begets the wife, permeating her through and through with his own self, so that finally they do indeed become "one flesh".

This is no doubt why the excitingly exotic side of marriage gradually gives way to the building of a nest, a family burrow, where the blood relationship becomes so intimate that it takes on the aspect of suckling, with the roles of infant and mother combined in a single person.

*

A silent old man, who has renounced the vanity of this world, clasping his hands, and overwhelmed by his memories: "Ah, wives, wives – they may have the kindness to lie with you every now and then! . . ."

*

In hospital:
"*So he*[1] *starts screaming his head off: 'Have you come here to look for a wife or to get treatment?!' and I say: 'I'm only made of flesh and blood'* . . ."

*

"*Let's kind of get married!*"

*

[1] Evidently a doctor in the camp hospital, reproving a prisoner for flirting with the nurse.

"Marriage is the end of the road."

*

"So then I got married to a widow – her husband was killed on a tractor."

*

"I had two wives and three sons . . ."

*

"Women are cleverer about these things than we are – what are you afraid of? – I ask. 'I am afraid you'll throw me over', she says."

*

"But mathematics I loved terribly – like a wife."

*

"What counts most in life? To my way of thinking your own happiness comes first and then your children. Not your wife – your children."

*

"She has two children. He turned out[1] *one of them. The other she got on the side."*

*

"She has a house in Rostov and a husband who doesn't drink."

*

"I was lucky to get quite a good husband, I do admit. I'd even agree now, she writes, to having one half as good. True, he was a pretty heavy drinker."

*

1 The word in the original means to fashion with a plane, like a carpenter, and hence has obvious sexual overtones.

"*My wife went off to work in the public baths.*" (The ultimate in degradation)

*

"*And the entire structure of my family life is broken!*"

*

"*Is this your little girl?*"
"*God knows! My wife writes and says she is.*"

*

A four-year-old boy – to girls a little older:
"*But haven't you got some kind of a daddy? . . .*"

*

To someone back from a labour camp:
"*You know, daddy, I was very afraid it wouldn't really be you who would come back and they would only tell me it was.*"

*

A scene from the past. Somewhere in Siberia prisoners sentenced under article 58[1] are being released after review by a commission. Women who have swarmed in from nearby villages line up outside the guard-house – to offer themselves as wives and to choose husbands. The security officer drives away a local whore: "This is not for your sort!" Just like trading at a market – all very prim and proper, no jokes or giggles, a due awareness of the importance of the business in hand. Prisoners sentenced under article 58 have a terrific reputation – real bargains. Some of them may stay behind, perhaps. A period piece, you might say, from the ancient Russia of Kievan times.

*

[1] Article 58 (now article 70) of the Criminal Code of the RSFSR covered "counter-revolutionary" offences. The scene described refers to the time after Stalin's death when political prisoners were rehabilitated by special commissions and allowed to return home. Some, who no longer had homes or families to return to, remained and settled down in the area where the camp was situated.

In the women's compound:

"Let me wash your shirt for you."

A phrase like this, when spoken in a pleading kind of way, as though begging for a favour, creates the impression of being the starting point of family life – love and the whole business of setting up house together begin with a shirt . . .

*

Sex can be construed in yet another way, this time with a plus sign to its credit: as a manifestation of trust. What can be more trusting than such intimacy between people who were total strangers only the day before and now give each other what they normally show to no one? . . .

A woman warder to a prisoner:

"Come to me when you are released. I'll take your trousers off myself." Yet he will be released – and she knows it – only in eleven years' time at the earliest.

Here we have a kind of destitute generosity with all defences down ("whatever I have is yours – there, take it!"), a devil-may-care impulse to establish kinship with a pauper spurned by all – as though to say: I am not greedy, what I have I share, and there's nothing more to it – like two people who meet on the road and just sit down to have a smoke together. What else can we offer each other? . . .

In general sex is nothing but a kind of weeping by the waters of Babylon.

*

. . . For some reason a man's private parts are more visible.

A man may also bear the additional badge of shame of being a Jew.

Every man is a Jew.

*

. . . I know I repeat myself and keep getting stuck in the same groove. I may say in my defence that a text, as a spatial entity, should be neither a static platform nor a tape moving in one direction only. It should be reminiscent, rather, of the circles made by a stone dropped into water. Antinomic concepts such as "winter", "sun", "women", "books", etc., impel words to radiate outwards in successive waves, creating eddies of speech round eternal enigmas which exercise us constantly and against which our reason washes in vain, always ebbing away again, powerless to take by assault things that are ultimately paradoxical (and would otherwise have only formal significance). These enigmas thus play much the same role as irony, never allowing the world to become set in a rigid posture of lifeless uniformity, to stare at us stony-faced and address us always in the same loud, monotonous way, but modulating our response to it so that our words seem to be in constant flux, first moving outwards and then returning to source, until at last it dawns on us: it is not our speech flowing back and forth, but the elusive reality beyond constantly returning to us to draw the strength needed for continued existence.

*

Two writers, Hoffman and Dickens, have shown to us that humour is love. They have revealed to us that God takes a humorous view of mankind. In humour there is both tolerance and encouragement: "Bravo!"

*

In the very name of Dante there is the sound of the Inferno: a palindrome effect.[1]

*

My impression is that Dostoyevsky's *Poor People* arose by phonetic analogy with *Dead Souls*[2], and by way of a reaction against it. "Not dead souls", Dostoyevsky seems to protest (getting hot under the collar as he does so), "but poor people!"

*

[1] The first two letters of Dante's name, if reversed, make *ad* ("hell") in Russian.

[2] Novel by Gogol, who was a strong influence in Dostoyevsky's early work.

It is always pleasant when, quite by chance, words or sayings to which we had attached no particular significance in ordinary conversation suddenly appear in a new light, so that we are astounded at how apt and pregnant with meaning they are. "You too, Brutus!", for instance, sounds so much more impassioned in Russian because Brutus is not far from "brother".[1]

We speak of "dying" of hunger, of fright, or of boredom, but this hyperbolic use of the word only comes close to the literal truth when we speak, in the novelists' hackneyed phrase, of "dying" of love. In love (understood as the set of primary psychological symptoms which we regard as its unmistakable manifestation), we are overcome by a rapturous urge to self-obliteration. We forget and reject our own selves, becoming filled with the light and presence of the object of our love, passing into a condition of weightlessness, losing our bearings and consciousness in a way which must somehow be akin to the sensation of dying. Our physical self on these occasions behaves accordingly: we sigh as if the soul were really about to depart, the heart "sinks", and the feeling of elation goes hand in hand with the prostration of an organism which seems ready to melt away as it approaches the source of light. I do not exist. I am you. "Oh, I am dying!"

*

An aphorism:

"If a woman has given a man her heart, she will give him her purse as well." (Balzac)

Good old Balzac!

13th March, 1963.

*

Art is a meeting place – of the author with the object of his love, of spirit with matter, of truth with fantasy, of a pencil line with the body's contours, of one word with another, and so forth. These encounters are rare and unexpected. Out of sheer joy and surprise ("You? – You?") both sides go into

[1] The Russian for Brutus is *Brut* and for brother *Brat*.

raptures and clap their hands. This clapping of hands is what comes across to us as "art".

*

It is difficult to say anything definite about the writer's craft. It is like love – which you carry with you everywhere and take along when visiting friends.

*

In a fairy-tale about beauty and love there is the phrase: "He was not himself any more." We long to be not ourselves. This is what matters most.

*

Cato, according to Plutarch, said: "The soul of a man in love lives in another's body." Probably said in disapproval, this was intended to suggest that love always implies a transference, a dislocation of one's own personality. One cannot, unfortunately, do without one's "I". It is the kernel, the essential condition and form of existence, of identity; it is the instinct for the continuation of the species, the measure of things, the basic reference point by virtue of which everything else provisionally stays in place and remains itself. Love does not believe in this and disturbs the order of the world for the sake of union and mutual interchange. Love is formless and it builds bridges, conceiving all things not in my likeness, but in yours.

*

"I" is exclusive, "I" is always exclusive – in the sense of excluding third parties: there is you and there is I.

*

Someone informs me as if it were the greatest cause for wonder:

"When I was a child I thought I'd never die! . . .", and he believes that he and he alone was granted this awareness which was really perhaps – who knows? – a premonition, an intimation, or a promise . . . The initial response is condescending pity: "Don't be silly, everyone has that feeling, particularly in childhood!", but then the thought occurs that he is essentially right: there really was a compact with him alone, and he received a guarantee: *you* will not die. Subconsciously everyone carries this pledge in his soul, and in fairy-tales it is honoured.

*

"You, too, were 'I' at one time! . . ."

*

Before execution by shooting or an attempt to escape some people think they will survive, that the bullet will miss them, or pass through them harmlessly. Someone says: "For *such* people there is no end, only a door: it will open at the last moment and they will not be killed – they will escape." (However, one man asked them not to aim at his face when shooting: a shot in the face is final, a death *with no way out*. The face is the soul's only exit?)

Perhaps the instant of supernatural stress, when a man "sees all", is like a key which unlocks the door, opening it just enough for the body's size and shape – enabling him to slip through before he has time to die . . . "I am the door."[1] (An opposite case: before his execution someone blinded himself – so as not to see death, like hiding under a blanket, or like the boy who clutched the leg of another condemned man as he was being led away: "Uncle[2] Shota, don't let them take me!" The other man told the story later . . .)

*

"When I first heard of death I didn't want to live".

*

"Thirteen times I shot at him. Point-blank. But the Lord must have protected him so well that he got up and walked away."

[1] c.f. John X, 9.
[2] Uncle: mode of address used by Russian children speaking to adults.

"*The Lord is taking me away out of love for me, I thought. So I shouldn't commit yet more sins.*" (Before facing the firing squad)

*

The fortune-teller looked at the water and said:
"*He will live . . . But it would be better if the Lord took him.*"

*

Talk about a probable transfer to another camp. An old man: "*I've reached the age, young man, when I think of a different journey.*"

*

"*He gave rein to his imagination and put up a note on the barbed wire of the forbidden zone: 'Do not fear death'!*"

*

Let us suppose a stranger tells you the story of an execution by shooting, and the way the narrative is developed implies that *he* is the man who was shot, but he does not finish his tale and simply goes away, leaving you guessing who it was you were speaking to.

Probably the big events of his life are behind him, and the present is merely their reflection in the twilight and semi-oblivion of prison, a memory of the past existence, the real one by which in effect he still lives and about which one does not ask and is not supposed to ask, but which furnished the cause, the starting point of this secondary life, giving endless food for thought to a man as he perhaps experiences in his personal destiny the full measure of our fall as a whole – and it could be that this mode of existence is the only right one, because it gives meaning to our dismal present by relating it to the big events that led up to it. (But one may well ask what sort of a conversation there can be, if every man goes on all the time about the main thing in his own experience, so that any dialogue grows into a repetition of grievances, addressed by force of habit to the world at large, a demonstration of one's single-minded capacity to live by the memory of the "main" event in one's life, and to classify and explain everything by reference to it.)

. . . A neighbour's laugh at night, a choking laugh under the blanket (I thought at first he was masturbating) on the bunk above me – by day he lives quietly, absorbed in his big "main" thoughts: the obtuse face of an idiot, and then such a full, meaningful laugh at night . . .

Hence, too the fear of release, of the free life "outside", purposeless and quite "empty" in the eyes of one who has experienced fullness. "But think of the women?!", people say to him. But what does he care about women? He will just keep his peace, smiling occasionally to himself. Lonely wanderers with past lives, silent because what actually have they to do with all "*this*"?

*

We came into this world in order to understand certain things: very few, but exceedingly important ones.

*

The man's face is incised, like the palm of his hand, with a fine mesh of extremely intricate lines. He is ensnared in history, weeping over the unreal life prescribed for him to the end of his days in the course of his interrogation.[1] Where should he turn? It is an existence between the lines of history. Who will give him back his prehistoric, ordinary, living face?

*

What capacity for thought and ability to plumb its ultimate depths they have, these creatures plucked out of life and put behind bars. The transcendental invades their minds and personality inevitably retreats into the background.

Indeed these are no longer people but open expanses. Not characters, but spaces, fields. Once he is in contact with the infinite, a man's natural limits are effaced. The biographical

[1] i.e. during which he was induced to "confess".

approach – indeed the very idea of it must be thrown to the winds. Let every man pass beyond the bounds of his own life story! Rely on a superficial notion of character and the ground will give way under you – personality is a pit, scarcely strewn over with the brushwood of psychology, of temperament, of everyday habits and behaviour. You blunder into this pit as you step forward to greet a stranger who comes up to you.

*

And what if the upturned soles of Buddha's feet in the Lotus Position are simply another projection of the hands joined in prayer? . . .

*

Sometimes, by their very intonation, people seem to be trying to reassure themselves that they have really existed, as though, if they failed to mention a certain particular about themselves (such as an address), they might never have been.

"*I was living in Moscow* – 28 *Kropotkin Street.*" This is said with great vehemence.

*

"*In my dream I saw a photograph of myself.*"

*

If we can dream in our sleep of a street with people walking in it, there must be plenty of room within us, as in a whole city, and our soul must be so spacious that we can wander through it and go down a staircase to the sea, and sit down on the shore and look.

*

We know our soul better than others do, and it occasionally gives the impression of being like a heap of worms or a pile of garbage. Only on looking around us are we reassured: not everyone is like us! By comparison with the decorous exteriors of the people round about, our inner squalor, of which we are only too well able to judge, is so staggering as to seem incredible and it forces us to turn away from our own selves and emulate the more reassuring outward appearance of friends and neighbours. Looking at each other we take courage, as it were, and try to conform to the model presented by our faces.

*

If you gather together in your mind all the grief you have caused to others and concentrate it on yourself as if those others had inflicted it all on *you*, and imagine as vividly as you can your own jealous pride wounded on all sides by your own malice – you will then understand what hell is.

*

"*The Devil does not need everyone. He only needs some people. He needs me. But I will not give in to him.*"

*

The camp Commandant:
"*You're an odd one, aren't you? Praying to God all the time, but coming to see Satan to ask for your parcel?!*[1] . . ."

*

A peasant says to a cat:
"*See how good I am? There – I've brought you something* . . ."

(Is this why we all do a bit of good? And why salvation cannot come from doing good alone?)

*

"*I only have to look at a wall for five minutes to tell that it has more evil in it than some other one . . . But I still haven't found out how to tell good.*"

*

[1] i.e. a parcel sent to the prisoner from home.

The Russian Apocrypha have a story about how the Devil inflicted seventy wounds on Adam with a cudgel but the Lord turned them inwards – "And He turned all his afflictions into him". ("The Story of how God created Adam".) If we pursue this further, does it not suggest an analogy for the banishment from Eden, and then for the torments of hell after death, when the soul, turned inside out, is plunged into the atmosphere of its own inner life, which will henceforth constitute its physical milieu, its environment? It thus creates its own climate in hell, and the punishment for sins, contained in the sins themselves, can be seen as something entirely material.

*

"*This insolent death* . . ."
"*This deathly man* . . ."

*

Fairy-tales interest me as a manifestation of pure art, perhaps the very first instance of art detaching itself from real life, and also because – like pure art – they enhance reality, remaking it in their own likeness, separating good from evil, and bringing all fears and terrors to a happy conclusion.

*

Is the wedding in the final scene of a fairy-tale really only an illusion meant to sweeten fate? It is more likely to be the actual, perfectly real denouement that finally comes about after the nightmarish story has reached its end and faded away . . .

*

"*God, life is hard.*"
"*And how did you think it was going to be?*"

*

Pain is needed for the complete, liberating feeling of happiness which it leaves behind when it goes.

*

. . . And devils were as common then as frogs in a bog.

*

Man is a communicating vessel joined up to God.

*

"*What I am grateful to the Lord for is that I've never killed anyone in the whole of my life. And the number of opportunities I had! . . .*"

*

"*I have only one relative: God . . .*"

*

In the night he hears a chorus of voices – of the spirits of the earth, perhaps, or of all the numberless tribes and peoples scattered over it. And as he listens he feels that if he were suddenly to understand but a single word out of this chorus, he would go mad. To understand is to go mad.

*

With what sort of a voice will we scream in hell? Not with our own – if even in an epileptic fit a man screams in a completely unrecognizable voice.

*

. . . And the coughing of two old men in the barrack resembles a dialogue. After listening to them for a while a third one joins in.

Or it could be that there was just one man, coughing as he talked to himself in two different voices – in a hoarse and fearsome one when asking questions, and in a calm, natural one when answering them.

*

And then there are also wall clocks which have a cat's head made of tin – the eyes go back and forth, ticking away with wearisome regularity.

30th June, 1967.

*

. . . This point about the all-absorbing role played by the plot is true of Dostoyevsky, and of the novel in general. The author rouses our curiosity, lures us into his domain, into which we tumble as though rolling down a slope, and by the time we collect our wits, it's too late: we're caught! A novel is a trap, a maze into which we are drawn by the plot until we are swallowed up by the narrative, becoming its prisoner and confidant. Is not this why beguiling stories of travel and love – with a wedding to be expected at journey's end – are so much favoured by novelists? This scheme of things – the story with an enticing bait at the finish – shows the novel to be an imaginary territory which you are forced to cross if you wish to know what happens at the end. But "what runs down the whiskers is not food for the belly", as we are slyly informed at the wedding feast in Russian fairy-tales – to bring home that our presence there is illusory, and to give the cue for the sudden disappearance of the author who, having let us briefly smack our lips over the long-awaited bait, is already beckoning us to a new wedding in another fairy-tale he is about to concoct.

*

It would be interesting to write composite sentences of which the first half was in one man's style and the second in another's, accommodating both into its overall structure and development, carrying them like two people on a seesaw, so that their co-ordinated movement encompassed a broader ambit than is generally possible. This is the charm of the artless "hanging participle" in such phrases as: "arriving at the station, my hat flew off". In fact, surely the function of language is to combine different perspectives not by stringing things out in a straight line, but by allowing the whole to grow and ramify, obedient only to its own whim? . . .

Speech must be trusted to lead the way itself – like the sculptor's hand as it carves wood following the grain, not knowing what will be achieved in the process, what knot (or word) may suddenly stick out and deflect it, causing a change of direction and structure.

*

"My soul tells me by sheer instinct."

*

"I am telling you in all honesty of soul! . . ."

*

"All you could do was quietly cross yourself in your soul and carry on."

*

"Me, interested in a cat?! I haven't even got it in my soul to live."

*

"The soul has forebodings of everything, but it can't actually foretell the future."

*

"What have you put that sweater on for? I can see by your eyes you want to escape, but I can't shoot – my soul won't let me. Take that sweater off!" (Old camp guard)

*

And our souls, as they fly up to heaven, will turn away from us.

*

. . . In the burial grounds of our Northern Neolithic Age children are never found – only skeletons of adults. Apparently, children were buried in a different way – just as until recent times among some Northern tribes dead babies were wrapped in cloth and birch-bark and put in the hollow of a tree or else hung up on its trunk or branches. We also know that according to Tungus[1] beliefs their ancestral spirits lived inside roots, while the top of the Universal Tree constituted the reservoir of the people's collective soul, ensuring the replacement of

Native Siberian tribe

each passing generation. May this have meant that children, since they had not had time for a full life, were despatched by way of compensation, not into the earth, but by a direct, privileged route – via the tree – to heaven, in order to be born once again as quickly as possible? . . . What a link with rain and dew, which evaporate and then soon fall again! What an unbroken circulation of souls in the air! . . .

*

I resemble a cockroach – not when it runs, but when it sits, rooted motionless to one spot, vacant and aloof, staring fixedly at one inscrutable point.

*

An epithet should not be too direct, but rather slightly out of focus in relation to the thing defined, not merely defining it, but also placing it on an oblique plane of meaning and hence directing the attention this way and that. The epithet's imprecision thus creates something of a flurry round the object, blurring its outlines in such a way that one feels its living connection and continuity with its surroundings. An epithet is required to look both out of the side and the back of its head, chasing several hares at once. Its effect on the observer must be to make his eyes dart from side to side.

*

It is interesting when your mind is restricted to a minimum of resources – when you have neither the books you need, nor the strength or means to consult them. All you have is a few lines, or one little picture, or a single musical phrase – and you immerse yourself in it and clean forget all about yourself.

*

Where does it eventually get to, this all-pervasive particle "I"?

*

And a tender voice will say:

"You don't exist. You understand – you don't exist! Forget everything. Sink into oblivion."

And I shall fall asleep.

*

"*I longed to work. Because it is like being asleep when you work. Because I don't exist when I work.*"

*

Strange: a man is entirely happy when he forgets about himself and no longer belongs to himself. Alone with himself, he is bored. One ousts the self by work, play, love, wine, etc. In our happiest moments we have no memory of ourselves, we vanish from our own sight. Sleep without dreams is a synonym for Nirvana (Lermontov: "I would like to forget myself and fall asleep!"). Thus moths fly into the fire. Oh, let me vanish in the splendour of Thy glory!

*

The "I" is a particle which, while endlessly crying out 'Give! Give!', at the same time searches mutely for a way to get rid of itself. The personality hovers in an unstable balance between life and death.

*

"*Even in his sleep he was all the time trying to prove to someone that he was not guilty.*"

*

The kind of dreams we have!

"I often fly in my dreams. In the morning you climb up on the roof, your head spins and you think: 'Now I'll fly'."

"And I always start guessing in my dreams how long I shall be kept here for. But every time I wake up at that point."

"You know, Andrey, I've seen both God and the angels in my dreams. Once I saw a great big fellow with a grey beard and a stick walking through the air. And he was driving a flock of sheep in front of him in the sky. He leant over to me and said something I couldn't make out. 'Remember it', he said, and then drove his sheep on. Soon he was far away, like a little cloud. Next, an angel flew by – little wings it had, just like in a picture. It flew up to me and asked: 'Did you understand what he said to you?' 'No', said I. 'All right, you'll understand it later.'"

(In this story, the usual obscene swearwords are dropped, without any effort, as a matter of course. There are marvellous stories of dreams about devils too, but these are told with plenty of foul language.)

*

"When you're asleep you don't sin, and don't swear . . ."

*

"In my dream I saw a sniper, shooting at me."

*

"I dreamed that two people were coming at me with knives, from either side. There was nowhere I could hide, so I flew away!"

*

"In my dream I was chased by a hermaphrodite woman I know."

*

Script for a film put together out of a dream sequence: A funeral and a coffin. We say our last farewells and set off home. In the bus who should we see but the dead man – alive and kicking. I don't know what to think. I am just about to speak to him, when what do I see, as I put my head out of the window, but clouds billowing up from under the wheels of the bus like smoke . . .

*

"I shall haunt you like a spectre,
I shall trouble you in your sleep."
(From a song)

*

In my dream a white hen gave me a shelled egg it was holding in its foot, and I ate it.

*

In my dream I saw myself from behind – a tiny little man.

*

There was nothing for it but to wait and hope for the gym shoes I had dreamed about.

*

Someone told us about a dream seen by a Latvian serving a 25-year sentence. In the dim and distant past he had been an athlete, and he dreamed he was a young man again, taking part in a 25-kilometre marathon race. He had a feeling of great physical well-being, almost of intoxication. But just as he had run half the course, the umpire suddenly appeared out of the blue: "Enough! It's time you took a rest." The Latvian tried to refuse, saying he wasn't a bit tired. The umpire gently but firmly insisted: "Take a rest!" His late wife was there too, and she joined in, saying: "That will do! Enough!" Next morning the former runner had no sooner told his dream to his friends than he dropped dead of heart failure. He had precisely 12 years and 6 months to go before the end of his sentence.

*

Strange that every time I wake up I turn out to be myself. What does this depend on?

*

Would I agree to go to sleep for the years I am here in order somehow to shorten my sentence and make it easier to bear?

Probably not. It is not something to be skimmed over lightly, but must be lived out, slowly and deliberately, step by step through every single day, one after the other . . .

*

Sleep is the watering place of the soul to which it hastens at night to drink at the sources of life.

*

In sleep we receive confirmation – I cannot find another, more fitting word. We receive confirmation that we must go on living.

*

How good that all people sleep, that we all have the gift of sleep and that after the follies of the day, we can plunge into it, our eyes protected by coverings of skin, and set off swimming in this ocean, together with all other creatures, and come up again washed clean by the miracle which nightly spirits us away, only to throw us back on the shore with the gentle reminder: Go and live, live again! . . .

*

We drown out that Voice with our own clamour, crying: "Help me!"

And it answers: "I am with you. I am with you, I say. Don't you hear?"

*

How amazing is God's dominion over us – total and despotic, yet painless and imperceptible; granting freedom without end, yet not allowing us to deviate by a single step from the predestined path. A King most manifest who never shows himself, who encompasses all and lets it be thought that He does not exist.

*

. . . Clouds producing the semblance of a drama charged with meaning.

*

And I understood: henceforth it will never leave me. Eschatology, the Revelation in my boot[1] – I march on, happy as can be.

How hard it is, how sweet, to occur only sporadically, to live in hope – in hope there is always doubt: will it get through the grille and the nets, up the fish ladders and over the dam? Always the sad sense of unfulfilment because of what gets stuck and fails to cross to the other side. How hard for it to be the keeper of its own wealth: the keeper always gets the blame.

*

We do not write a phrase – it writes itself, and all we do is to clarify, as far as we are able, the accumulated meaning concealed within it.

*

. . . Perhaps genuine art always reveals incapacity, lack of skill. When an author does not know what the "rules" are, he starts writing in a way all his own, at variance with the accepted models. In any event, there is occasionally something bordering on downright incompetence about works of genius.

*

Nothing is worse than when the words advertise the subject-matter. Words must not shout. Words must keep silent.

*

When the rains pour down endlessly, you can begin to feel quite cosy – not sitting in the warm, but actually getting frozen and wet through, and experiencing a strange lost sensation,

[1] 'It' in this and the following paragraph refers to art. The words 'Eschatology, the Revelation in my boot' refer to the hand-written pages of the Revelation which the author kept inside one of his boots, as the Bible, both Old and New Testament, is forbidden in labour camps. (*Author's explanation*)

enlivened only slightly by tenderness – for whom or what is not clear; perhaps for this raw damp, for this downpour so oblivious of people. Let it rain.

27th September, 1967.

*

Someone went up to an aspen tree:
"*Still trembling? Ever since* then? *Well, go on then, go on.*"[1]

*

A clairvoyant at an open-air market, to a woman:

"Be on your way! I shall say nothing to you."

Two hours later she was run over by a lorry.

He told a young fellow where his wife had a birth-mark (no one, of course, apart from the young fellow himself, could have known about it), and to a girl he said:

"Once you tried to hang yourself, and once you tried to drown yourself. Don't worry, next time you'll manage it."

*

I noticed that my shadow walked beside me, but moved independently of me.

*

"*There seems to be something unclean and shameful about mirrors.*"

*

Why are people so fond of fixing a mirror shaped like a river or lake beneath pictures and photographs, thus duplicating them with a reflection which is usually thought to be more picturesque and almost more vivid than the original? . . . Anything paired with its image in a mirror or in water appears to be much more intensely itself. It is not divided in two, but doubled, multiplied by itself. Juxtaposed in this way with its own illusory projection, it seems all the more complete and self-contained.

[1] Allusion to the legend that Judas hanged himself on an aspen tree and that its leaves have trembled ever since.

The important thing about a reflected image (besides the fact of being reversed) is that it may ripple in a breeze or mist over, flow and breathe, gleam in the dark or from the bottom of a pool. The reflection is, so to speak, the object's light, its psyche, its idea (in the Platonic sense), and once invested with it, the object rises up even more solidly on the dry land above. The mirror image confirms and identifies it, at the same time introducing a hint of forlornness, of longing, of the unattainable beyond – that is playing the same role in relation to the real world as the legendary City of Kitezh.[1]

*

. . . Anna Akhmatova's poetry resembles a pond or a lake edged with trees, or a mirror in which everything seems less real, yet stands out in sharper relief than in actual life. A bright sky and glittering clouds are reflected, becoming brighter still, in a dark and haunted pool, but on the surface there are neither ripples nor lapping of water: all is bathed in the silence of unseen depths, illuminated by a dark, subaqueous light, like the first coating of paint on a canvas: white on black, a strange effect of blackness coated in whiteness; a background smooth, deep, and funereal, like a mirror, in which objects are sharply outlined and have a hint of something disturbing and magical – where can this come from, you wonder, when there is really nothing there?

Add to this the deep, velvety timbre of her voice, so resonant when she read, and her dress – neat-fitting and austere. Also: her love of tradition, her attachment to the classical mirror of poetry in which she peers intently at herself and where, on the still background of the lyric poetry of centuries past, both the present day and the living melody of its speech are solemnly and magisterially reflected like the streets of Venice in its canals. Her poetry always conveys the impression that others have just passed by there before her – the same as when you suddenly

[1] The legend is that at the time of the Tartar invasion of Russia in the 13th century the City of Kitezh sank into the earth and a lake was formed over it. The sound of its church bells can still sometimes be heard tolling under the water.

glance at a mirror and have the feeling that someone has flitted past a moment ago and things are still nervously alert to a presence which has been and gone.

A mirror is the emblem of her style: the frozen immobility of gesture, the sign of her august and muted manner. And the colour is always black. Ask anyone you like: what is Akhmatova's colour? and they will invariably say: black. When she uttered the challenging words: "Out of the darkness of enchanted mirrors" she must obviously have been mindful of Pushkin's "enchanted crystal", through which everything shone so clearly. But *her* mirrors are dark and no one peers out of them; instead, patrician reflections glide over the surface of the glass. Such also is Akhmatova's own aristocratic nature – a diamond mirror framed by St Petersburg and Tsarskoye Selo[1] (Versailles), to match her pose, her eternal pose, which plays the role of background. Or to put it more exactly: her role and the background against which she acts – so unhurriedly and gravely, lest she disturb the bewitched water – have merged in her pose, in the immobile, mirror-like stance of a Queen.

In the diamond mirror of mute waters
shine the living shapes of clouds . . .

*

Of all implements the nearest to a constellation is a trident.

*

Cats, for some reason, give the impression that their blood is blue – in the literal sense that it would stain things this colour.

*

Metaphors and similes are based not only on the likeness or closeness of the things compared, but even on their remoteness from each other. It is this that makes it possible for us to indulge our fantasies by means of language – stare hard enough into the obscure depths of some object or other and it will grow

[1] Small town with the Tsar's summer palace, near Petersburg. Akhmatova lived there as a child and it provides the background for many of her poems.

a funny little face. It is such little faces, claws, wings, tails, tongues, fleetingly glimpsed in things, that probably attract me most about metaphors – they can turn the drab page of an exercise book into a flowing, ornamental pattern, full of wild beasts.

*

"*Solnyshko*" ("little sun") is how women usually begin letters to their menfolk, who bear no resemblance whatsoever to the sun. But the moment I saw that venerable old man he immediately struck me as being exactly what is meant by the word. His beard resembled a grey nimbus from which the sparse hairs stuck out like rays, and through which you could clearly see the outlines of his ever-grinning face – or "snout" as he once modestly called it himself. Goodness, solemn and somewhat austere, roamed over those features, liquefying there, and round smiles constantly fluttered from the silent lips out into space. I only once saw him grieve deeply. This was when one of the big men in charge of us died – an event all of us obviously greeted with nothing but malicious glee. "Is there anything to be upset about?" I asked, surprised at the tears of the old man who had suffered a great deal in life at the hands of the official in question. "Oh, but of course there is! After all, his soul is now straight on the way to hell!", he said in measureless sorrow, but still smiling.

. . . In contrast to him there was the Moon, round-faced, clean-shaven, tearfully compassionate in the way peasant women are, slightly pockmarked, with a nose like a potato and eyes shyly cast down – buried in the puffy cheeks they indeed looked like the "eyes" of the potato. But he was a closed book to me, until one evening I began talking about the thief crucified together with Christ. Not about the thief that repented, but about the other one who, as we know, refused to believe in Christ and was damned.

"But you know," he said mysteriously, and shivers ran down my spine, "he was also saved . . . oh yes, he was saved too . . . Only no one realizes it . . ."

And a tear dropped from his all-knowing eye, and he looked down, and suddenly I realized that he was speaking about himself, that I was face to face with the other thief, who had been saved in some inscrutable way, or with one of those prophets who are yet to come or have already come – Elijah or Enoch . . .

On old pictures and engravings the Sun and the Moon were shown at either side in the shape of human faces. Sun and Moon, two Testaments, two Churches, two prophets, two olive branches . . . No matter that the Sun is older and higher, the young Moon is given to him for the sake of symmetry – to serve as a light at night when people sleep.

And from such raptures as these I wake up.

*

Before interrogation in prison she had a vision. Nikita the Martyr and John the Warrior[1] came to her in a dream and said:

"Raissa, do you remember the words 'I don't know?!'"

*

"The thread of life." For the sake of that "thread" people lived a long time: John the Warrior for 114 years, Nikita the Martyr for 95. You must not die, "lest it break", said the Old Believers of the Solovetski monastery. In 1732 Nikita, returning from a visit to John at Lake Top, was going to Yaroslavl and happened by mistake to turn off into the village of Sopelki, where 30 other Old Believers had gathered at the time. They fasted for a week and cast lots to elect a leader, but none of them was sure of himself, each fearing he might have been spiritually "damaged"[2] by praying for the unbaptized. Nikita alone was

[1] "Old Believer" saints. The Old Believers are schismatics who refused to accept the reforms of the Russian Orthodox Church in the 17th century. Another name for them is "Stayers" (*ostaltsy*). There are a number of different sects of Old Believers (such as the "Runners") which are still active today, and whose adherents are often persecuted and sent to labour camps by the Soviet authorities.

[2] "Damaged": a sectarian expression referring to a fall from Grace or to a State of Sin brought about by action contrary to the Church's (or sect's) teaching or traditional beliefs.

"undamaged" and it was thus from him that the "undamaged" thread of Old Believers' piety began and still continues with the sect known in popular parlance as the "Runners": the church of the "truly Orthodox Christian pilgrims".

*

The "Stayers"! The loyal remnant! . . .

"The remnant shall return, even the remnant of Jacob, unto the mighty God.

For though thy people Israel be as the sand of the sea, yet a remnant of them shall return: the consumption decreed shall overflow with righteousness." (Isaiah X, 21–22)

*

"*He has a lump on his forehead and a running sore on his shoulder through praying all the time. He makes the sign of the cross over the lavatory seat before he sits down on it. In a word, he is up to his neck in Christianity.*"

*

"*This* starets[1] *is so radiant that sometimes his very clothes start gleaming white as you look at him.*"

*

"*When he first started taking God's name in vain, well, I thought, he'll be struck down by lightning in a minute, the roof will fall in. I even ducked down . . .*" (At the first interrogation)

*

"*He listened to my explanation of the Revelation, about the beast and the dragon, and about the meaning of the number six hundred three score and six ('Let him that hath understanding count') – he listened carefully, for about two hours, without interrupting. Then he got up, stretched himself, went round and stood at the back of my chair and said:*

[1] A man – sometimes, but not necessarily, a monk – popularly revered for his wisdom and holy life is known in Russia as a *starets* (literally, an elder, plural: *startsy*).

'Oh, if you had only come into my hands two years ago I would have skinned you alive![1]'"

*

"They all laughed at him. Particularly a lieutenant-colonel, one of the *bytoviks*[2]. 'I am a lieutenant-colonel', he said, 'but I've never met any God in all my life. Where is He, your Christ? Has anyone ever seen Him?'

'I have', he said, 'I see Him every day.'"

*

Science does not believe its own eyes and keeps asking: "What is all this about?" But such prying and probing only thickens the walls that separate it from the truth. One would have thought air was transparent enough, but no! – it consists, so they tell us, of oxygen and nitrogen, plus carbonic acid gas; at first sight this seems to advance us a good deal, but in fact it only brings us up against a new, still more substantial range of questions, and when we begin looking into nitrogen and oxygen separately, we find that oxygen by itself is denser and thicker than air, that it is not just O, but O_2 – to say nothing of the nitrogen! In the meantime, both mind and body receive ample nourishment from this wall of matter that just gets thicker and thicker, growing all the time . . .

*

. . . I am now beginning to realize why the veil used to be worn. It played the role of a theatre curtain, to be drawn back on those rare days when a play was given. In the course of the four hours[3] during which we kept almost silent and merely

[1] The speaker is evidently an interrogator in the period of reform after Stalin's death when the secret police was curbed and physical torture forbidden.
[2] A prisoner sentenced for a "white-collar crime", such as embezzlement or some infringement of discipline or regulations. Owing to the Draconian nature of Soviet law this is a large category in the camps, distinct from both "politicals" and common criminals. Because of their generally "loyal" attitude they are relatively privileged.
[3] i.e. during a visit to the author by his wife.

looked at each other, I became utterly convinced that the face is a window, a kind of port-hole through which you can look or enter, and also out of which a soft light is shed on the earth. And therefore a face has double perspective; it beckons you in and at the same time sallies forth and advances on you, and looking into it, you do not know which world you are living in, and which is the bigger; eagerly swallowing what flows out from it, you can be engulfed and swept away. (And if people looked more carefully at each other's faces, they would treat their neighbour with greater caution and respect, for they would notice that every man is like a palace of crystal – in which he dwells with his own inner access to the kingdom we seek . . .)

In short, the face violates the laws of nature. It seems to serve as a kind of very thin screen which allows the light to pass both ways, back and forth between spirit and matter. Our faces enable us to lean out, as it were, from within – thus showing ourselves to the world and flowering on the surface of life.

Apart from its likeness to a window, the closest analogies to the face are fire and water – at which one also never wearies of looking; the face is constantly in flux, and it burns without being consumed by the flames . . . A thesis could be written on portraits or icons under the title "The world seen in a face".[1]

*

"We live between the fingers of a giant graven image!", he said, in explanation of why we now have such a bird's-eye view of world history. The effect of distance is not to make it all more remote, but rather to clarify events in the same way as people become long-sighted with age – the thickness of time serves as a magnifying glass, concentrating ancient Judea, Egypt, or Babylon in our field of vision and making them more obvious to us than if we were looking from close to.

*

Our fate after death may depend entirely on the placing of a

[1] Title of a mediaeval Russian book of wisdom.

comma, as witness the arguments about a line in St Luke (the story of the malefactor who was forgiven, XXIII, 43): "Verily I say unto thee, today shalt thou be with me in paradise." Those who deny life beyond the grave and recognize only the last Resurrection on the day of judgement (Adventists, Jehovah's Witnesses and others) maintain that the punctuation here is a later emendation and suggest that the phrase should be read differently:

"I say unto thee today, thou shalt be with me in paradise." In other words the promise is transferred to the Day of Resurrection.

A crucial issue is also raised by the argument with the Old Believers about the wording of one phrase in the Creed: "shall have no end" or "hath no end". Very much indeed depends on that "hath" – in particular, what view you take of the millenial Reign of the Saints which, according to the Old Believers, had already come to pass on earth – before the first Schism of the churches. Then there are those who see the entire Middle Ages and what came after – in effect, the whole of historical Christianity – as the Reign of the Antichrist.

That's where an argument about words can lead you . . .

*

"*A Stake driven by Seven Blows of Truth's hundred-ton Hammer into the Throat of every Spreader of Lies and Calumny concerning Jehovah and all his Friends, male and female.*" (Title of a book)

*

"The first Mystery and the greatest, that is – the Book descended from Heaven.

Eleven years before the destruction of Jerusalem or in the year AD 62, Jehovah or the God of the Holy Prophets sent a Book down from Heaven signed by his own hand, together with an Angel, to show His servants what would soon begin to happen, to wit: in the second century, through the agency of Papias and Origen, Satan would compose a Christian Holy Writ such as would give rise to 666 hellishly hostile Christian faiths, and with these Satanic faiths he would bring darkness to all peoples and nations.

. . . Lest any man and particularly lest any of the Jews should discover that this Book came from Jehovah, Satan called it 'a work by the Apostle John'.

. . . And he put the Lutherans up to writing, instead of 'Jehovah', a dog's angry snarl: 'Grr-grr.'[1]"

(From a manuscript book written by the Peacemakers or Ilyinists: *The Revelation of the Twelve Mysteries from Jehovah's last Battle with Satan*)

*

According to the doctrine of the Peacemakers, also known as Ilyinists, or Jehovists (not to be confused with the Jehovah's Witnesses), the "Creator of All Things" – father of Jehovah, of Satan and of other Gods dispersed among the solar systems – also has a father, who in his turn has a father, and so on. As they put it, God has "a grandfather and a grandmother", and to the question: "From whom then is the first original God descended?", they reply: this is not known and, in actual fact none of them are really gods at all, but men possessed of secret knowledge and great powers, descended "perhaps from some mosquito" (this by way of an ironic concession to the theory of evolution). Religion thus assumes the guise of science fiction or an adventure yarn: Satan rules over Earth and the whole solar system (his rightful domain), and Jehovah is fighting against him with the support of "his people". They are both of them gods – one the god of mortal and the other of immortal men. There is no discernible moral distinction between them. Calvary was not Atonement, but a cunning manoeuvre: Jehovah died on purpose, reckoning that Satan would follow him and not return to earth, while he (Jehovah) would be resurrected by virtue of a prior arrangement. Original sin: Satan seduced Eve and thus begat Cain, in answer to which Jehovah started his race – also through physical intercourse – from Abraham.

[1] i.e. "Herr" (written and pronounced *Gerr* in Russian): reference to the German word for Lord.

For this reason preference is given to the Jewish tribe which, headed by the Peacemakers, will lead those worthy of immortality along the true path – that of Jehovah. The world was not created, but put together by magician gods out of eternal and uncreated matter. The Jehovists appeal to reason, to material advantage, to the possibility that human beings may have god-like powers. It is a kind of popular anthroposophy, and it seems that I have thus stumbled on the traces of a rare sect that was thought to be virtually extinct. I would frankly speaking have preferred to come across *khlysty* or *skoptsy*[1].

"If beyond the thousandth sun you walk for another quadrillion miles, you won't find your God even there, but my God walks on the earth and visits his friends and sups with them, just as He visited Abraham, supped with him under an oak tree and then went and stood with him near Sodom . . ."

*

A man, almost certainly from the Urals, who knows what's what in matters of religion. He looks rather sly and self-possessed, is well-built, though a little round-shouldered, with bandy legs and a thick-set torso. There is a touch of the skilled mechanic in his proficient handling of questions of faith. The line of reasoning is speculative: "But perhaps He had a powder in His pocket?" (on the raising of Lazarus) and scientific: Elijah's chariot of fire was a rocket in prototype. All this with the knowing smirk of one who understands. Attributes which are patently "unreal", such as Divine omnipotence, are dismissed out of hand: if He could do *anything*, He would have organized things differently! What matters most is how everything is organized, the mechanics of it. He distrusts words, abstractions, book learning. Obviously everything has been carefully concealed or disguised, and to get at the truth you must uncover the secret of how it works. His method is not to denounce the mechanism, but to dismantle it. Tales of magic

[1] Russian sects. The *khlysty* believe in the ability of every man and woman to incarnate Christ and the Virgin Mary; the *skoptsy* castrate themselves to save themselves from sin.

he tells as if they were true stories: here everything is contrived in a way he can understand, and a mystery can be seen for what it is: sleight of hand, a trick. A miracle is a clever hoax, a stratagem. Golden apples and flying carpets have the same appeal as science fiction. What counts above all is not righteousness, but know-how and skill. ("I know how it's done all right!") The gods possess the secret of production. The world is ruled by competing "wizards" who have superseded the improbable "gods". This is scarcely Christianity, but rather a form of paganism based on technology. There is neither morality nor mysticism here, but fascination with an exciting tale of adventure and discovery, in which the cogs of the mechanism are gradually revealed. He treats the spirit as he treats electricity – with respect. But who would ever pray to electricity?! It is the dream of an earthly paradise.

*

"The Fourth Mystery . . .

In a thousand years' time Jehovah will utterly destroy Satan and all the men that belong to him. He will make a new earth a million times bigger than this one, but without oceans and seas, and will dwell in it with His immortal men for 280,000 years; and after this He will again make a new earth, much better for them to live on. As time goes on he will constantly transform the earth, making it better and better, till it reaches a perfection beyond our understanding, and will live on it for ever and ever, together with immortal men.

And the city of Jerusalem will be lowered to the transfigured earth from heaven, and it will have been made by men from the heavens, that is, by the inhabitants of other planets; it will be adorned with precious stones and the streets will be paved with transparent gold. In the middle of the city Jehovah's palace will stand, but there will no longer be a temple or any sacrifices. A river will flow under the palace and along all the streets, and on its banks wondrous fruit trees will grow, bringing forth new fruit every month, and by eating this fruit human beings will neither grow old nor die, and for all of everlasting eternity they will remain immortal, men at the age of 34 and women at the age of 14 . . .

He will not only make you immortal in body but will also cause you to shine like a star."

*

"*The whole of our life is but the trace of a long-extinct star!*"

*

What are the stars to us? What have we to do with them? Why do our minds dwell on them so obsessively? Why do we imagine them to be addressed to each one of us personally, each soul individually, and why, as we say, do they "look down" on us, while the moon, though brighter and bigger, does no such thing and seems quite aloof? After all, with its influence on the tides, the moon surely has a deeper bearing on our earthly existence; yet it exists quite apart from us, as it were. The stars, on the other hand, are aimed directly at us, straight at our hearts – hence, no doubt, our reciprocal interest in them and the feeling of inner dependence on them which impels us to draw pictures of constellations and compile horoscopes? . . .

*

"*I sit on the sofa in nothing but my underwear and to make sure I'm not just hearing things, I ask whether there is life on Venus.*

'There is no life on Venus', the voice answers back to me out of the darkness."

*

A joyous companion on the journey.[1] "Keep up your spirits! . . .", he would say, gently raising a finger. His words were always significant and his advice always had a kind of prophetic meaning. I later had reason to be surprised at the accuracy of one of his predictions which was of practical importance from the point of view of my life in the camp.

"*And just wait till we start flying through the air – that will teach people! . . .*"

*

[1] i.e. to the camp.

"*And so the Lord said:*
'Listen, My people, do not go out of the barracks . . .' And by now machine guns were chattering away out there . . ."

*

"O my people, hear my word: make you ready to the battle, and in those evils be even as pilgrims upon the earth.

He that selleth, let him be as he that fleeth away: and he that buyeth, as he that will lose;

He that occupieth merchandise, as he that hath no profit by it; and he that buildeth, as he that shall not dwell therein;

He that soweth, as if he should not reap; so also he that planteth the vineyard, as he that shall not gather the grapes;

They that marry, as they that shall get no children; and they that marry not, as the widowers.

And therefore they that labour, labour in vain;

For strangers shall reap their fruits, and spoil their goods, overthrow their houses, and take their children captives for in captivity and in famine shall they get children."

2 Esdras XVI, 40–46.

*

"*I read Sienkiewicz's* Quo Vadis? *and cannot see the letters for my tears.*"

*

"*And so they just messed around all night long.*" (The fisherman-apostles who came back without any fish)

*

The text of the Gospels explodes with meaning. It radiates significance, and if we fail to see something, this is not because it is obscure, but because there is so much, and because the meaning is too bright – it blinds us. You can turn to it all through your life. Its light never fails. Like the sun's. Its brilliance astounded the Gentiles and they believed. There is no art here – despite all the parables. Feeling is conveyed directly, without intermediaries. Art is always secondary, allegorical. But here all is directness. An emanation of the spirit and of the miraculous. The parables have only an auxiliary role – to help us in our lack of understanding. The "aesthetic" approach is not possible. It is easier to conceive the world as an allegory than this book . . .

*

"*'If they shorten my sentence'*, *says he*, *'I'll . . .'*
'The Lord will do it', *I reply*."

*

An inspired orang-outang. A Pentecostalist.[1] An archetypal, rather wild Mordvinian. Among other things, he has been a circus acrobat, and has travelled widely, even spending some time in Paris. He knows what he is talking about:

"And all the sewage is washed away down porcelain pipes and not a drop goes to waste! . . ." (On West European toilets)

He gives one a sense of what I would call the physics of the spirit: the main thing is to breathe (because "air" means "spirit"?).[2] His advice to me:

"Breathe as much as you can – and you'll survive!"

He does not get on with his brethren in the faith – they find him too eccentric, too different in his cast of mind, and he lives apart from them. An old buck. He plays with etymologies, trying to master the "breath of speech" and to get to the root of things through words. Eden is the same as Adam (which means "man" in Mordvinian). The organs of sex – the tree of Sin and Knowledge – are located in the middle of Eden-Adam. It is here that the apple was plucked. Carnally, as it were. He does not mince his words in pursuing analogies. But such earthiness can give a more real and palpable sense of the spirit. Mystical experience and the descent of the Spirit he compares to drinking and fornication. It is one thing to indulge

[1] Pentecostalists are an Evangelical sect, an offshoot of the Baptists. (*Author's note*)

[2] The two words are etymologically the same in Russian.

every day and quite another to do so once a month – the same applies to communion with the other world, which is of similar intensity.

In the evenings he prays aloud in angelic tongues, standing behind the barracks. He makes prophecies and is free in his interpretation of the texts. His thinking is so amorphous that it gives him the power to judge everything fearlessly and on a grand scale. He addresses me as *man* (with emphasis).

"*Man*, there is greater need for you here!"

This flatters me.

When he talks of his revelations – with his raised arms, and curly beard – he looks like Samson embracing God and the Cosmos in an ecstasy of self-immolation:

"Let them throw all their bombs – atomic, hydrogen, the lot! – down on me alone!"

He longs to perform a great and noble deed. At these moments he seems to merge with the Universe and talks of himself as having just been in a state of trance:

"The heavens opened. I roared like a steam-engine. My hands reached out in all directions and clutched at the walls."

He sees himself as a forest.

*

In the night he dreamed that his tongue had caught fire in his mouth and that same day, as he started praying he spoke for the first time in other languages – after undergoing Baptism by the Spirit.

*

Singers (almost as in Turgenev[1]), showing off not themselves, or their talent, but the *songs* as such – to see whose song has the most effect. The superiority of a rival is acknowledged, in a tone of slight regret, by saying not: "You sing well", but: "The song is good". The only desire is to excel, to win on the strength of the actual words of the song. They may be doing

[1] Reference to Turgenev's short story 'The Singers' in *A Huntsman's Sketches*. This passage refers to a group of religious sectarians in the camp.

their laundry or quietly getting on with some little job, but in that case they put their work aside for a while, and listen rather warily while a song is being sung.

One "defeated" man burst into tears. Not because of his defeat, but because some lines in the winning song gave him a lump in the throat: "It had something about our brethren . . ."

They are very much affected by the words and take them to heart as being literally about themselves. The tune is not all that essential. If they choose, they may simply recite or read their favourite couplets, and – since the meaning counts so much more than the quality of the performance – even re-tell them in their own words.

*

I have been trying to find an explanation for the icon of the Tricheiric Virgin[1], but none of the old men here can recall anything about the Virgin Mary having plucked flowers with a third hand. Apart from the story of John Damascene whose hand was cut off and grew again thanks to the Virgin's intercession (which possibly served as a basis for the iconography of the Tricheiric Virgin), I have, however, managed to turn up another, probably apocryphal, source for it. Once, as she wandered round the world, the Virgin went into a smithy to spend the night. There she found the blacksmith and his daughter, armless from birth. This is how it is sung in the style of a wandering minstrel's spiritual:

On a smith's door one ev'ning
Mary shyly knocked and said:
"For one night please give me shelter,
Far's my home, my Son's asleep".

When the smith the door did open
God's own Mother stood and looked
At the furnace belching fire,
While she nursed her little Son.

[1] The three-handed Virgin, a motif in Russian iconography.

Sparks flew high and, hammer swinging,
Tired and breathless toiled the smith,
Oft with horny hand and grimy
From his brow he wiped the sweat.

Next to him a little maiden
Also standing by the fire,
Sadly hung her head in silence
For she had no arms at all.

Some of the stanzas, despite the mannered turns of phrase, are magnificent. But on the whole these verses detract from the theme, treating it in the sentimental vein of one of those popular little songs of the last century ("Blue with cold and all a-shivering, Trudged along the little mite"). In itself the song is good, but in this particular case the subject is somehow larger and stronger than the verbal structure in which it is embedded. The smith is forging nails and suddenly starts prophesying. Terrified, Mary drops the Babe, but the armless girl makes a movement to catch Him and save Him from falling and – actually does! The verse, unfortunately, rather weakens the effect of the miracle:

Said the smith: "This is my daughter,
She was born a cripple, see.
Her mother's dead, but she is with me,
I must work in grief and tears.

Nails I now have started forging;
Four strike terror in my heart –
Someone's body will hang from them,
On the Tree condemned to die.

As I forge I see a vision
Of a tall and heavy Cross,
On that Cross your Son is hanging
Crucified and all in blood".

With a cry of pain and horror
Did the Mother drop her Babe,
But the girl leapt quickly forward
Just in time to save the Child.

In the arms which God had given
Christ lay down with blissful smile.
"Smith, oh smith, you now are happy.
But for me there's naught but tears".

It occurs to me that in the old days smiths were regarded as sorcerers. I see the scene rather in Rembrandtesque style – with the glowing forge and the nails burning like candles, all mixed with the flying sparks and the cryptic chant of the sorcerer . . .

*

The snow is coming down thickly again. And it is beyond anyone's power to stop it.

I like the labour camp winter more and more. The soul lies deeper and deeper under one's *bushlat*[1].

26th November, 1967.

*

. . . Take the North again, for example. We felt that their authenticity could be felt most keenly of all in what lay beyond the actual monuments themselves. In that sense Kiy Island and Pustozersk[2] proved to be the farthest points in our search, the extreme limit of space – an ultimate source located outside the realm of history. And the point is not, of course, that out there, in Kiy and Pustozersk, there is nothing (though this, too, is important), but that the spirit dwells in such places with far greater intensity than elsewhere.

[1] A heavy, padded winter jacket issued to prisoners.
[2] Region in the far north of Russia which the author and his wife visited before his arrest, and where there are many old wooden churches.

The darker the night
The brighter the stars.
The deeper the pain
The closer to God.

Where does one look for a source? According to the law of contrast (the law of pain) it must be located not in the metropolis, but well away from it, on the periphery – whether of a literature, a city, society, or civilization as a whole – in the same way that monasteries situated beyond the city border, in the desert, at the edge of the world, were in ancient times spiritual and cultural centres – none the less so for being far from everywhere, or even, for that matter, entirely inaccessible. Prophets appear among the lower classes, in out-of-the-way places and in any case certainly not among the élite. The reason is surely that, coming from below or from afar, it is easier to rise above the general (and even the highest) level and to stand outside the bounds imposed by any given culture. Were the Apostle Paul, Jan Hus or Nilus of Sorsk[1] spokesmen of their respective cultures? Hardly. But they sprang, perhaps, from the *sources* of theïr cultures – sources far removed from culture itself, more a creation of the wind than of human agency; focal points of pain rather than of success and achievement. Culture consists of books, pictures (these flourish!). But take away the root of pain and pictures too will blow away like autumn leaves . . .

In short, the circle of civilization (of the life of a nation, of history) is drawn round a centre which, paradoxically, is itself located outside the perimeter and is hence related to it only tangentially.

*

. . . In a drawing of an aircraft carrying a hydrogen bomb he sees the shape of a cross raised over the earth. A man with fire in his belly, as though he has a furnace going inside him. Who stoked it up, I wonder? Red-faced and grimy, a red

[1] Nilus of Sorsk: Russian religious reformer (1433–1508).

glow on the wall behind him.[1] The height of simplicity and honesty. The very picture of a proletarian standing at his forge, ready for anything. No murmur of complaint, except to ask: How long? No emotions, but spirit, ideas, flaming intellect. For him the material form of things is merely the vestment of thoughts. Ideas have clothed themselves in flesh and iron. The body is an instrument of the spirit.

"When you are released, buy an apple, Andrey, an ordinary apple and cut it in half. And in the arrangement of the pips you will see the head of Adam. Understand?! Death is in the apple. And you'll see other things too . . ."

Here people think and philosophize more intensely than in the world of scholarship and science. Ideas are not culled from books, but grow out of a man's very bones. Nowhere is the life of the spirit lived at such a pitch, with such zest, as here, on the edge of the world. Heady stuff.

*

"Save me, Oh Lord, whether I want it or want it not, for like stinking excrement, I desire sinful wickedness, but because Thou art good and all-powerful, Thou canst prevent me. For if Thou showest mercy to a righteous man there is no greatness therein, if Thou savest a pure man there is no wonder therein, for they are worthy of Thy mercy. But rather, Oh Lord, in me, accursed and sinful and wicked, reveal the wonder of Thy mercy, show Thy charity for I am a beggar in thy sight, beggared of all good deeds. Save me, Oh Lord, for Thou art merciful and blessed for ever and ever, amen."

*

In Rembrandt's *Return of the Prodigal Son*,[2] the father's hands are different from each other, and the right hand quite literally does not know what the left is doing. The father's hands correspond to the son's feet – a Christian version of the

[1] The author's conversations with this sectarian took place in a boiler-room where he worked as a stoker.

[2] This painting is in the Hermitage in Leningrad.

lotus with the soles of the feet turned outwards. The interplay of gestures is richer here than in Leonardo's *Last Supper*. Looking at Rembrandt's picture, we are confronted by the son's bare heel, which is more expressive than a human face – filthy, peeling like an onion, as scabby as a convict's pate, exuding repentance. Nothing in the picture is directed towards the spectator. Like the main characters in it, it is turned to the wall – into itself. Verily: everything is within you. As a result no picture could be more relevant to the theme of the Church.

All is submerged in that munificent cathedral darkness more deeply than Sadko sitting on the bottom of the sea.[1] And it is a good thing that the paint has become so dark over the years. When it becomes so dark that we can no longer see it at all, then the Prodigal Son will rise from his knees and reveal his face.

*

Once more everything is thawing. Full circle again. And it was so nice and quiet, the winter. There is something in us of bears settling down to hibernate, or of ships lying to for a long time.

"*But I don't advise you to wake a sleepy man!*"

Someone sits and discusses what he would do, and how he would live if he had five wives. And he hasn't even got one.

A man's life is like a statue: with all its ramifications it can be described and taken in at a glance.

The cat miaows piteously at the door, hoping someone will open it.

"*Every grave costs four roubles fifty – to dig it and put a mound of earth on top . . .*"

The light is so weak in the barracks that you could gladly fall ill. If you coughed – your teeth might drop out. I suspect that tomorrow morning I shall be looking back with surprise at this evening's feeling of impotence . . .

*

[1] Reference to the Russian folk tale of Sadko, a merchant of Novgorod.

I can't make out – is that smoke curling along the wall, or the shadow of smoke?

*

Part Three

"*Get up, fellow! Your country needs you!*" (Warder to a prisoner in his cell, calling him out to be put on a transport for the camp.)

*

. . . A gypsy with her cards, a hard look in her eyes,
An ancient necklace and a string of beads . . .
I hoped my fate would say the Queen of Diamonds,
But once again I get the Ace of Spades!

Why, then, once more do you, my luckless fortune,
Lead me along a road of pain and tears?
Rusty barbed-wire, a window's solid bars,
A prison railway truck and rattling wheels . . .

*

"*I went through hell and high water.*"

*

"*Society's an interesting set-up and real fun too!*"

*

"*It's nice when people nod in agreement with you.*"

*

"*He does not say 'Sorry', but only implies it . . .*"

*

"*You don't know when to say 'Good morning', or when a plain 'hullo' will do.*"

*

"He lives alone with himself."

*

"He's such an isolationist that no one drinks with him."

*

"We must live, mustn't we? And smoke, mustn't we?"

*

"You have to keep giving life a leg up."

*

"Life is a proper bag of tricks."

*

"Ah, well, life's just a transit jail."

*

"His one wish was to get home to his mother. 'Four times', he said, 'I didn't make it. If only', he said, 'I could reach my mother. I'll try a fifth time'."

*

"He took his stripe off as soon as he arrived." (i.e. back from the special régime camp where the inmates are called "stripers" or "zebras", because of the stripes on their clothing.)

*

"I'm just in for questioning, but Vasya's in for stealing biscuits."

*

"Conditions are tiptop."

*

"I've set myself up like a king."

*

"There was five of us. All intellectuals except me . . ."

*

"Of course there is a difference! He is a soldier, a fellow with a home and family, but I am a tramp, a mere nobody."

*

"We seem to be fated to live amid noise and shouting . . ."

*

They stood and swore at each other, ringing the changes on the words "swine" and "dog".

*

"Don't you lovey-dovey me – I'm not a child!"

*

"To my way of thinking you're both of you filthy swine and nothing to pick between you!"

*

"It's just because I'm so bashful I don't tell you to four-letter off."

*

"I'm a frantic kind of fellow!"

*

"I'll beat the daylight out of him: he'll have straw to sleep on and only his teeth to scratch himself with."[1]

*

"So I just let him have it on the cheek-bone! . . ."

*

[1] i.e. I shall take all his possessions away from him (straw is a symbol of poverty) and beat him so hard that he will become a cripple and will have to scratch himself with his teeth because his arms and legs will be broken. (*Author's explanation*)

"*If he didn't swindle you, he'd rob you. I did some finagling, too, out there. You've got to live!*"

*

"*We had an easier time of it – we foraged around like wolves.*"

*

"*Say what you like but at least it pays for the booze.*" (Gambling at cards)

*

"*She's so dressed up you could drink for a week if you robbed her.*'

*

"*The man who takes no risks never goes to jail.*"

*

"*You sharpen the knives in the day time, and go to work at night.*"

*

". . . *Good heavens no – never laid a finger on anyone! It's only by gambling.*" (Dostoyevsky's "Mr Prokharchin" – new version)

*

Russian misers do not hoard money so much as weave fancies round it. Porfiriy Golovlev, Plyushkin[1], Pushkin's *Covetous Knight* – all these are very Russian characters. For the most part they merely give rein to their imagination, sitting on their coffers. They get all worked up about trifles, but don't really give a damn about profit or loss.

*

"*I had one mania – to get rich.*"

*

"*Money is such a temptation that no one resists it.*"

*

[1] Golovlev: character in *The Golovlev Family*, a novel by Saltykov-Shchedrin; Plyushkin: character in Gogol's *Dead Souls*.

"You have to have money for your girl, too: she can tell by telepathy whether you've got anything in your pocket or not."

*

"The old woman was saving up to buy the kid a motor-bike."

*

"'But I don't need any money', I said, 'I am made of gold as it is'."

*

"I'll get my release, and then learn all about black magic . . ."

*

"What really matters is the kind of luck you have . . ."

*

Memories of a luxurious life:
"I fed on nothing but sprats and eels! . . ."

*

"And the store sold anything you like except the Elixir of Life. Provided you had the money."

*

"A roll of white bread with blisters on it. Tinned 'Crabs' – kind of white worms in bits of paper."

*

"An express train sort of all streamlined."

*

"People with a capital P."

*

"A wallet made of pedigree leather!"

*

"They are given all the freedom in the world! . . ."

*

"That goblet was big enough to hold half a litre of vodka!"

*

"In Leningrad all the houses are architectural! Go up to any entry and get an eyeful of the angels without any clothes on."

*

"I took out a roll of white bread, may I be shot dead, and a half litre bottle as well . . ."

*

"You could even see a few glasses of champagne here and there!"

*

"All the drunks were clinking glasses: 'Here's to you! Here's to us!'"

*

"A drink that cheers you up."

*

"I'm nice and kind when I'm drunk, so she liked it when I was drunk."

*

"But my thoughts develop when I've drunk a lot."

*

"It's like lying on the moon – sheer bliss! . . ."

*

"They dragged me out into the street, and it looked to me to be spinning round like a windmill, with people walking about on their heads and going snip-snip with their legs as if they were shearing sheep."

. . . And all beaten-up as I was, I pulled my cap down over my eyes and started out for the station, pretty well switched off and my mind wandering somewhere else . . ."

*

"*If I was President I'd pass a law telling people to drink hard for the first sixty years, to cut down gradually for the next forty, and then to kick the bucket.*"

*

"*No, you have to work as well, or there'd be no interest.*"
"*But I both drank* and *worked.*"

*

"*Some people cried, some giggled, and others got into a state about something. There were some terrific moments. How can I put it to you? You just come all over goofy. You switch off.*" (Smoking *plan*[1])

*

"*Yes, I had a drink on purpose so as to speak to you properly! . . .*" (Having things out with the boss)

*

"*I rambled a bit, but I stuck to my point: 'Now, don't you try any of that hypnotism business on me, gentlemen,' I say to them!*"

*

The art of telling a story depends to a considerable extent on spinning it out and introducing the detail only very gradually. Your account must be slow, deliberate, and broken up by pauses into thematically significant sections.

It is no good saying: "I go to the bath-house."

Better to draw it out, let things sink in:

I go – to the bath-house. I grab a . . . (what do I grab?) a cake of soap. All right? Then, after a further moment's pause

[1] A drug like hashish.

for reflection: a towel. Finally, with an effort, almost triumphantly: a sponge!!

And everyone listens – fascinated. Pity one so often lacks self-assurance and starts gabbling too fast for the good of the story. It helps even if you can just break up a sentence into its basic components, for instance:

"A woman. A real Russian bitch. Big tits. Tamara."

Then there is the law of composition. The beginning must be insinuating. You plunge the knife in only at the end of the first chapter.

*

Another thing: words should have their own special fragrance or sparkle – so that you are drawn back to them again and again. Each phrase should breathe secret joy and excitement. As one reads, one should want to toy with it in the mind.

*

So all is back again where it started, and once more the wind brings a February snow with it, and turns up our *bushlats*, and no sooner does it seem for the tenth time as if the thaw is setting in and we are going to have rain than a swirling snow-storm begins again. But someone will soon come in, banging the door, and announce in a voice hoarse from smoking:

"It's March."

The words will ring out – damp, categorical, brooking no argument.

"It's March."

And everyone will cheer up.

And our cat sits out in the snow, managing to keep warm, listening to its animal sap rising.

14th March, 1968.

*

"*My heart used to thump away like a machine-gun, but now it's like a fish and just goes flip-flop.*"

*

"*I was young, physically healthy, afraid of nothing.*"

*

"*Your cock is still crowing inside your pants!*"

*

"*And he kicked the bucket in the morning, the swine.*"

*

"*She's a real window-smasher.*"[1]

*

"*Grandad was released as a particularly hardened criminal.*" ("Grandad" is a nickname)

*

"*Hit him in the eye – turn him into a clown!*" (A standard phrase during fist fighting)

*

"*They had no way of getting us off their backs!*"

*

"*They backed us up against the carbide factory.*"[2]

*

"*Bar-bar.*" (A foreign language)

*

Precise definitions:
"*A full-length bust of Pushkin.*"
"*Three Knights: Minin and Pozharsky.*"[3]
"*I let myself in for a fiasco!*"

[1] i.e. a determined woman who sticks up for her rights. (*Author's note*)
[2] Reminiscence of an episode during the war. (*Author's note*)
[3] Confusion between two heroes of the war with Poland in the early 16th century and a popular painting of three legendary heroes of Kievan Russia by Vasnetsov.

"*Not a gram's worth of a hangover.*"[1]
"*Something like a couple of nurses.*"
"*In the first place, there are three reasons.*"
"*To the bones of the marrow!*"
"*The whole autobiography of his life.*"
"*Provisions are not accepted with the exception of money.*"
"*I received a sum in the dimension of 120 roubles.*"
"*You have a bourgeois streak in your mind.*"
"*Howls like a mare.*"
"*He's as long as a hare, the swine.*"

(And it occurred to me that hares really are disproportionately long.)

"*He thinks everybody is called Nick.*" (About a madman)
"*They were all dolled up in hats.*"
"*An immorally stable man.*"
"*Faced by an absence of energy.*"
"*All this is illusory eyewash.*"
"*And there I stood – like a book-keeper's ledger.*"
"*The cook stood there with his great big ugly mug 40 by 90.*"[2]
"*I have a 45% diminished responsibility.*"
"*One of those hundred-rouble whores.*"
"*Or we'll have a real stand-up fight on our hands.*"
"*I was dressed in khaki from head to toe – trousers, jacket, and cap.*" (While on the run)
"*A herb to cure the nervous system.*"
"*Terrific fellows they were – Pushkin and Goethe . . .*"
"*He knows four languages: German, French and that there English.*"
"*And what should I see but a female captain.*"
"*A lady judge.*"
"*A little bitch from Baku.*"
"*A slip of a young thing born in '42.*"
"*A Chang-kai-shana.*" (chaikhana)[3]

[1] In the Soviet Union drink is sold and ordered by weight: e.g. "two hundred grams of vodka".
[2] Centimetres. (*Author's note*)
[3] Chaikhana: a tea-room in Central Asia.

"*Campanella, the Italian dance.*"
"*Somewhere in Kharkov or Odessa, or thereabouts . . .*"
"*And every little verse in that album had* "*The End*" *written after it . . .*

*

Set expressions:
"*As dumb as a felt boot.*"
"*As uncouth as makhorka.*"[1]
"*Mangy dogs! Stinking goats!*"
"*Good*-auskas[2]*!*"
"*For the* refuseshtein."[3]
"*Nothing but* wasser."[4]
"*Why are you wriggling like a snake in a frying pan?*"
"*Spineless semi-snake!*"
"*Jabber-blinkies.*" (Drugs)[5]
"*As tired as a battle horse.*"
"*I worked like a lion.*"
"*Sea sausage.*" (Cod)
"*Pure eyewash – nothing to catch hold of.*"
"*A blabbering idiot.*"
"*A face like a leper's.*"
"*Red tabs in fur caps.*" (Colonels)
"*Belted with a crow-bar.*" (Of a strong, powerfully built man)
With growing inspiration:
"*I says to them:*
Whores!
Sodomites!
French letters!"

[1] Makhorka: a very cheap and crude kind of tobacco.
[2] *auskas*: a typical adjectival ending in Latvian. (*Author's note*)
[3] *refuseshtein*: an imitation of a German word. This type of jargon is the result of Russians and non-Russians all living together in Soviet prisons and camps. (*Author's note*)
[4] *Wasser*: German for water. The reference is to excessively weak tea or watery soup. (*Author's note*)
[5] Drugs: the Russian is *kaliki-morgaliki*, from words meaning "to jab" and "to blink". A man whose brain has ceased to function properly after he has given himself a "fix" with a needle just sits and blinks his eyes. (*Author's note*)

Sometimes the use of words drives me to despair. No creature could be more abstract than a cat. Yet this man must needs say something nasty – in a gentle voice – even to a cat:

"*Come here, then, you little whore.*"

His words stick to things and fester there. He infects everything he touches with them. To name something is to swear at it so far as he is concerned.

*

There was so much foul language while this stove was being built that after about six months it started falling to bits. Things do not like to be sworn at while they are being made.

*

A man swears in order to curse someone, to insult him. A woman swears in order to get her tongue round a salacious word.

*

"Go on, just swear a bit – then you'll feel more at ease."

Not better, but more at ease. One of the boys. A means of establishing group familiarity. Swearing as a way of creating a homely, family atmosphere, a cosy shelter for the soul.

*

An unfortunate Estonian living in the labour camp assumed Russian swear words to be normal speech. In hospital the old man rather put his foot in it:

"Well, how are we feeling?"

"Fucking awful, doctor."

*

A Catholic Pole to a supervisor:

"*Don't pester me – I don't want to swear on one of my holy days.*"

*

"*I hadn't yet learned how to weep in Russian.*"

*

A stray cow is usually called in a kind of mooing voice, with cajoling sounds coming from the belly. It is, one feels, an attempt to find a common language with the errant beast.

*

Foreign words in Russian. Aeroplane, electricity. Should we be ashamed of these words, or even shun them? The fact is that having entered the language and taken root in it, they have assumed a fuller and richer sound for the Russian ear than many a native word. The simple, home-made and nowadays generally used *samolyot* (lit., "self-flyer") says less to us than the borrowed term "aeroplane". Along with all the other similarly constructed words – *samokat* (bicycle), *samovar*, *samogon* (home-distilled vodka) – it is much less graphic, conveying nothing except the information, for the benefit of the simple-minded, that the thing flies by itself. Combined with *kovyor* (carpet) in the sense of "flying carpet" it is not so bad, but otherwise it's a kind of bare bone, picked clean of all its meat, rather than a real word.

*

Mayakovsky's "ladder"[1], apart from the obvious rhythmical and structural patterns involved, arose from a desire to instil energy into the text by exhibiting it in a special and striking manner. In principle, anything set out in this way can be read with a particular declamatory emphasis and made to sound like poetry. But under this continuous heavy stress it eventually begins to flag.

*

In Turgenev's *A Huntsman's Sketches* there is precious little about hunting as such – it was only needed as a pretext to bring master and peasant together. How else were they to meet? Nekrasov[2] used the same device. At that time a man

[1] Mayakovsky's way of printing his verse on the page so that it was broken up into units for special emphasis in declamation.
[2] Nikolai Nekrasov (1821–78): Russian poet.

out on a hunting trip was like today's special correspondent exploring life in the raw. Before Turgenev, contacts were limited to chance encounters at coaching inns and took place to the sound of jingling harness bells. People talked to their coachmen too. But there was a limit to the number of journeys one could make from Petersburg to Moscow and back[1]. So the master stepped down from his carriage and went a-hunting. Pushkin anticipated this development in his story "The Mistress-Peasant".

*

A volume of Leskov[2] has come into my hands. His sentences – unkempt, scampering hither and thither like dogs – appeal to me greatly. The style is craggy and almost semi-literate: "Our captain was an excellent fellow, but a nervy one, hot-tempered and real tinder." Such rough edges! – "against all the laws of architectonics and economy in the construction of a story" – as he writes himself in "Interesting Men".

In "The Immortal Golovan" Leskov has something to say which will stick in the gullet of all who think that descriptions should be true to life. To me, however, it seems extremely important:

"I am afraid I shall be quite unable to draw his portrait for the simple reason that I see him all too well and clear."

For the simple reason that he saw him all too *well*! And yet people are always urging you to depict only what you know well!

This phrase is a declaration of war on all *deliberate* attempts to be "life-like" and sums up in a few words the essence of the truly creative mind which in practice always concerns itself with the unfamiliar – it is this that rouses the imagination

[1] Allusion to Alexander Radishchev (1749–1802), whose *Journey from Moscow to Petersburg* (1790) was the first attempt to describe the condition of the Russian serfs.

[2] Nikolai Leskov (1831–95): Russian writer.

and spurs it on. "Truth to life" only makes it shy away. A thing too familiar does not surprise and therefore need not be copied. Art always first turns reality into something exotic, and only then starts making a representation of it.

Going on from here, Leskov, by his particular style of speech, creates a sensation of bewilderment and inability to describe events, strewing words about in clumsy disarray and hoping that this chaotic language, as it blunders around in blind confusion, will finally run up by accident against something which will spring to life and soar up – under the impact of so much incoherence – in "dense and headlong disharmony". How to describe a suicide, not in such a way that it comes to resemble a police report, but so as to convey all the horror and senselessness of the event? The first thing, he evidently thought, was to renounce any attempt to give a precise description of it. And so he steps back, spreads out his words like the fingers of his hand, and waves them about, dismissing the very idea of narrative but informing us of the occurrence and getting to grips with it by a much better method – by allowing himself to flounder helplessly in a profusion of language which does not even try to depict what has happened:

"It is very difficult to give an account of such incidents to people listening in cold blood when you yourself are no longer as worked up about them as you were when they first happened. Now that I must tell what the upshot of it all was I feel powerless to attempt a description of the events in all their immediacy – to convey the speed, density and urgency, so to speak, with which they crowded in, jostling and piling on top of each other – all so that I may glance down from a great height at such human folly and then merge into the background again."

By refusing to reproduce the events he did so very well indeed!

*

It is extraordinary to hear on the radio songs like "Glorious sea – our Sacred Baikal" or "In the wild steppes beyond the

Baikal".[1] Nothing so special about them, one would think. Yet the way they sound here, and the way we listen to them! . . .

*

"*I find even alcohol difficult to bear. Give me a quiet morning at the edge of a wood! I would go out into the fields and drop down in a faint.*"

*

"*I swear by freedom!*" (Almost an expletive)

*

"*And they never caught you?*"
"*How could they?! They had a million roads to choose from and I had only one.*"

*

"*I had a home-made cannon: a rocket launcher with the barrel of an automatic – all welded together with lead. Without any sights on it. You hit a man between the eyes and they popped right out of his head.*"

*

"*The judge asks: 'Tell me, witness, why do you say in your evidence that this man used his gun when you didn't see it yourself and, in fact, weren't even there at the time?' And the old girl answers: 'Oh, I thought they'd give me a pension'.*"

*

"*At the barber's I looked out of the corner of my eye and I see the fellow in the next chair – he was getting a shave as well and squinting over at me.*" (Man on the run, seeing a security guard at the same barber's shop)

*

"*It's stiff with security out there – like a spider's web. Then there's the* taiga. *And the winter. And not a soul living there.*"

*

[1] Popular songs about escaped convicts in Tsarist times.

"I felt drops of cold sweat on my temples."

*

"'Choose a star to guide you,' he says, 'and make a break for it. Keep the railway on your left.'"

*

"I take my bike and ride off in the other direction."

*

"The dame I was going around with threw herself on my neck." (While on the run)

*

"I was amazed when she started putting over a line about turning myself in."

*

"A wolf eats branded sheep as well." (Proverb)

*

"Don't try to wrap spaghetti round my ears, you snakes."

*

"Why are you trying to pin the whole shoot on me?"

*

The doctor says:

"I can either certify you're mad or say you're perfectly all right – either way it's the high jump for you."

*

"They all marvel at me as if I was a tiger."

*

. . . If there is too much noise in my part of the barracks, I put on my cap with ear-flaps. There is clearly some law at

[1] i.e. don't try your soft talk on me.

work here: the lower a man's mental or educational level, the louder, the more strident he is in most cases. It is a kind of mania for filling the air with noise. Some people, even when they tell a story, yell at the top of their voices – as if they wanted to shout someone down.

They never switch off the radio – they say they sleep better to the sound of it. This background of constant noise probably creates the illusion of a life full of meaning and events. Or is it a way of exorcizing the emptiness which, like a disease, gnaws at the vitals of people in this kind of plight? With silence all round they would go mad.

*

Know what I did yesterday? The sky was very starry. At night I came back from work and hung a clean towel over the head of my bed – as if tidying up for the Holy Day. Life sometimes seems to centre on small things like this – for me it was almost the equivalent of a spring-cleaning.

21st April, 1968. Easter.

*

. . . or simply to sit quietly, resting with the whole of the body.

*

He loves the night because there is too much light in the daytime – with his poor eyes he can only *listen* to the landscape.

"If I could just clothe myself to look like the sky, I'd make a dash for it across the forbidden zone as if they'd rolled out a carpet for me!"

He came to believe he was invulnerable because he had got away with two attempts to escape and thought he was bound to succeed the third time:

"The soldier won't dare shoot – his arm will drop off together with the gun . . ."

*

What should a man do to earn his supreme reward? Perhaps it is enough if he feeds the birds, when he is hungry himself – and then forgets all about it.

*

A sheet of paper is for me what the forest is to a man on the run.

*

"*A forest is better than a field: you can hide in a forest.*"

*

"*You just take a stick in your hand, and go on and on.*"

*

"*Go, Andrey: an unfinished page is waiting for you back there!*"

*

Leskov may have written *Enchanted Wanderer* by way of thumbing his nose at Pushkin's and Lermontov's disenchanted noblemen.

*

"*Write to her, then, and say – not that I am dead, but that I have simply gone away.*"

*

People say: as many as there are stars in the sky. But in fact there aren't all that many of them. They can be added up on the fingers. How many are there in the Great Bear? Seven at most. And then they keep track of each other – every single one is accounted for.

*

"I could go on talking to you for months on end, without a break!" – this from a lonely man who is particular about the company he keeps. Funny how some people become infatuated by the sound of their own voices and are deaf to everything else – like black-cocks during the mating season. Better listen to the whistling of the wind. I keep very much to myself. In the evenings I go out for a walk on my own for half an hour or so until bedtime. It's nice to be alone.

*

This is because of the crowded conditions. They write in books and magazines that every man needs some space to himself and that if you are constantly surrounded by people it can make you ill. Automatically you lower a kind of invisible veil over your eyes and, with your vision blurred in this manner, you look but do not see – except that the cat has stuck one leg up in the air like a factory chimney and is licking it: a nice enough thing to watch.

*

Nothing has changed – everything is the same as last year. I am sitting at the same table, under the same birch tree and all sorts of catkins and seeds keep dropping on the paper, as if it were only yesterday. The speed with which the leaves unfold and the sun sets course for summer reminds me of those sequences in films when they want to show that so many years have passed: snow falls and thaws, and the cherry blossom comes out, all in the twinkling of an eye. One cannot even help feeling sorry that time flies by so fast.

10th May, 1968.

*

The music of Mozart and of Haydn still has something of the same significance as the ringing of church bells – except that it chimes in celebration of love and spring. When we hear this sort of music over the radio, we find it hard to believe that the composer can have died.

*

While waiting for the timber to be unloaded I admire the forest which comes up close to the forbidden zone. Such a luminous texture, a grainy and phosphorescent surface. Apart from Claude Lorrain I can think of nothing to compare it with.

It brings on a pastoral mood. But when one looks over a long period of time at the same insistently beckoning landscape, watching it change rapidly against the background of a static everyday existence which proceeds at an infinitely slower pace – when nature is thus more light-footed and articulate than man, giving so much food for heart and eye even in this wretchedly confined space that one wants constantly to thank it – then one cannot help but keep turning in one's thoughts always to the same tree, endeavouring to take in the dense cloud of foliage that bulges out at us like an eye, and marvelling at its goodness, at its calm superiority over us.

*

The most interesting people in West Germany are said to be the policemen – at least they treat the likes of us with more humanity and decency than anyone else does. It would seem that a certain contact, demanded by the character and spirit of their profession, with the fantastic, with the extraordinary and exotic in life, makes them more responsive and understanding as far as we are concerned. A Russian tramp and drunkard wandering through Germany was regularly able to rest for days (and sometimes weeks) on end in German lock-ups where the policemen would feed him and occasionally even give him a hair of the dog that bit him – at their own expense. Once he was picked up in the street and put in the cells. All of a sudden the *Schutzman*'s kindly fat face appeared in the food hatch and he handed his prisoner a mug of beer, grinned from ear to ear and greeted him with the words:

"*Smert nemetskim okkupantam!*" ("Death to the German invaders!") – the only Russian words he knew.

*

"*The Germans' aim was to* capitulate *Russia.*"

*

"*My whole chest was* occupied."

*

"*Aufstehen!*", joked a little man, coming into the smoking room.[1] But he said it in such a threatening voice that I was horrified: he still remembers! And he laughed unnaturally in a sort of demoniacal way. It's amazing how hatred corrodes people's hearts. How weak and helpless are those that hate, how defenceless . . .

*

On Hitler:
"*It was the way he treated people that proved his undoing – his utter undoing. Our people don't like it when they are kicked in the teeth.*"

*

"*Dreaming of Yids?!*"

(The usual joke when someone groans and screams in his sleep. The "Yids" come at night to strangle and torment the sleeping man who, presumably, had taken part in atrocities against them at some time or other. Of course, he saw nothing wrong in helping to "liquidate" them at the time, but now they come back – in dreams . . .)

*

. . . In a cell a lad is sitting
Aged sixteen or something like.
"Tell me now, my little fellow,
Have you bumped off many men?"
"Just eighteen of them were Christians,
Plus one hundred Yids and ten."

[1] Room set aside in the barracks where prisoners could smoke. The "little man" was probably a Russian collaborator of the Germans during the war who still remembered German words of command such as *aufstehen*: stand up!

"For the Yids we shall forgive you,
For the Russians we shall not,
And at dawn tomorrow morning
In the court-yard you'll be shot."
(An old song)

*

Man is always both much worse and much better than is expected of him. The fields of good are just as limitless as the wastelands of evil . . .

*

"*And if a man is a monster, do what you like – he'll always be one!*"

*

"*Would I have enough strength of will and courage to burn a cat in a furnace?*"

*

"*For the sake of my idea I have despatched more than one man to the next world.*"

*

A Russian does nothing but tempt God with various rational proposals about the best way to run the world. Russians give a lot of trouble to God.

*

"*All those who are not of our set I would exterminate!*"

*

"*If I had only taken his gold watch, I would have been released ages ago . . .*"

*

"*I have two dead men to my credit.*"

*

"I let him soil my hands."

*

"I says to him from the other side (at a ford)*: 'Stop, Vasili Ivanych or I'll shoot.' But he keeps on going and laughs: 'You won't shoot . . .'*

What could I do?"

*

"'Okay,' I replied, 'I shan't tell anyone about your case. But how could you have done it to children, tell me, to children, after all, three or four years old, to the whole lot of them still in the kindergarten?'

'Yea, but they didn't belong to anybody . . .'"

*

"I want, he says, to be murdered by clean hands . . ."

"And tell me, did you feel any pity?"

"What pity can there be, Andrey?"

*

A murderer, even if he is more sinned against than sinning, always makes a mess of things, doing the job not in the way he intended, or even killing the wrong person. This makes it all the harder to decide whether the murderer is simply evil, or whether he is just a victim of fate or circumstances. In nine cases out of ten he will say he didn't do it, but that it "just happened". But isn't that precisely what we all say when something really bad has happened? Isn't it true to say that any "good" man is capable of any evil, and that it is merely a matter of chance whether he actually *perpetrates* it or not? Isn't it therefore enough merely to *think* of killing someone to be a murderer?

*

"I have so much anger in me that if you were to lay me on some ice it would thaw to a depth of four feet."

*

"I'd sooner die than kill."

*

He looked at the cat and said for no reason at all:

"It must be killed" – with no malice, calmly, as people say – *"it's time for breakfast"*, or *"it would be good to shave"*.

*

"He could hold out no longer and bumped him off."

*

He never brought any run-away prisoner back alive. He would steal up to the man at night, as he sat by his fire in the forest, and pause for a minute or so before pressing the trigger: "Let him live and dream his dreams for just one tiny bit longer . . ."

*

"I see him as a moral leper!"

*

"And so he perished at the hand of a peasant – like a pig."

*

"But you are more a bandit than me."

*

"And she feels now, the viper, that her candle is burning out."

*

"What a man thinks means nothing."

*

A few months before proclaiming himself Tsar, Pugachev[1] did not even think of doing it. He does not sound at all like a man who was bent on evil. In the record of his interrogation of

[1] Emelian Pugachev (1726–1775): Pretender who claimed to be the murdered Emperor Peter III, and leader of a peasant revolt.

16th September 1774, for example, we find him saying the following in connection with his stay in the Kazan jail: "Meanwhile some money of mine had disappeared – I do not remember how much – and many people learned of this and wanted to look for it, but I did not grieve for it and said to the others: 'I regard it as alms: if someone has taken it – good luck to him!' I drank no spirits at that time and occasionally prayed to God, and therefore the other prisoners and also the soldiers considered me a good man. At the time I had as yet no intention of calling myself Tsar and the life I led did not come from a desire to curry favour with people so as to be able, after calling myself Tsar, to refer to that virtuous life."

This was winter 1773, and in the following summer it all started. Pushkin mentions that Pugachev was good-natured, as well as being roguish and artful. Pugachev himself noted that during the Prussian campaign, Denisov, a Don Cossack colonel, took him on as batman "for my great dexterity in the service".

Pugachev was most probably that usual type of Russian adventurer who is both the plaything of fate and also not averse to seizing any opportunity it presents him, becoming now good, now evil, without being by nature either, but simply adapting himself to circumstances which were themselves merely a matter of luck, the caprices of a shifting "fortune", as in the episode with the money he suddenly gave away to just as casual and light-fingered a thief.

*

An arm as narrow as a sword and the fashionable word "airliner" – and there's the whole man for you.

*

"Ever since I was sixteen I've been like a fish in water."

*

"In school me and my brother finished two and a half classes between us."

*

On success:
"*I managed all this without a father or mother!*"

*

"*How many are you?*"
"*Eight – and all through no fault of ours!*" (usual joke)

*

A gambling man will have no compunction in telling the vilest things about himself. He will even do it with gusto: that's the sort I am! He stands aside from himself and examines his own outrageousness in the third person – like an artist. Fate for him is merely the subject-matter for a tale which needs to be entertaining. But how much trouble he causes with this tale! . . .

*

"*My life and biography contain nothing but services rendered to humanity . . .*
Such men as I are everywhere only rewarded . . .
I make bold to assure you that you have never yet met such a disinterested person as myself . . ."
(From "A Complaint to the Prosecutor General")

*

Occasionally one meets people of a dreamy disposition:
"*Why isn't Moscow in Sukhumi*[1]*?!. Now, if only Moscow were in Sukhumi! . . . A most beautiful spot!*"

*

"*Moscow is a capital city: people from all over the world arrive there in hats.*"

*

"*Buy yourself a nice pair of shoes – and you'll feel just like King Lear.*"

*

[1] A resort on the Black Sea coast.

"*Life is sad, and so I sit sadly in sad reality and await an existential illumination.*" (Inscription on a photograph)

*

He got his mistress into the habit of smoking and sitting on his friends' knees – so she could tell him afterwards how they had behaved.

"*I cut her hair city-fashion, to make her look like a witch: a fringe in front and hanging down behind – the way they do it in the West.*"

*

"*I keep to the Japanese principle of politeness.*"

*

"*What is Western culture? It's carrying snot around in your pocket: you blow it into a handkerchief and carry it about with you.*"

*

"*Oh, I did laugh in '59: a man fell down a hole, and then his wife fell in after him!*"

*

"*When you suddenly realize there is nothing to eat – you can't help laughing.*"

*

. . . At some stage you realize the frivolousness of all you have done and lived by, and this feeling is capable of driving you to despair, until it occurs to you that the whole of world history is pretty frivolous too.

*

Everything he ever wrote he did so about and by means of himself, pulling it all out of his own – very insignificant –

person, as a conjurer pulls a duck or a gun out of an empty top hat, all the time marvelling at his own resourcefulness.

(Abram Tertz).

*

. . . I am pleased our small son has become fond of the expression "it turns out that". I do not know how often I actually use it myself. But my meaning always boils down to something of the same sort. This is why my style is overloaded with such conjunctions as "thus", "therefore" and "hence", which only seem to provide logical explanations, but are in fact more like the devices of a conjurer – on the lines, for example of: therefore (or hence) an omelette in a hat suddenly popped out from behind a screen. There is no proof here, only a sudden appearance – out of thin air, out of nothing: it turns out that . . .

*

While washing I touched my head and was suddenly surprised how small it is . . .

*

I simply can't imagine why mice should have tails.

*

Whenever one sees Australia on a map, one's heart leaps with pleasure: Kangaroo, boomerang! . . .

*

A sparrow is very funny when it bathes: it bends forward to wet its breast, and then spends a long time shaking the water off. And the fact that it has no arms is then particularly noticeable.

*

I wonder what mice make of birds, and beetles – of butterflies? They are obviously able to see each other. But what do they think?

*

I am rather sorry that here in the camp I have begun to take a poorer view of dogs.

*

I suspect that old men are more child-like than appears at first sight. They are fond of the same things as children – going to films and stuffing themselves with cake, for example. And they skip around on one leg – at least in their own imagination – much more frequently than we think. To see that old men are children, you only have to look at dwarfs.

*

A cat of three colours – and smeared with green paint in the fourth place.

*

. . . When green leaves turn black against the background of a dawn as pale-pink as a carrot.

*

One must know how to twine rope out of a phrase. And then walk on it as on a tight-rope. In the air. Without holding on to anything. Outside one's own body. Without form. Like a pure spirit.

*

Verses:

> "To hunt and shoot is my delight
> And toil I do respect
> I take up any work in sight
> And culture don't neglect."

It is interesting that hunting and shooting have pride of place.

*

Poetry parodies everyday life, expressing itself with an exaggerated courtesy and a great many circumstantial details:

"The frost was bitter when I left the forest that icy cold and freezing winter's day . . ." But all the time, poetry inwardly shakes with laughter: "Just as if I were real! What a joke!"

*

It would be worth while to wander round the Tretyakov Gallery[1] and look at the paintings for what they may really be: pantomime. Hogarth, while assuring us that he was copying life, lets the cat out of the bag in his autobiographical *Anecdotes* – quite unaware that he is giving away both himself and everybody else who was in on his secret:

"I have endeavoured to treat my subjects as a dramatic writer: my picture is my stage, and men and women my players, who by means of certain actions and gestures, are to exhibit *a dumb show*."

This kind of treatment leaves very little room for "realism", since it is based on the use of various effects and devices.

The first is that of drawing the viewer's attention to things that he then instantly recognizes for himself – rather in the manner of museum guides who understand very well the principle involved: "Look over here," they tell you, "and now over here – see how that elderly gentleman is opening his mouth and putting his finger to it as a sign that he wants to eat, while his young wife feigns hysteria allegedly because they have no money, but in fact to cover the retreat of a hussar she has just been entertaining: see him there, jumping out of the window, leaving behind one of his boots under a chair – note how worn it is because of all the campaigns he has been in". And so they go on, passing from one detail to another, till finally – and hereby hangs the tale! – they point out how the cat is meanwhile eating up the master's lunch. The viewer is delighted to see that everything fits together so neatly – which it does, not because it has anything to do with real life, but because this is how the painter has programmed it. One is pleased to be able to "read" the situation so clearly from the precisely formulated and meaningful touches that make up the

[1] Main art gallery in Moscow.

picture as pre-conceived by its creator. Sceptics are completely won over by the boot and the cat – it is such details that serve to dot the "i"s in the story of the development of "realism" in art.

The second effect is that of *holding* the attention, of "entertainment": the canvas is contrived like the plot of a novel – everything is joined together and finally tied up with an intriguing little bow. And look what odd tricks are played by pure coincidence: a cat and a boot side by side! (That boot is the crux of the whole picture . . .)

"Typical characters in typical circumstances"[1] nearly always turn out to be there by pure chance – it is like the luck of the draw in a card game. The art of imitating reality ("realism") boils down to an ability to excite curiosity, to devise a puzzle with a key to its solution. As in real life? Not at all – as in art, where everything is always pre-conceived and invented.

Thirdly, there is the effect of surprise: one moment of time is suddenly picked out from all the others and stopped in its tracks – as in the final scene in *The Government Inspector*, when everybody on the stage is literally struck dumb. This gives it a peculiar intensity; indeed it is less like a moment of time than a bolt from the blue causing everyone to freeze in the posture of a culprit caught in the act, like a pickpocket. The author constantly surprises his characters red-handed: Aha, got you!

Of "truth to life" there is little in "realist" art except, perhaps, some of the raw material snatched from under the viewer's nose: a street, poverty, the squalor of everyday life, the habit of peeping through keyholes. But the actual painting and composition are based on artificial tricks, including the technique of close-up. Genre painting was essentially micro-cosmic. The very modesty of its subject matter (a major's courtship scarcely lent itself to the same grand treatment as the last day of Pompeii[2]) imposed a smallness of scale which was admirably

[1] A standard formula used by Soviet critics to describe the essence of the official doctrine of "Socialist Realism".

[2] *A Major's Courtship* (1848) genre painting by P. A. Fedotov; *The Last Day of Pompeii* (1828–30) by K. P. Briullov, now in the Russian Museum, Leningrad.

adapted to achieving both the effect of instant recognition and that of entertainment – the story always has to be figured out, and this requires a close examination of detail. Hence the clarity of presentation, the clear and precise readability – stemming not at all from realism but from the need to make quite plain the exact interrelationship of everything in the picture.

For the same reason, deep chiaroscuro is abandoned, colours are less rich, and the brush is applied much more finely; since everything must be scrutinized so carefully, the colours are lighter and the lines sharper – the cat and the boot have to stand out clearly. So there you have it: if you want to paint pictures that are "true to life", study the art of pantomime!

*

Grown-ups are just the same as children. If they are not kept busy with work, they play all the time – cards, dominoes and other games. There are special games (always designed to trip up the new boys) to while away time in the prison cells: "The Sawmill", "Geese", "Button" (played with a drinking mug), "The Cunning Neighbour". All of them very amusing.

*

"*I am older than he is, and yet he hit me!*"

*

"*I love looking at people's mugs when they play cards – a real farce!*"

*

. . . I have always been irritated (and even now I am sometimes roused to fury) to see how vacuously people play dominoes for days on end, banging the pieces to make everything shake and jump, while repeating mechanically the same swear words – it is essential to bang the pieces with the words: "Go on, go on" – otherwise there can be no play. But on looking closer, you see concealed behind this a second reality – something which provides the inarticulate not just with relaxation, but with a badly needed substitute for a proper existence; it enables them to live through the drama of victories and defeats, and to feel the hand of fate upon them at a point when it seems to have abandoned them altogether. After working a while at the factory bench, a man will play a game of draughts to break the monotony, to plunge into a round of adventures or events of a kind lacking in his daily routine and now conjured up on the board, with "men" made of wood. It is the same kind of reality as, say, creative writing or reading – like immersing oneself in a book as though it were real life, and thus leading in a game or in words a parallel existence which is more interesting and thematically richer than one's own. The board on which one plays, with its intersecting planes, simulates the intricate pattern of human existence, its multi-dimensional quality. It seems ordinary and commonplace enough – yet how unlike one's own drab daily round!

*

Literary speech in the old days seems to have been freer in the syntactical sense, allowing turns of phrase which tied together, as it were, different currents and layers of being. The principle involved in combining letters and words is perhaps best represented by book ornamentation. Here we have all kinds of embellishments and tracery: beasts with interlocking tails and men leaning on swords, or a single unbroken line drawn to form a maze-like pattern of intertwining plants which invites us to follow it with the eye through all its twists and turns. In this manner, by means of a kind of sacramental knot, the head-piece joins the initial word of the chapter to the book's title or table of contents, making the whole into one large, common letter with numerous scrolls and rebuses needing to be deciphered, i.e. read. In earlier times people were hence always much more mindful of the fact that as we read we join the letters of the alphabet into coherent speech, and because they delighted in seeing them woven together, the very designs of the letters inevitably led them to express themselves in a high-flown manner natural to literary language – always more elaborate and measured than spoken language, as was pointed up and illustrated in a book's ornamentation. I always used to think that these decorative motifs were meant to convey verbal images, but now I understand that their main effect was to demonstrate the intricacy of the process by which words are strung together.

*

. . . and, as if to emphasize my point, autumn has arrived, invading the summer with many inconveniences and driving rain. The clouds which now cover the sky like smoke are a forceful reminder that later landscape painting became prosaic or merely picturesque, losing its theatrical quality. It would be good if people went back to the older tradition, painting landscapes as battles used to be painted, with the sun, torch in hand, rising over the fields and casting the light of day upon the scene.

21st July, 1968.

*

. . . It suddenly also occurred to me that this vast amount of timber for building, the "wooden" quality of Ancient Russia, corresponds very well to the spirit of the people and the character of our history, conveying both its colour and what it was like to the touch – a combination of angularity and roundness, a warm, full-bodied materiality which was yet none too durable, and easily mouldered away or burned to ashes, so that nothing remained but an empty field, where everything then grew up again like grass. Compared to the stones of the Western Middle Ages, our wooden antiquity thus had greater kinship with life as such: it was more formless and precarious, and little of it has survived, since it was indifferent to the idea of storing up for the morrow. So we have nothing but gaps, schemes never brought to fruition but always started from scratch over and over again, vague outlines – and just here and there in the ocean of timber, an occasional stone cathedral juts up like a rocky island; and among all the voices singing to us indistinctly, suddenly we hear an Ivan the Terrible or a Nilus of Sorsk. Its face is blank and amorphous, ready to wear the first aspect that comes along, whether coarse or delicate, otherwordly or brutish, but always lacking precision. Compare the Caucasus: a metal die, its mountains starkly etched against the sky, and men to match – hooked noses, spiked moustaches, and their food sharply spiced and peppery, not like our stodgy stuff – a *kasha*[1] into which you can mix anything and it will all be taken in and absorbed: Finns, Greeks, Tartars, Vikings, French jargon, Petersburg dissolve in it like butter; and all the time we remain as formless as ever, unconcerned with the purity of our blood, assimilating all and sundry, with noses like potatoes and slanting cheekbones – and we get away with it, sometimes producing a Socrates in birch-bark shoes, a philosopher looking for all the world like a village idiot; even our beauty has a matt, wood-like quality – a face such as yours which blurs under the glance of the beholder, or a landscape with a greyish tree on the background of a faded sky. Timber is both heavy and light – such gossamer lines and fibres, all warmth and impermanence, quite the reverse of stone; and one's little house in the town was built of logs and caulked with the dung that had been raked together and spread in the yard where it lay with one's mother's old cast-off rags – a soft, warm place to lie down in and cover your head . . .

*

"But maybe you will say a few words of thanks to Russia one day – not now, but in about a hundred or three hundred years' time, from your distant, free and by that time perhaps flourishing and prosperous Europe, for whatever good things you may sometimes have seen or read, or encountered in this country? If only a couple of words, and no more . . ."

"I want to put it out of my mind and forget it."

*

[1] A standard Russian dish made of boiled buckwheat, to which butter and other ingredients may be added.

It is pleasant to hear somewhere in the distance the clucking of a hen, the mooing of a cow – voices of a peaceful world. It is practically August by now. There is already an August darkness about things. The days are bright and hot – it is high summer. But on looking a little closer you see that the shadows in the evening are more opaque and sombre, and even at midday the vegetation, now in full leaf, and the blue sky seem to have a fine gauze cast over them, a kind of darkish haze that drugs the senses and makes the air look as if it might come out at any moment in inky blotches. It is not in autumn or winter that death lays the eggs whereby all things will be wormholed, but now, in August. The job is done, the eggs are laid – in August.

27th July, 1968.

*

. . . All around there are people swearing at each other as they argue about who gives orders in the air force in war-time – "And we immediately change direction and start bombing!" They shout terribly – always, as usual, about things of no importance and it is difficult to write to such an accompaniment. And if we go on like this, winter will soon be upon us. That same winter which I had no time to savour last year. How much it has shrunk, this concept of one year.

At times I have a great hankering after milk for some reason. Whole milk and a lot of it. But no matter, I'll wait – and go on waiting.

*

"Obviously she comes from an upper-class family – the kind that needs no filtering."[1]

*

"With a name like that he elbows his way right into the best society."

*

[1] Meaning that it has such pure blood that any filtering for impurities (as milk is filtered, for instance) is superfluous. (*Author's explanation*)

When all is said and done one must be grateful to one's stomach. Here we are, whiling away our time without a thought in our heads, but it just goes on digesting day and night, attending to our needs. It could fall ill, or start playing up and say "that's enough as far as I am concerned", but it carries right on, the nice fellow, always on duty.

*

Think, when you look at people, of their recent birth, their childhood, or their imminent death – and you will love them: such frail creatures!

*

. . . Babel[1] exhibited a trait common, perhaps, to all writers: he was not merely an observer, he was also a snooper. All his life he spied "through the keyhole" in the hope of seeing something interesting. As an author, he was always himself off stage, looking from outside at the bizarre scenes he picked out from some squalid area of life – hence his reticence about his own views and the elusive quality of his biography. What kind of views, indeed, can a man have if he is entirely engrossed in the search for outlandish things and subjects buried among the rubbish? And his biography is that not of a living person, but of one seconded to life (his job of clerk in the Red Cavalry suited him admirably), who could fit into any surroundings or situation and look at it without prejudice. He was a spy in the service of literature who ferreted out wonders in everyday existence, a *déclassé* secret agent who once rented a room in the house of a "finger man" in order to write his *Odessa Stories*. His non-Russian origins were also a convenience for him.

*

An ex-soldier to a journalist:

"*I paid for this with my blood, and you want to write about it?!*"

[1] Isaac Babel (1894–1941?): Russian-Jewish short story writer; author of *Red Cavalry*. He was arrested in 1939 and was presumably executed or died in a camp.

How impossible to describe life! How shameless of literature to poke its nose in everywhere! How can you use a pen to write about – blood!

*

"*You ought to tell us about animals! Stories about animals never did any harm.*"

*

"*What an ugly beast the camel is, but the meat's good to eat . . .*"

*

I've just been told something new about wolves. A wolf, it appears, has the habit of seizing a horse by the tail:

"It's in the nature of a horse to run, and the wolf has to grab it from behind. If he sees he is too light to stop it, he eats a lot of earth – some fifteen or twenty kilos – and goes after the horse again. Then, when it's all over, the wolf spews all that earth out of himself."

What marvels they are, these animals!

*

"And who'd have thought such wild and bloodthirsty creatures would want to stick so close to human beings!" – this apropos of two kites – nicknamed Vaska and Katenka – which kept bringing the carcasses of hens into the camp. Sparrows they gobbled up feathers and all. "There they'd sit, the beauties, all blue-eyed!"

And then there was the hare which would come running up at the sound of an accordion; and the bear which saved a small girl, a security guard's daughter who had fallen into the river, but was killed for its pains while it was carrying her back to her home in its paws! Everything wants to get close to man!

*

"*And afterwards I saw that dog in a dream one night: with eyes as big as that!*" (About a dog that had been eaten)

*

"*It doesn't expend its calories at all.*" (About a cat)

*

"*We ought to put it inside a boot – and make it sit there!*" (About a cat)

*

"*But we were just curious to find out: once you've had one in your hands it's supposed not to be afraid any more! . . .*" (A mouse)

*

"*We trapped it under a rail – a stinking weasel, a lively little devil!*"

*

"*The cow just went on swelling up. People said we should give her a live frog to eat. So we did. She swallowed it in one go and licked her chops. And then she was as right as rain again. After that she could eat anything – clover, lucerne, anything.*"

*

"*And so I spread my* bushlat *out on the ground and then I saw a bird flying around. It did a circle and came down. I was just settling down on my* bushlat *when another one suddenly starts up from underneath it. It turns out I was lying on a nest. Real cunning things, birds! Before I knew where I was they'd all fucked off and there wasn't one left.*"

*

Lions on cheap oleographs seem benign rather than fierce. Not because the artist has never seen a lion in his life or because he wants to play a joke on us. The humour lies in the very appearance of animals: they *look* so comic. Even the sight of a dog fills us with amazement: just like me, but with a tail and four legs! In the popular idea of the lion you can clearly see the fable-like quality of all animals. The Creator himself has commanded them to imitate us. At the court of man, they play the role of jesters. What snouts, what horns! With them our life is more like a theatre.

Someone told us about a rooster which was made to drink vodka. In his usual state "he was as lazy as an elephant. But after a bit to drink he was like fire!"

Women also do a good deal to make human life more theatrical – always dressing up and painting their faces. Woman by her nature is intended for show.

*

"*She was married to some lousy Armenian . . . And it's the second time she's been loaded by him – I don't know how much, but she's pretty far gone by now.*"[1]

*

From a song:

"My little Katie, my crack-pot matie,
My Katie darling, you're my ideal,
My next job will be audacious and bold –
On my return I'll dress you in gold
Katie my darling – honest I will!"

*

After over twenty years in a camp – by which time he was forty – he went to a zoo for the first time in his life. And what did he like best there? The giraffe!

*

Only one Pharaonic Decree (and a good thing, too!) has come down to us from the days of the Old Kingdom in Egypt – to an official who was being sent South on an expedition. And what does the Pharaoh write and show concern about in this one and only Decree? About a dwarf who must with all haste be

[1] i.e. she has been made pregnant by him ("loaded" – like a rifle) and is now far advanced in her pregnancy. (*Author's explanation*)

conveyed to Egypt as the most interesting and precious prodigy: "My Majesty desires to see this dwarf more than the treasures of the mines and of Ethiopia." (*Historical Anthology of the Ancient East*, p. 31)

Passion for art (the exotic), for puzzles (and miracles) is apparently in our blood.

*

"*Do you know what an egg-plant is? It's like a bull's ball, but it's blue and grows out of the ground!*"

*

A consumptive – proudly:
"*I've got little sticks coming out of me!*"[1]

*

"*And at that moment my prayer failed to reach God, because I couldn't take my eyes off that dirty Jew.*" (At Christmas)

*

"*And the fellow says: 'Let's go and watch – they're going to carve someone up now'.*"

*

The old man would traipse over to the cinema with all the others and doze off there from time to time. After a good sleep he would go back to the barracks with all the rest. When people made fun of him and asked why he bothered to go, he replied:

"Oh, I just sit and look at my own films."

Sitting there in the crowd he probably has a greater sense of being a spectator – this requires a feeling of shared cosiness, the warmth of being together with other people. Attention to sound or to images, the work of visual or auditory perception, inhibits the will and intellect. In the theatre it is not at all essential to understand; it is more important to see and hear. It might even be possible to use the theatre as a means of

[1] *Bacilli* is translated literally into Russian as "little sticks".

therapy – like hypnosis. Is one's mind actually engaged at all? Only in a very subdued way. Just as meaning is swallowed up by rhythm in poetry, so on the stage life is engulfed by display.

*

"*A concert group of one Georgian and a woman of God knows what race – her hair was all grey, and she played an accordion.*"

*

"*And I made a little hole with a nail so I could see the whole thing.*"

*

"*They were all crowding up against the iron bars.*"

*

"*Iron bars are our stage and screen.*" (From a song)

*

"*There used to be more fun in the camp in the old days. Someone was always being beaten up or hanged. Every day there was a special event.*"

*

A kitten plays on the floor with an invisible mouse. By the look of it, the mouse can't be any bigger than a fly. But there is no fly either. The kitten is just daydreaming.

Intellectuals have the same ways as crickets. They chirp so loudly that the whole drying shop[1] resounds with it. As soon as the machines stop working you can hear them trilling away like mad. One new prisoner can hardly speak for joy:

"But you have *crickets* here!"

Just as if he had suddenly run into old friends.

*

I wonder why it feels so good to wear an overcoat, or even a

[1] See note on page 46.

jacket simply thrown over one's shoulders? Probably because it forms a kind of roof over our back and we feel so snug and sheltered – like a snail in its shell or a peasant in his hut.

*

We really have little idea of the roundabout ways in which art affects our senses by suggesting all kinds of smells and noises – never directly, but obliquely, by means of goodness knows what remote effects. Take, for instance, the splendid tinkle of gold sovereigns in old-fashioned novels. They gleam as we run them through our fingers; or as we weigh a purseful of them in the palm of our hand and fling them at the villain's feet. How would those novelists have fared with banknotes or a wallet stuffed with receipts? Half the poetic charm of their writing resided in the glitter and ring of gold. Doubloons, ducats, "I wouldn't give a farthing!" Ecus. Oh, what wonderful sport with words . . .

*

"*Tell Sonia that her Goldie is off to Kolyma to do his five years' hard.*"

Rolling the words on his tongue and toying with them like the cards he runs through his fingers in virtuoso fashion before flipping them at a single go from one hand over to the other, all the while revelling in the sterling worth summed up in his name, he sent out his call sign as he paced his cell in the big transit prison, and pronounced over and over again, without a thought for anything but the pure poetry of it, this epitome of his own destiny and of the noble art of thievery:
"*Tell Sonia that her Goldie is off to Kolyma to do his five years' hard.*"

*

". . . And now the "pigeons"[1] are twice as rich
Who can touch them with an untried hand?"

How well this song expresses the dejection and anxiety of the professional hoist by his own petard after losing his touch through a long absence from the scene.

[1] Pigeon (*frayer*): the victim of a criminal; any non-criminal.

(I must confess that I have similar thoughts about the practice of literature.)

*

One thief to another, smugly: "I've never held anything heavier than a purse in my hand!"

This is his way of saying that he could never stoop to any form of work, and that the greatest prestige is enjoyed not by the burglar, the armed bandit or the mugger, but by the pickpocket with his subtle specialized skill – the thief in the true sense of the word, in its metaphysical meaning of conjurer.

Bandits and murderers are not well regarded in these quarters. A murder – a "wet job" as it is called in the language of the underworld – is frowned on not so much because it usually involves serious difficulties with the authorities (though this, too, may be a consideration), but because it shows a lack of the professional touch and is a sign of the bungler. A "pigeon" must be "rolled" so that he does not even notice.

In theory one would think that power belongs to brute force. In fact, this is not the case at all: power is wielded by the magician, by the man with subtle sleight of hand. It belongs to the light-fingered cutpurse. Power belongs to art.

Almost as in the case of poets, what counts most in the thieves' code of behaviour is style, the ability to project one's personality in terms of a show, a spectacle. Contempt for "pigeons", that is, for all not subject to thieves' law, for all "non-thieves", who do not even deserve to be called men ("Any *men* here?" – total silence in a vast, thousand-strong crowd making up a prisoner transport: only two *men* could be found . . .) is to a considerable extent due to the fact that the average person – particularly the educated one – is incapable of the kind of theatrical exploit, gesture, or the spectacular death which so impresses thieves. The expression "like a greedy 'pigeon'" has become proverbial among them: "Greed is the 'pigeon's' undoing."

Two warders once came along to take a thief to the SDB[1].

[1] Strict Discipline Barracks.

He was unwilling to go and threw a temper (he may simply have been in a bad mood). Taking out a knife, he pointed it at himself and threatened to run it through his bare chest, if they didn't leave him alone.

"We've seen your sort before!"

"You've never seen my sort!"

And with a quick, slashing movement he showed them exactly what sort of a man they had in front of them.

The thief's theatrical panache has given rise to hundreds of legends, which even now, when the thieves' law is not what it was, make up a good half of all labour camp poetry.

*

"They were decent, fair-minded people . . ."

This was said by a *moujik* (I use the word in its specialized sense[1]), of whom a good thief would say ironically:

"I'm really grateful to him – he puts his purse near me."

But other people speak very unfavourably of them indeed. Both kinds of opinion are perfectly justified and relate to the concept of the thief as the embodiment of ethical rules which took shape in a moral vacuum. We have here the visible outcrops of a code of behaviour: order, caste, etiquette, hierarchy have arisen where previously nothing had reigned but arbitrariness and a lack of any sense of limit. A thief, properly speaking, is not an immoral character, but a man who believes in élitist principles of morality far stricter than the nobility's code of honour, since the slightest misdemeanour is here punished with instant death – something considered less fearful than infringement of the thieves' law.

A former thief once explained to me that according to the standards prevalent in the old days, if a foreman or a barracks orderly had lost his temper and called me a "bitch"[2] without any evil intent, then he – the thief – would have been obliged

[1] *Moujik* (peasant): a non-criminal who performs various services for the thieves in the camp and is protected by them.

[2] "Bitch" (*suka*): a thief who has betrayed his comrades or collaborates with the authorities, and a general term of abuse.

to kill the man, even if I had begged him not to, because he "drank with me", i.e. put his lips to the common mug of tea, and if my dishonour were not washed away in blood it would mean that he was calmly drinking with a "bitch", something which would automatically put him in the same class – and if he had not murdered my defamer on the spot, he would himself have had to be murdered at the earliest opportunity as a "bitch" by some other guardian of the moral code who happened to hear of this breach of it.

By these earlier standards I would thus have been counted among the *moujiks* who in the labour camps always used to enjoy the protection of the criminal fraternity and paid a fixed tribute in return, just as in ancient times peasants were liable for the upkeep of, say, the Prince's body-guard.

Seen in this light, the thieves' "fraternity" with its "law" appears to have resembled an order of chivalry (stood on its head, perhaps, but not less of one for that) which, apart from enforcing a stringent code, set the highest store by *spirit* – a word also used by the thieves in a special sense:

"To string yourself up you need spirit."

"'If you've got the spirit,' I said, 'take a knife and ram[1] him.'"

"Spirit" and scrupulous attention to one's obligations were such a matter of pride that, for example, a thief leaving a labour camp was quite likely to go up in ritual fashion to another prisoner and ask: "Do I owe you anything? Take it." This was considered good form, and a "creditor" was entitled to settle a debt by killing the man who "owed" him something – but would himself be killed if he did so without justification.

A kind of saying has been preserved from those days which is now said more in joke than in earnest when people want to make sure that the person they are talking to is satisfied and bears no grudge:

"Mind now – no talk at the transit camp! . . ."

A transit camp used to be the cross-roads where many

[1] "Ram": the word used is a wartime pilots' expression for suicide missions against enemy planes.

paths converged, where reputations were discussed and reviewed. There the names of famous men were constantly mentioned and passed from mouth to mouth – "Pushkin", "Spartacus"[1] and other heroes of the epic tales which are told in the labour camps.

*

A God-fearing Orthodox peasant talking about thieves, with a shrug of the shoulders, as one talks about a social necessity:

"*It's a busy life – there's always a shop or a bank to rob. And where would all those judges and lawyers be without them?*"

*

The way to rob a shop: do it in the lunch hour, or better still in the evening, just before closing time, when they latch the door on the inside. The main thing is to show you mean business by your tone of voice:

"I'll count to three and then shoot the door open – one, two . . ."

You must say "One, two" very quickly, without drawing breath in between – in one go, like a gust of wind. They never hold out till "three": they always open up.

In court the sales-girl readily identified him:

"That's him, that's him. He's got eyes like a wolf . . ."

But all the customers who had been in the shop were full of praise when they gave evidence:

"So nice and good-mannered he was. We thought he was an actor . . ."

*

Accused, with a critical glance at his counsel (evidently an unimpressive figure):

"*You're my lawyer? You're going to* defend *me? Me? And what with, pray? With papers?*" (Nodding at the guards behind him): "*They brought me here with bayonets, and all you have is papers?!! . . .*"

*

[1] Nicknames of legendary criminals.

Dreamily:
"*A good thing – the F–8.*" (A make of hand-grenade)

*

"*If you want to make a noise, I'll make one too.*" (Standard warning to the victim of a robbery)

*

. . . During his many years in camp he turned a number of schemes over in his mind till he finally settled on one which he felt certain was absolutely sure to work. Late one evening he and his partner would go into the restaurant car of a train, bar the doors at both ends and grab all the money in the till and of course any loose change people happened to have on them. Then he would order everyone at gun point to drink all the liquor in the bar to the last drop. Naturally, they would all get drunk as lords, and by the time they slept it off and came to their senses, the two of them would be far away.

(This plan, in fact, appeared to me to be very comprehensive indeed: a nice combination of alcohol, theft and trickery.)

*

This is how they got "Spartacus": three men wearing gauntlets went for him with red-hot crow-bars – nobody could get anywhere near him with a knife. "Spartacus" grabbed at the crow-bars and got his hands all burned. Then they killed him.

"*It was a rather remarkable death.*"

*

"Pushkin", they say, was sitting one day at a camp-fire with another young fellow from his mob when a guard came up and told them to get back to work. The young hoodlum just swore at him. The guard shot him dead. "Bastard!", Pushkin said, groping behind him, where he was sitting, for a stick or a hatchet, but he couldn't find anything, so he got up very slowly and started walking up to the guard: "Bastard!"

In the corner of his mouth he had a lighted cigarette.

"Stop – or I shoot!", the guard shouted and took aim, but then he began to back away. He was as white as a sheet and his hands were shaking.

"You won't have the *spirit*!", Pushkin said, coming up very close.

And taking the cigarette out of his mouth, he stubbed it out against the guard's forehead. Then he turned round and calmly walked away. The guard didn't shoot.

*

I work very hard at my job of polishing chairs, and my chairs shine better than anyone else's, but I cannot cope with the output quota – it is hard for a slow person like me to move my hands with the necessary speed from one thing to another, reaching for a piece of leather, a scraper, or putty to fill in cracks and scratches. A good style (whether in writing or in chair-making) can only be achieved through lack of self-assurance, as I have observed. A stylist is usually a very diffident person who tries to compensate for his sense of inadequacy by careful attention to every word. A diffident man cannot allow himself to work badly, in slipshod fashion – as a genius can.

*

It's a good thing when the title of a book shines or glitters in some way: *The Silver Prince*[1], *Treasure Island.* Later on names like these appeared only on postage stamps, such as those of Borneo or Brazil. But the very first novel in world literature was pretty resplendent: *The Golden Ass.*

*

Mystery Island, *The Three Musketeers* . . . such titles used to have a wonderful music about them and were, perhaps, more full of meaning than the books themselves. I remember how we spoke of them with bated breath, and I remember the smell of their pages and bindings, and the silvery gleam of the yet

[1] By A. K. Tolstoy.

unread *Silver Prince*. The pregnancy of words in childhood! Who will restore it to us? . . .

*

The first lines of some verse, addressed to his fellow-writers, by a poet from among the criminals:

> "Your brother and your son in spirit
> Hastens to tell you – none too soon –
> That we are naught but lice they've squashed
> Or phlegm just fit for a spittoon."

Unfortunately I do not remember any more of it. But he had a couple of nice lines about being a prisoner:

> "For him the heavens above are rent,
> The sky falls down upon his head!"

*

Literary turns of phrase from an autobiographical novel composed by someone here:
"*We plucked flowers, etc.*"
"*The gramophone was pouring forth songs.*"
"*The melody went round and round in my head.*"
"*I knew nothing, then, of the brevity of life.*"

*

Clichés, I now realize, have more than merely stylistic significance – they are crucial to the development of the theme since they guide the narrator's mind through the plot of his familiar tale and enable him to reel it off. Utterly inane turns of phrase, such as "like a bolt from the blue", "I shake all over, but preserve my self-control", or "I take her clothes off and she gives herself to me", will have been so often repeated in the telling of the story that they now constitute the cog-wheels or the machinery which keep it moving. "A fine figure of a man", "picture of health", "in the prime of life", "in a coat of navy blue" – such expressions skip from branch to branch, from one event to the next, from the hero to the heroine (who is "like a doe", or "like a gazelle") and thanks to them everything happens naturally, of its own accord – as in real life.

Cast doubt on someone's clichés and he will tell you indignantly: but that's how it was in actual fact (and, indeed, it was). A man with a "life story" is happy because he can at least say he has "seen a thing or two" – it is his accumulated capital, and he fancies he need only describe all this wealth in his own words for "a great novel" to result (it will not).

Clichés are the signposts of art, its milestones. By following them life, hardly noticing as it does so, turns into a fairy-tale or a legend.

*

. . . The violin sang my favourite song,
The accordion set my head in a whirl,
Vodka and wine did the rest before long
And I fell for a pretty young girl.

To love pretty girls you need plenty of cash,
And I brooded on this in my mind.
So then I decided, for cutting a dash,
I would steal anything I could find.

I burgled and stole, and I dressed her in mink,
And threw money about left and right,
But one misty night I was caught in a trap,
And this was the start of my plight.

When misfortunes arrive they come by the score
It's good-bye – and for ever, my cuty!
Greetings, cell and high walls, iron bars and hard floor!
All hail, mother prison, my beauty!

*

"He was a nice, simple fellow and he never made trouble. He liked a good laugh and a joke. That kind are all dead now."

*

I am getting *kasha* again and feel very much better. Funny how one depends on such small things, but it's all to the good – it brings home how terribly vulnerable you are, held together by nothing but snot, and liable to kick the bucket if someone pokes you with his finger. Yet, my God, how tough with all that!

29th November, 1968.

*

. . . When I felt really bad, I lay down on my bunk and to keep up my spirits borrowed some stories by Edgar Allan Poe which my neighbour happened to have. In *A Descent into the Maelstrom* I chanced upon a passage that very much caught my fancy as just the thing to put a man trapped in a whirlpool in the right frame of mind. I cannot refrain from quoting:

"It may look like boasting – but what I tell you is truth – I began to reflect how magnificent a thing it was to die in such a manner, and how foolish it was of me to think of so paltry a consideration as my own individual life in view of so wonderful a manifestation of God's power. I do believe that I blushed with shame when this idea crossed my mind. After a little while I became possessed with the keenest curiosity about the whirl itself. I positively felt a wish to explore its depths, even at the sacrifice I was going to make; and my principal grief was that I should never be able to tell my old companions on shore about the mysteries I should see."

*

When the "bitches" laid "Pushkin" out on a sheet of metal plate and started roasting him over a camp fire he shouted to the bystanders and said something I could not improve on as an epigraph, if I felt myself worthy of so using it:

"You 'pigeons', tell everybody I am dying a thief! . . ."

*

Part Four

A silver crescent and next to it a silver star, both straight from a Turkish mosque, are etched in the black sky.

*

Do you know how I spent the New Year's Eve? Turning over pictures cut out of old magazines, one after another: unforgettable pictures, chosen quite haphazardly . . . Giorgione's Sleeping Venus, a glass decoration for a Christmas tree, a trinket. It seems very likely, I may say, that the art of painting originally consisted in drawing and then colouring some object which fascinated people not because of any connection with real life, but rather as something in vivid contrast with the drabness of its background, a bright patch which caught and held the attention. Such pictures as these, however, restore my sense of reality, giving the mind something to hold on to, so that I pull myself together with a start, waking up, as it were, and remembering that *this* is reality, that I actually seem to be alive, and am not just appearing to myself in a dream. In that sense a patch of colour, by attracting our attention and gladdening the eye, overcomes the insanity of formlessness and non-being and proclaims the actual existence of a world in which beauty and reality eventually converge at some point on a higher level. The element of colour, interwoven in its primary form with nature and made manifest in art, testifies through its simplest properties – those of being able to attract and retain the attention, of activating feeling and mind – that it is relatively more "real" than all the dreary greyness which leaves no memories, fading away once we wake up and blow on it . . .

*

While Odysseus sails the seas, Penelope spins. Yarn – hair – waves – bride – spouse – destiny, and, to cap it all, a wedding, because the fairy-tale spins the yarn of destiny's fulfilment. The spinning wheel is the oar and the boat and the sail of destiny in the house.

*

They say the Sun has a radius 106 times greater than the Earth's. This is fine. But how much nicer to think that this great big helpless planet of ours depends on such a *small* sun up there – it looks no bigger than a stove, really. The other day, I was asked by someone as we shifted sawdust together:

"Is it true that the Earth is a sphere?"

I found this difficult to answer and said:

"I don't know exactly."

*

If one reflects on one's life and the encounters of which it is composed, one becomes dimly aware that it does not arise from a casual concatenation of circumstances which might equally well never have come about, but was foreordained from childhood when it already existed, as it were, in preliminary outline, only later taking final shape as one's "destiny" – a destiny which, for all its strangeness, seems not fortuitous, but rather something that could have materialized only in this and no other way. As we look deeper, however, we perceive that not quite everything which is thus made manifest bears the stamp of pre-destination fulfilled; much is random or adventitious and seems to have no direct relevance to us, while other events are clear landmarks, of an obligatory and inevitable nature, and when we come face to face with them it is borne in on us that we have long ago anticipated them, or seen them before somewhere. In the course of a considerable part of our life we in fact come up against much that is already familiar to us: we did not know what would happen, but the moment events take place they reveal an aspect that in all essentials we recognize at once, in the twinkling of an eye. As we live, we learn how we were fated to live, and though in minor matters we may have somewhat muddied the waters of our pre-ordained destiny by getting up to all kinds of little tricks through the exercise of our own will (which is a secondary one), the most vital part of it always makes itself known and comes to pass exactly as it was supposed to.

30th January, 1969.

*

I ask myself: to think of the bird Sirin[1] while carting sawdust – is this really how it should be?

And I reply: Yes, it is.

*

"Play on, guitar of mine, play on,
And my song – like a bird forlorn –
Is seeking a lost paradise."

This is the definition of art. In its broadest and most general sense.

*

I had always thought (and other people on whom I tried it out agreed) that the sirens in the Odyssey must have looked somewhat like water-nymphs. But then one day I saw that on an Attic Vase of the 5th century BC they were made to look just like our Sirins. So even that far back they were thought of as birds. Can it be, incidentally, that their singing is a way of signifying union with Heaven in the hour of death, when the "I" dissolves in beautiful sounds and the soul, forgetting all, leaves the body? There are inscriptions on old Russian chests which say of the Sirin and Alkonost[2] (in terms reminiscent of the theory of music in Ancient India): "When it raises up its voice in song, it no longer feels its own self". And the same applies to a man who hears it: "And his mind is so

[1] Half-bird, half-woman of Russian mythology, evidently going back to the Greek *siren*.

[2] A legendary bird of paradise in mediaeval Russian tales, eventually deriving from the Greek *halcyon*.

captivated thereby, that a great change comes upon him". Self-consciousness has ended – the delights of paradise begin.

*

"*When you come out, you're like a new-born babe . . .*" (About a village sauna bath, where the steam is so hot that people wear a cap and gloves to prevent scalding of the ears and hands, but the rest of the body gets used to it.)

*

. . . I always wanted to ask Yegor: "Where have you come from?" But he hadn't learned to speak yet. And if we were now living together, I would be badgering him – instead of the other way round – with questions such as "what for?" and "why?" Like this I would get him to help me rediscover truths which we grown-ups have already managed to forget. I think he could teach me more than I could teach him. We are too used to thinking of childhood innocence as an absence of something, as a *tabula rasa*. But suppose the reverse is true and this applies rather to those who have lost their innocence?

*

A sign:

There are three men in a death cell. In the night a tiny spider descends from the ceiling on a thread it has spun, lands on the chest of one of the men and stays there. This means the man will be shot in the morning. The next night the spider lands on the chest of another of the three. This man too was taken away. When the third of the condemned men remained alone, the little spider came down in the daytime, hung over his bunk just above his nose and climbed back to the ceiling again. This it did three times over. The man was pardoned.

*

. . . The snow is falling in large flakes and somniferous spring winds are blowing. Why does wind make us sleepy? Because it is breath.

*

In Lithuanian the words "life" and "snake" come from the same root: *gyvate* (snake) – *gyvybe* (life). The Russian *zhizn* (life) seemingly goes back to this "gyv" root, but *zmeya* (snake) is connected with *zemlya* (earth). A rather remarkable bouquet.

Another thing about Lithuania: they say you can still see there roadside posts, later topped with crosses, which originally represented the Tree of Life.

Until quite recently the Letts still kept up their knot writing. Songs and fables, and the more important domestic dates and events, were recorded on a thread which was gradually rolled up into a ball. Thus a book was made.

There we have it: the spider's thread of the spinning wheel that spins the yarn of fate and at the same time the fabric of literature.

*

Beard, dear. The sounds go together perfectly. Hence we can say: "a dear old man with a beard". The opposite would be: "a nasty, cleanshaven old man". "Dear" and "cleanshaven", "Beard" and "nasty" do not form pairs, but clash with each other. How can a man possibly be nasty if he has a beard?

*

A warder to a young Russian fellow:

"You a Jew or something, letting your beard grow?"

I was astonished. Everything is topsy-turvy: beards, once typically Russian, have now become a sign of outlandishness. But then how deeply ingrained and ancient it is, this sort of thing! Among smooth-faced, uniformly shaven folk a beard is a sign of foreignness, almost of perversion. Time was when to shave was considered well-nigh equivalent to Jewishness; now this applies to beards. The principle of distinguishing between "our kind" and others is an ancient one. The very word "Jew" has a nasty, unsavoury ring: Jew is a stranger, an enemy, "not our kind". In Russian fairy-tales devils are sometimes referred to as "not our kind". The names of several peoples originally derived from words meaning literally "our men". And now here we have the same thing again: "You are not one of us." But why must I be "one of you"?! For the simple reason that everyone here is "our kind", "one of us", and anything "different" smacks of the outsider: Jew!

*

We have been seeing people off again. A man looks very odd when he puts on a proper jacket, ordinary shoes and neatly pressed trousers – the whole ritual of sprucing oneself up seems absurd and pathetic against the background of snow; the prisoner's quilted jacket shows off to much better advantage. Then there are the signs of irrevocable parting which begin months before someone leaves – the double barrier of awkwardness both for the man who is leaving and for those who remain behind: it is an effort for him to speak with us because he is already living in another world; and we feel somehow uncomfortable because of a sense almost of estrangement when at every other word he suddenly checks himself, remembering that we are now people apart, and gazes listlessly somewhere into the distance with faded eyes; we see him off out of a sense of duty, but only his body – and even this is already unlike him. We yawn: the soul is far away . . .

19th March, 1969.

*

The sort of things people write in letters "from outside":

"*In the street where our infancy was spent practically no one is left of the boys who went jointly through childhood, and those who are still alive have long ago settled somewhere in the family circle of a comfortable apartment.*"

"*I had to study hard and learn a lot of science, particularly in the category of work I am now working at.*"

*

We and they. *Them* I can only liken to spectres, or phantoms. They hover somewhere behind the scenes, watching for a chance to intervene – though in fact they seldom do for the simple reason that there is no cause to. To all intents and purposes life passes them by. In so far as the stage is occupied by us, the actors in the drama, they are shoved into the background, forced to play the role of "extras" in the wings. People pay little attention to them and, though fearing them, do not believe in the reality of their existence. Hence even outwardly they belong to a category which somehow tends to fade into non-being. Their very features and their dress have an unreal quality: their glance conveys a formal expression of interest, but whenever one of them appears in the compound, there is something spectral about it, as though he were not really present among us. And another thing: they may well feel much more dependent on us than we do on them. At any rate, we never wonder how our uninvited visitors spend their time off duty. But they are very curious about us, constantly looking into our eyes, or trying to engage us in conversation, conscious of the fuller mode of being which they cannot help observing and envious, without realizing it, of people that have lived more varied and richer lives than they – whose only function is the parasitical one of watching over their fellow men.

*

Apropos of the "Declaration of Human Rights" a guard in charge of a work-party said:

"*You don't understand. It's not for you. It's for negroes*".

*

A foreman to a prisoner:
"*How can you be happier than me! I don't believe it!* . . ."

*

A sentry (Georgian), outraged:
"*I am not human!? I?! As if you were humans!* . . ."

*

"*He's watching, is he? That's his job – watching.*" (About a warder)

*

A scene from the past: when everyone was being released from the camps on the island of Sakhalin, a security officer's wife howls at the top of her voice, quite unabashed by the prisoners standing there and listening:

"But, why my God? What have we done wrong ·Why couldn't they be kept for just another four years! The children would finish school. My husband would retire on his pension. What have we done to deserve this?! . . ."

*

Also from the past, in Komi. Prisoners are being taken somewhere on foot in the winter. A batch of them are spending the night under guard in a peasant hut. The woman of the house, with her skirt over her head, crawls about on the floor on all fours, imitating a bear – she growls and frightens the children, all excited by the game, with her bare bottom. Yellowish hair covered with dried urine. The children are terrified. Scrawled on the stove – a four-letter word. The eldest son, now in his second class in school, had written it by way of a present to his husbandless mother. They wanted to rub it out, but she wouldn't hear of it. With confidence and good-natured delight she repeats: "it's a good word!"

*

The *taiga* is your law, and the bear your prosecutor. (Old proverb)

*

A warder, talking to some prisoners:
"*Our dogs will never do anything, if yours do not tell.*"[1]

*

"*An informer even sleeps with his ears pricked up.*"

*

[1] The warder is, in effect, telling the prisoners that informers from among themselves ("stool pigeons") are worse than the worst warder and do them more harm than anyone else. (*Author's explanation*)

"People with venal blood in their veins."

*

"Maybe he's selling himself cheap, the bastard?"

*

"The lowest scum of the lot."

*

"His eyes are a picture of innocence."

*

"He snarled at me like a wild beast."

*

"He has the ugly mug of a pirate and smiles like a rose."

*

. . . And I could feel my neighbour's eyes on me like spiders crawling over my face.

*

The landscape is gradually beginning to look like stage scenery to me. I was warned this would happen. Sky and forest are nothing but pasteboard imitations, as I now notice in my fourth year. Yet, despite this, I am, if anything, becoming more charitable, more sentimental even. I am no longer embarrassed by direct expressions of feeling. When we are young, we are afraid of looking silly and put on an air of cold aloofness. To think how beautiful this very same landscape might seem if one wished!

. . . River and field were soft and mellow as though a singer's body had melted away in them at dawn. Some such thing happened long ago to Canenta on the banks of the Tiber. For six days she neither ate nor drank while seeking her lost husband, and then in her grief she sat down and sang, and as she sang she dissolved and was dispersed in the air, making a morning haze just like this . . .

*

"Eskimo women, whenever their husbands were away for a long time, used to make a figurine to represent him. They dressed it and undressed it, put it to bed and looked after it in every way, as if it were alive. Such figurines were made, too, whenever a man died. The dolls Eskimo girls played with were also frequently representations of the dead . . . A doll was thus made into a repository of a dead man's soul and his 'representative' among his kinsfolk. The soul enclosed in the doll was supposed to pass into a woman's body and be born again to new life. It was thus considered to be both the soul of the dead relative and the soul of the future child." (A. P. Okladnikov)

I have never read anything of greater significance about dolls, though it is written in such dull text-book fashion. Could it be that our present-day dolls are the last relic of those emissaries between dead and living bodies? And perhaps this is also how art began? Perhaps portraiture – including modern photography – now valued only as a memento of the dead or departed (whom once we dressed and fed with our own hands!) also owes its origin to those dolls which used to serve as intermediate links in the chain of life. Without them – without dolls, that is – the world would have crumbled or fallen apart, children would no longer have resembled their parents and the whole tribe would have dispersed like dust over the face of the earth. Art is thus the intermediary between generations – though now it links them in a figurative instead of a literal sense. But once upon a time the grandfathers literally turned into their own grandchildren after living for a while in the transitional form of dolls.

Similarly with the butterfly: it changes from a caterpillar only after going through the pupa[1] stage. (The Russian for *butterfly* is almost the same word as *babushka* – "grandmother"; another word for "butterfly" in Russian dialect is *dushichka* – "little soul": a "butterfly" is thus the soul that has flown out

[1] The Russian for "doll" (*kukla*) is also, as in Latin, used in the sense of *pupa*.

of a dead body.) Mummies, too, were swaddled to resemble dolls and put into coffins similarly shaped. Or – as it has been put in verse:

> Children play with coffins,
> Dolls rot in the earth.

And now what about the body? Well, the body was also a doll – made of clay. The soul's temporary abode was a "whited sepulchre" or painted coffin. And then there are those little wooden dolls, placed one inside the other, called *matrioshka* in Russian. Where have they come from? There must be some distant connection with Egypt and the pyramids, where coffins looked like a *matrioshka*, a body, a doll, a doll inside a doll . . .

*

In the past people did not cling to life quite as much, and it was easier to breathe.

*

Your thoughts should be so deep that you neither hear nor see the world around you.

*

Just imagine: Hesiod lived right back in the Iron Age.

*

"And then it suddenly dawned on me."

A little door opened up within me, and I saw . . . This is how words come to us, and our understanding of things. All else in art and science is incidental – mere embroidery.

One waits in a state of passive receptiveness for the "door" to open, hovering on the brink of a passionate, all-consuming urge to open it oneself and look (for fear of missing it), and yet at the same time one is somehow relaxed and withdrawn, unwilling to make the slightest move to force the issue: it is essentially a paradoxical state combining tension and mental activity with the lack of them, and for an artist it is the only starting point, and indeed perhaps even the final point in his work.

The sages must be referring to this crucial moment in the process of grasping a new truth when they tell us that experience, memory, learned authority, training, tradition and even the very wish to understand things are fatal hindrances which simply hypnotize us into falsely supposing that we are nearing the truth, whereas if we cast everything aside and empty our minds, ceasing to expect anything at all, we can hope that the door may open a little, suddenly and of its own accord . . .

*

How pleasant (and terrifying) to take a really deep breath and dive, not quite sure of the right place, into a sentence which numbs you at first as it opens up and closes behind you again like water, and which seems quite foreign to you, until you enter it completely and all at once begin to feel borne up by it – by the external momentum of the very speech into which you have so rashly plunged – and let the current carry you along, even at the risk of floundering and going under in this river which now appears mercifully to have taken you in hand, edging you, as you think, towards the subject you had meant to write about – when suddenly you notice that it is no longer the same and evening is drawing in and you must just keep on swimming like a good little boy silently obedient to his mother who is still willing to be patient with him, and like it or not, you must make no fuss, but sink to the very bottom where, hardly mindful any more of what you were talking about, you at last say something commensurate with the force which, by propelling you back to the surface, bears witness less to your proficiency as a swimmer than to its own kindness of heart. You come out of the sentence a little abashed – and dazed by what you have succeeded in saying.

*

. . . And once again I must admit to liking the ancients more than I used to. But not the Romans. I dare say that Greek art has suffered very much through being copied in late Roman times – the form in which we now largely see it. Realism in the bad sense (interest only in recording externals) started with the Romans. They turned the living tissue into a mask and adapted the sacred subjects of the Greeks to their own bleak and barren history. Not for them the dualism of the vase paintings about the Trojan war, where the heroes do not fight so much as look over their shoulders – the ambiguity of this posture, so dynamic and yet so full of awe for the will of the gods, is breathtaking. But the Romans had nothing like this of their own, as far as I remember, except the she-wolf that suckled Romulus and Remus – and even she belongs rather to the Etruscans.

*

In their admiration for Helen of Troy people somehow leave out of account that she was the daughter of Zeus – hence all the fuss about who was to possess her. She is brought, like a doll, from one acropolis to another, but does not herself seem to care where she is or to whom she belongs. She is like the wooden "Palladium", the statue of Pallas Athene, which had been sent down from heaven by Zeus to protect the city of Troy. The city fell when Odysseus and Diomedes stole it, putting in its place the wooden horse filled with warriors. They thus acted for the same motive as Paris did when he stole Helen from Menelaus – she conferred the protection of Aphrodite on anyone who possessed her. It was less a fight over a woman than over a guardian statue – and hence opened an era in which gods and cultures began to circulate.

*

. . . You are wrong to criticize our son for his drawings. His little men now have hands and arms growing at the waist out of their stomachs. This is as it should be: we wave our arms about starting mainly from the elbow, and if we look at them from above (as we do), they seem to swing somewhere at the waist. Who ever heard of arms starting at the same level as the chin? Aren't they at our sides? Children copy nature more faithfully than we do by looking at themselves instead of at what is in front of them.

11th May, 1969.

*

Some scholars think that the stone images of Turkic origin on the Black Sea coast – as distinct from the Polovtsian figures of goddesses there – represent not a dearly loved person buried somewhere in the vicinity, but an enemy killed by him. This unproved theory is based on the fact that certain peoples (Yakutians, Tungus, etc.) considered the souls of the dead dangerous or hostile to the living, and in order to render a dead man harmless they imprisoned him for all eternity in this manner. They naturally sought to put as many enemies as possible out of action and turn them into graven images. If this hypothesis is in any way correct it throws new light on the epic poem (*bylina*) about how the heroes (*bogatyri*) of Ancient Russia met their doom. All the *bogatyri*, as I remember, suddenly turned to stone under the influence of mystic forces, that is, in terms of this scholarly theory, were killed by nomads and immured (i.e. sculpted) in stone. The Turkic image-makers thus ensnared and sealed up the souls of the last *bogatyri*, effectively putting a stop to any possible process of self-renewal. I do not know whether anyone has ever studied our *bylinas* for a possible connection with the stone images scattered over the Altai region, Kirgizia, Mongolia, etc. But it would be rather nice if it turned out that they are the *bogatyri* of Russian legend, and that they had strayed so far afield!

*

As late as the 19th century it was still quite commonly believed in this country that the soul of a man took up its abode in any picture of him, and the art of portraiture was therefore thought of as something magical or baneful. But there is another point of greater interest: an archaic image is in no way a portrait, but a dwelling place for the soul of the person represented, whether a deceased kinsman, an enemy or a demon. This is why an idol could be so rough-hewn, massive and faceless – closer to unfashioned stone than to the image of a man. It is a repository, a shrine, a prison for the soul, not the representation of a body, and may best be compared with a burial urn. There is almost nothing on the stone's surface to identify any particular person and, looking at it, we are not supposed to see a likeness, but to call to mind whoever dwells secretly within, mentally projecting his image on the rough exterior, which will then quiver into life under our eyes. Just as the occupant's name is not written up on a building and only the initiated know to whom it belongs, so one looks in vain for a "portrait" in the face of an idol. It is like the wall of a house. How could you feel comfortable in a house whose outside wall exactly depicted your features, reflecting all their incidental peculiarities of expression and temperament? No, we would choose a rather more appropriate way of representing ourselves. Apollo Belvedere, for instance, is perfectly life-like, but no one lives inside him. As he stands there in his dancer's posture you would never want to bow down and worship him, as you might a Scythian stone idol: here there is somebody sitting inside. The dominating idea in ancient art was not representation, but the provision of a dwelling place. In later times the graven image conceived as an abode for the soul gave way to the loftier and more "visible" idea of the icon, where the face is a window.

*

The past says to us through its burial mounds: "Do you think I was less real than you?"

*

Is it not odd that in this country all we have left from the funeral rites of the past – Egyptian pyramids, burial services, sacrifices – are those slippers made of black paper which are sold, without any belief in God, by undertakers' establishments, so that the deceased should find it easier to go to the next world . . .

*

Old men used to say: "You'll spoil your boots!" But I paid no attention to them . . .

Man loves his boots: boots are reality. But the main thing in a boot is not the toe, but the top. It clasps the leg, holding it like a vice. With his boots on a man feels spruce and smart. That is why military men like them so much – not as protection against mud and dust, but because they give an inestimable sense of one's own worth. In the same way, a tight leather belt or a Sam Browne makes you feel more inclined to strike out, or to issue orders. For exactly the same reason ladies used to lace themselves into corsets: driving out to a ball was like riding into battle. The body is thus saddled and harnessed. In boots a man is more self-assured – and is no longer alone. They grip him as firmly as his hand grasps the hilt of his sword.

*

. . . Summer, stretching out before us like a road through the desert, will become less dreary only when we actually start out along it and the heaviness of heart we must expect descends on us and envelops us, instead of merely looming ahead somewhere on the horizon. Summer, like any other business, is not so bad once it is begun, but with the weather we are having just now it seems to be moving away, chuckling softly as it goes: "I am still a long way off, but when you see me, you'll be surprised how big I am!"

*

. . . I should write sentences as long drawn-out as sobs, and match the length of the days by the prolixity of my text.

*

Mandelstam is splendid. Given how much he disliked to philosophize, his sense of life as something endowed with meaning was quite astonishing – as was his view of the world as a settled abode when one considers how totally he failed to achieve any form of domesticity for himself. Everywhere he found harmony and order – but hadn't a penny to bless himself with. The passionate interest in biology which he indulged during his wanderings sprang – as one sees in his notebooks – from a longing for the kind of structures and hierarchies offered in such liberal profusion by science, to the basic idea of which he was, however, indifferent or neutral. He was interested in the stylistic properties of life rather than in theoretical or applied knowledge about it. He was selflessly devoted to cultural values, not in a spirit of academic piety, nor out of a desire to enlighten or command, but because of the call of his blood – which is, after all, sterner stuff than mere water. Just as Esenin called himself the last poet of the country-side, so Mandelstam could justly claim to be the last poet of the intelligentsia. But he was fully aware of how important it was to be "like newcomers even in the midst of woe", and casting aside all the panoply of social origin, material comfort, "Bryusovism",[1] the authoritative weight of centuries and academies, he stood naked – not before a world equally naked, but – always mindful of whence he had come – before the sweeping vistas of history.

*

A child's ultimatum to his mother:

"I'll bring home a wife with painted fingernails."

"Bring anyone you like, only come back yourself."

What else could she say?

*

One of my fellow-prisoners tells me that on the day his son was born he went round and bought all the newspapers of that date, so that when the boy was eighteen, he would be able to give them to him and say: "Look what happened on the day you were born!" But it didn't work out that way. His wife married another man and his son does not know his father, and the parcel with the old newspapers has probably been thrown away.

[1] "Bryusovism": V. Bryusov (1873–1924): Symbolist poet whose verse was sometimes heavily erudite.

The wife had no imagination. But it was a good idea! . . .

*

Someone has been telling us about a prisoner who for many years now has never bought anything in the camp store. Not because he is saving money, but simply, he says, because his body has grown used to the ordinary camp food and he does not want to throw it out of gear. Suppose the store closed down and you found you couldn't survive without it? It is like conditioning yourself to live in extreme cold or adapting yourself to the rigours of travel in remote areas.

*

People adapt themselves in various ways. There was one man who spent ten years in the punishment barracks on reduced rations rather than work: it was easier that way and he got used to it. When he left the camp he borrowed forty copecks from somebody: "I'll soon throw my papers away and I shan't need any money, either, once I get to the railway . . ."

*

While he was being beaten all he thought about was how to lose consciousness as quickly as possible. But independently of his will his body twisted and turned, trying to avoid the blows and put off the fatal outcome as long as possible.

*

One man pretended to be dumb throughout the ten years he spent in a camp. On his release he said to the camp authorities: "*Really fooled you, didn't I!*"

*

"*A fine fellow: never heard him say a thing during the whole five years except: 'Heave!' and 'Steady on!'* "

*

"*The doctor was standing there in his white coat and I said: 'I'm going blind.' 'It's just mania', he said.*" (In the madhouse)

*

"*Well, while we were just sitting around and laughing, he slipped away . . .*" (A suicide)

*

Life is more significant than we think, oh yes, more significant than we think.

*

There are people who realize only about half the potential given them by nature, or even less. They are the sort who could have lived (or might still live) an alternative life somewhere else and for a different purpose, and so they exist at half-capacity, as it were, and somehow non-committally. They are hence rather inconspicuous and taciturn, and even seem physically inferior or underdeveloped as personalities. They are merely glimpsed from behind as they merge back into the obscurity from which they come with no other purpose than to pass among us without leaving a trace and then disappear unrecognized. Only a small portion of them is visible on the surface of our life.

Others have realized and "found" themselves up to the hilt, and impinge in more than full measure as they function in our midst, entirely at home – dynamic, talkative and giving their all, but they are a trifle pathetic in the very completeness of their personalities: they have nothing beyond what is already on display, and this will vanish without a trace when their time is up.

*

. . . A man so emaciated, so withdrawn in every respect, that nothing is left of him but his sexual organs which give the impression of having grown to monstrous proportions. (In the bath-house)

*

. . . *Hamlet*, it would seem, is a variant of *Oedipus*, and how curious that both are on the same subject of patricide and incestuous union – equally taboo – with the mother. The Oedipus theme, which in the ancient version had to do with ineluctable Fate, is in Shakespeare lifted out of this context into one where the protagonist appears to be independent, able to fight against circumstances and exercise freedom of choice. It is this freedom of choice that makes him such a guilt-ridden and enigmatic figure over whom we have racked our brains for centuries, wondering whether he is a hero or a weakling – all because fate has given him the freedom to respond in his own way to a situation which essentially precludes all choice.

*

How should we define the characters of 20th-century prose fiction, where there is such a distinct tendency to put all the emphasis on a person's state of mind? Are we moving back to something like the conventional figures of 18th-century classicism – personified vice, virtue, etc? Tolstoy's characters are already no longer contained within the clearly defined limits of types which – like Pechorin or Bazarov[1] – could serve as the exemplars of a whole social group or attitude of mind, and even as generic names for them. We cannot say: "You are a regular Anna Karenina!" "You are a real Levin!", in the way we use the names of such more compendious figures as Khlestakov or Oblomov. From then on the characters of fiction became less and less sharply delineated as "types", turning rather into imitations of "real life" individuals.

Dostoyevsky goes even further. The main thing about his characters is that they are *possessed* in an elemental, all-pervading way, and their ideas and behaviour are manifestations of a pestilence, of a hurricane sweeping over the human race: the sinuosities of the psyche, its very cartilage, are consumed by the spiritual fire of a maniacal world conflagration. Raskol-

[1] Pechorin: main character in Lermontov's *Hero of our Times* (1840); Bazarov: hero of Turgenev's *Fathers* and *Sons* (1862).

nikov, we are told, "thought feverishly, by fits and starts. And he was hardly aware of having a body at all . . ." The body is now a light outer casing – it burns from inside and cracks like an egg-shell under the pressure of the spirit which has taken up its abode within and at times issues forth, ravaging the borrowed flesh as it does so.

And then, after the body, the "character" inside it also falls apart ingloriously, revealing itself to be as ephemeral in its newly discovered "typicality" as a carnival mask made of plaster. It is already a thing of the past by Turgenev's time; and very soon Turgenev, with his meticulously assembled portraits, becomes obsolete, and the realist novel about characters gives way to the novel about man's condition and state of mind.

We now find that not only the principal figures, but even a purely episodic one such as Kalganov[1] (in the scene at Mokroye) are endowed with features and characteristics which are quite unstable and may change without apparent reason: "Occasionally a rigid and mulish expression appeared briefly in his (Kalganov's) face: he looked at you, listened and yet seemed to be brooding obstinately about something all of his own. He could be listless and inert, or he could suddenly become agitated for reasons which sometimes seemed quite trivial."

We are told nothing further about Kalganov, but his moodiness shows that he is ready to develop from his embryonic state into a fully-fledged medium like any other of Dostoyevsky's personages – reaching out into space, rigid (as antennae), inert, and then all excited in anticipation of the fit which is nearly upon them . . . And here it is! Off they go, whirling round in the grip, not of life, but of a tempestuous spiritual frenzy.

The creation of a literary character is, it would seem, an attempt to reduce a man's immanent qualities to the visible aspects of his temperament and then to build up from these a more or less clear-cut and immutable psychological cliché, a self-contained system like the body itself. Of course it is realistic and natural – as are vice or virtue personified (though

[1] Character in *Brothers Karamazov*.

no less conventionalized for that), and we find all the hallmarks of it even in Zmey Gorynych.[1]

But the idea of the literary character really came into its own and began to flourish in ever more complex forms only when the time was ripe for man to assume the sovereign role of a Hamlet or a Don Quixote – that is, when he ceased to be an auxiliary, dependent creature and turned into an autonomous individual subject to no commands other than those of his own "I", now free in every respect. In this sense literary characters were henceforth created simply by way of giving the promptings of temperament and destiny a humanist rationale – which took as its starting point the notion of the individual personality and, like any other, was valid only within the strict limits of its historical framework. From now on the literary character began to act in obedience to his own will: "Here's what I am like – better watch your step", and the function of the novel, when it appeared on the scene, was to give a full account of his independent life and to show that, subject though he was to the pressures of external forces, environment, heredity, and so forth, he easily assimilated them to his own self – the primary unit in the existing state of things, the supreme authority in the world order as he conceived it.

Before this time it had been unknown for a character's motives to spring from within himself. The heroes of antiquity were not "characters" in the full sense, but rather victims of circumstances: a man might, for instance, be born of a goddess and a mortal, or find himself called upon to fulfil a predetermined purpose. What King Oedipus was like as a person is of no importance – he was just an ordinary, decent sort of man who despite himself perpetrated an evil deed. What mattered was the *nature* of the deed, the kind of trick played on him by fate – which in those times was the decisive factor in the life of an individual; it was not his own psychology that he had to come to terms with, but his predestined lot and his lineage.

The feeling of "truth to life" or realism inspired in us by all

[1] The mythical dragon of early Russian epic poetry.

those characters of 19th-century literature is probably no more intense than what people felt as they read the old chronicles or the Lives of the Church Fathers. When we say of a literary personage that he is "life-like" we mean that he lives out to the full his own character – which for us is an absolute reality intrinsic to life and needing no further proof. But under a different system of values the same personage would appear truly life-like only if his actions could be put down to a predetermined fate or the instigation of the Devil, rather than to the workings of a fictitious psyche. In talking of truth to life in literature ("this is how it is in real life"), it is important to specify exactly how one is using the word "life": in what ontological sense, and with reference to which particular literary manner?

*

. . . Perhaps the quarrels among the gods were the same, in principle, as what in modern parlance is called psychophysics? Man thus comes to resemble a landing field constantly used by helicopters. In and by himself he is meaningless – simply an empty space, an airfield . . . (God! The furies that hover over our heads!)

*

He was no longer a man, but a pile of fallen rock or a heap of rubble; not a prisoner, but himself a whole camp looming up before us as primordial as chaos – a camp in which by now other people's lives doubtless bulked more largely than his own character as he told his story in the first person – it was just so much timber floated downstream, with the logs piled up in a jam, bristling like the hair on one's head: his "I" had been scooped up and tossed in with all the rest, not as a lesson to others, but just for people to look at . . .

*

. . . A second life is being played on the tape of my everyday existence – this, with its routine work, lights-out and reveille has an appearance of unreality, and gives rise to a feeling the reverse of solipsism – namely, that everything around me is more plausible than I am myself. I find it easier to suppose that I do not exist, only this other busy life.

*

"*And so little by little he began to go wrong in the head.*"

*

"*I woke up one morning and heard the cosmos shrieking!*"

*

A former criminal dreams of writing a poem which would send people into a dead faint, but when they came to they would find that the scales had dropped from their eyes. This ultimate poem with the power of transforming human nature (no less!) is just that philospher's stone which our civilization has, without knowing it, always been looking for and is still looking for now.

*

"*Man points in as many ways as the rays of the sun. But who regulates him?*"

*

"*When I'm in my psychic mood . . .*"

*

"*That's my nature – the way I got it with my mother's milk . . .*"

*

"*When I heard this I saw red inside me.*"

*

"*I saw x's and y's in front of my eyes.*"

*

"*Then he took to thinking and his hair started coming out.*"

*

"*What we really need is to think everything through right to the very end!*"

*

"*He's so brainy it's enough to scare you!*"
(The inadmissibility or immorality of being too intelligent.)

*

Is it possible that a lunatic is someone with too firm a hold on his own mind? Here he is, living in calm expectation of the moment when he will be called to the throne of Russia – and so sure it will happen that he does absolutely nothing to try and bring it about! It is the people in charge of him who fuss and fret, disconcerted by his inactivity. If the truth were told, he is more balanced, more normal than all these myrmidons who are baffled and driven insane by him and demand his abdication. It is as if they were afraid he might prove right in his unshakeable certainty, and they, not he, might have to be made to see reason and accept the fact of his exalted and legitimate status.

*

"*Degenerator.*"

*

"*Schizofrantic.*"

*

"*He could read and write, but he was slightly round the bend.*" (And had played so much on the harmonica that both his eyes permanently squinted towards the bridge of his nose.)

*

. . . Oh, what an unending flow of beings! Say what you like – the river Lethe is absolutely essential!

*

I have never taken much of an interest in Shevchenko[1] and never even read him properly before now. And leafing through an odd volume in Russian translation I did not, quite honestly, have much expectation of finding anything new. All too firmly entrenched in our minds are the stock phrases enchanting, perhaps, to the Ukrainian ear, but provoking only a condescending smile in us. They are certainly there in plenty, the familiar clichés describing the beloved country and just waiting to take their place as inscriptions under some wearisome oleograph or other. But apart from this there are unique things not to be found anywhere else.

Shevchenko is so little known because he was outside the mainstream of the 19th-century tradition of Russian poetry, which was nurtured for the most part on smooth and regular verse forms. In some ways he is closer to the 20th century, a direct forerunner of Khlebnikov,[2] who was half Ukrainian and saw the Southern steppes as the ancient Scythian heartland, as an epic territory with untapped reserves of linguistic material closely related to Russian and as rich as the black earth of the region. The element of popular tradition in Shevchenko is not merely decorative, but is the genuine article inherited from his ancestors together with his own roots. His sense of ethnic and social (peasant) distinctiveness, the search for his own people in history and in everyday life led deeper into the wellsprings of folklore than was thought proper by Russian poets at that time – though these too were just then very much engaged in "looking for the people". Indeed, it is for this very reason that Shevchenko at his deepest level was overlooked by the 19th century. He was seen primarily as an untutored genius of humble origins who suffered for his beliefs and wrote a few stirring calls to action. But as a poet he was thought uncouth and simple-

[1] Taras Shevchenko (1814–61): Ukrainian poet.
[2] Velimir Khlebnikov (1885–1922): Russian futurist poet.

minded, and people turned up their noses at him, even if they were loath to admit it because of the universal adulation of the peasant (Belinsky,[1] however, was not ashamed to own up to his dislike of, or rather deafness to, Shevchenko's rude muse). We had Koltsov,[2] and Nikitin[3] as his Russian counterparts, but they were always looking bashfully over their shoulders at the gentry, while Shevchenko charged ahead with all the primitive force and dashing spirit of a Cossack – which meant that, although he fitted in well with the ideas then in fashion, his verse stuck in people's gullets. Rather than listen to his wild strains, the Russian reading public mentally consigned Shevchenko to a provincial stamping ground of minor importance – something in which he himself seems gladly to have acquiesced, content to think of himself as the poet of his ill-starred borderland. In this unwavering attachment to his favoured part of the world Shevchenko is rather insistent and monotonous – like the artless lilting measures he borrowed from Ukrainian folk poetry, which he clings to with might and main, as though afraid of straying from the familiar path and losing himself for ever in the ocean of iambics so dear to the gentry class.

But while endlessly repeating in effect the same lessons he is as deep as a well in his dark and narrow faith. It is frenzy and raving that hold sway here. Any theme is an occasion for a witches' sabbath. A woman seduced or parted from her beloved goes out of her mind and wails for pages on end. The very first known work by Shevchenko is called *Under a Spell* (1837) – an excuse for women and girls, possessed, or throwing fits, to cavort wildly like creatures bewitched from poem to poem. Occasionally changing to non-rational speech or lapsing into glossolalia, Shevchenko plainly feels the urge to express himself in language that wells up from the depths of a brain overpowered by its subconscious. Madness serves him as a way to his own dark sources, where freedom, merging into the fever of ancient magic and sorcery, borders on a craving for total

[1] V. Belinsky (1811–48): literary critic.
[2] A. Koltsov (1809–42): poet noted for his stylised folk songs.
[3] I. Nikitin (1824–61): realist poet.

destruction in one wild outburst:

> "Oh let me breathe,
> Shatter my skull and tear my breast asunder!
> Worms dwell in them and serpents – bring release!
> Oh, let me quietly, forever go to sleep!"

It is hard to make out whether we have here a plea for one's own release or for the release of the devil *in* one, an appeal to drive him out – both meanings merge in this violent bid for freedom and each successive outbreak of frenzy on the part of a victim serves as a prologue to the bloody carousels of *haydamaks*[1] who have freed themselves from all restraints of authority and reason. By associating social rebellion with an instinctive, subconscious explosion Shevchenko came closer than anyone else to anticipating Blok's "The Twelve" and Khlebnikov's elemental poems "The Present" and "The Hot Field" . . .

Experts, by the way, are amazed that Shevchenko who had lived very little – almost not at all – in the Ukraine and had never studied ethnography, should have shown such a deep understanding of myths, of the archaic substratum of folk beliefs. It must be assumed that his irrational nature was spontaneously responsive to all these influences. Besides, it cannot be excluded that the people (and folklore) of the Ukraine are linked at a deeper level than we are with the primitive currents and images of the subconscious, so that fairy-tales here possibly make a more distinct and immediate impression, as living facts of psychic experience. Apart from Shevchenko, the example of Gogol[2] would seem to bear this out.

*

I have never seen any other poet worshipped in quite this way – by weatherbeaten peasants gathered together in the *kapterka*[3] before a portrait of him draped in embroidered cloths,

[1] Ukrainian Cossack revels in the 17th–18th centuries
[2] Gogol was from the Ukraine and used folklore themes.
[3] Store-room in camp barracks.

as though standing before the icon of a saint in church, celebrating his anniversary in secret and chanting in chorus: "Batko![1] Taras!", like the Lord's Prayer.

*

In answer to a question about Christianity and the New Testament – with a hurt expression:
"*Why weren't the apostles Ukrainians?* . . ."

*

What a wind! Pillars of dust, as in a typhoon, whirl over the face of the earth: "Didko" (Grandad) is celebrating his marriage.

("Didko" is the Devil in Western Ukraine. You can't call an old man "didko" – he would be offended.)

*

Getting ready to leave.[2] Good-byes. Last meetings. Last books. Books, too, will be off to various other camps and I would like to finish them, look through them, copy or clip passages out of them. I should go round the compound, by myself, saying good-bye to all the corners that have been congenial. But I won't be able. Too many people. At moments like these, they say, it is a good idea to read Plutarch. But the Byzantine chronicles will do almost as well. The images go with the background, alternately blending or clashing with it. All is uproar, helter-skelter, and there's nowhere to sit. Much talk and many farewell speeches. This morning I got up at five, to have time to finish Byzantium.

A strange remark to the effect that evil brings salvation, that it purifies the soul – not, as might be thought, through repentance or punishment, but by virtue of the crime itself:

"I have worked off the evil in me and don't worry any more and have no regrets. Otherwise, it would always have weighed on my soul."

[1] Ukrainian for "Father".
[2] i.e. prior to the author's transfer to another camp.

I thought of G. – the same psychological type. From this it again follows that the soul is something extraneous to man, and that our soul is good – only we ourselves are bad.

I have collected many cuttings over the years: a whole pile of stuff on ethnography, archeology. Where shall I pack them all? My padded jacket I'll throw out. It won't last another three years anyway. What a gipsy encampment. I can't help thinking of the *tyubeteykas*[1] (embroidered skull-caps), which were so fashionable in the early '30's, when they were worn by shaven-headed Moscow executives. They were made, it was said, out of abandoned church vestments. How many epochs and peoples came together and intersected in those *tyubeteykas!* . . .

27th June, 1969.

*

In his *History* Ammianus Marcellinus has this to say about the Huns:

"They all have strong, compact limbs and thick necks, and look so monstrous and mis-shapen that they could be taken for two-legged beasts or be likened to the roughly hewn piles used in the building of bridges."

Ancient art is in general indifferent to individual features, paying much more attention to the distinguishing marks of tribes, peoples or age groups. The same thing with icons – as we now realize, these give a much truer idea of infants than the paintings of a Raphael who turns the Child Jesus into a three-year-old Cupid. In the same way, Russian wooden dolls render the typically Russian cast of face more exactly than Repin.[2] And the more representatives of foreign races I meet – Gothic Germans, Assyrian-looking Armenians – the more clearly I see the truthfulness of ancient art which conceived of human's in terms of tribe and stock. Ammianus's comparison of the Huns to wooden piles gives us a clearer picture of the "Heathen

[1] Worn by some Moslem minorities in the USSR.
[2] I. Repin (1844–1930): Russian realist painter.

Idol"[1] of the *bylinas* – he must have been inspired by the sight of real life Tartars. As seen by Mediaeval Europe (Alberic, 13th century) Tartars looked just like the "Heathen Idol" in the eyes of the hero in a Russian *bylina*:

"They have a large head, a short neck, a very broad chest, big hands, small feet and amazing strength. They have no faith, they fear nothing, believe in nothing, worship nothing."

*

Looking at a train: so that's what Zmey Gorynych must have been like, twisting and turning, all lit up, among the hills!

*

Art is possessed by a sense of reality never even dreamed of by "practical" people. For them – indeed for all of us in the cold light of day – the distant past does not exist. We know, in the abstract, that there have been Goths and Huns at some time or other, but we don't really believe it. Art believes it.

*

I have been made into a temporary night watchman. It is difficult to imagine a better job. I guard iron which nobody steals. Large frogs hop around on a stone gantry and on seeing me immediately turn into stone themselves. They gobble up large black beetles and jump far away from each other; how is it they don't lose their way? . . .

This put me in mind of the mouse I saw back at Camp Eleven. It was sitting on the window-sill when I entered the deserted smoking room at night and switched on the light; it was so panic-stricken that it forgot the way down, and even though I stood motionless, it ran away in terror along the hot radiator, burning its paws, until it somehow tumbled back into its hole.

*

[1] Monster in Russian folk sagas (*bylinas*).

"But the worst of it is that there's nothing here you can eat. If it was a meat factory or a confectionery . . . But there's nothing apart from a lot of old iron."

*

"Repair these machines – they won't complain."

*

"In the mines a man develops a dreamy kind of mentality."

*

"The peasant was barking at a tractor."

*

"The containers are all wavy – like the hills in Manchuria."

*

"He wore down the thread on his heart."

*

Peasants will now talk about an engine – how many tons it weighs or its horsepower etc. – just as gravely as they must once have discussed the weight of a *bogatyr's* mace or of a magic sword.

*

"They have this radicational equipment: it sends out a wave and by the time it comes back from out there it's been photographed. So they've got every object right in front of them."

*

"Work on an open object."

*

"He worked as a soup-ladler."

*

"She worked in light athletics."

*

"She worked as a chef because there was a vacancy."

*

"No, you just think of it! It works without any physical effort!"
(Miraculous functioning of a machine)

*

"And this is metal! Cold metal at that! And it spins round and round! . . .
(With eyes popping out, referring to the coldness of machinery.)

*

Sarcastically, about a machine:
"It squeals like a piglet . . ."

*

"Not every woman is so difficult . . ."

*

"In the twentieth century everything is mechanized. Only mating is done by hand."

*

"You read magazines and newspapers and everything man is provided with. Tell me: what is science? Science is diesels, compressors, tractors. It is books and things like that."

*

"Why should I listen to a scientist or scholar? He is just the same as me!"

*

"*He is a scholar. But he is a good man.*"
(It is difficult for someone to be both a scholar and a good man at the same time!)

*

A peasant, speaking with admiration about Pugachev:
"*An uneducated man sent all those educated people into a fit!*"

*

. . . For the sake of distraction I've been reading Stevenson. Curious things do happen: if you think a lot about something, it turns up of its own accord. This has happened before – with Pushkin.[1] You have none of the sources you need, yet the necessary references and quotations suddenly appear from somewhere unexpected, out of the blue. This is what has happened again now. I heard from someone that Stevenson had written a work called *The Strange Case of Dr Jekyll and Mr Hyde* and the title alone made me long and yearn for it: the very title, it seemed to me, promised something, had the ring of mystery about it. Months later I learned that a boy here had a five-volume edition. I asked about Jekyll – no, I was told, there's nothing like that. And so I stopped thinking about it. Then one day I opened one of the volumes and could hardly believe my eyes: *The Strange Case of Dr Jekyll and Mr Hyde!* (Those English really know how to choose names that make your flesh creep just to hear them!) The story is indeed pretty remarkable. True, I had expected even greater things, for some reason. But I was grateful all the same. And it contained one page which had long been waiting for me, something that bore out a particular conjecture of my own:

". . . With every day, and from both sides of my intelligence, the moral and the intellectual, I thus drew steadily nearer to the truth, by whose partial discovery I have been doomed to such a dreadful shipwreck: that man is not truly one, but truly two. I say two, because the state of my own knowledge does not pass beyond that point. Others will follow, others will outstrip

[1] i.e. while the author was working on Pushkin.

me on the same lines; and I hazard the guess that man will be ultimately known for a mere polity of multifarious, incongruous and independent denizens." The way everything falls into place . . .

8th August, 1969.

*

A work of art teaches nothing – yet it teaches everything. It does not work to the advantage of this, that or the other. Not even to its own advantage. It is reversible in its value, in its effect on the mind. What is served by Lermontov's *The Demon* – atheism or mysticism? First one, then the other.

*

The weather has improved, but it is cool in the evenings, and the sunsets remind one of the Far North. Where does all that pressure come from? At some juncture over ragged cloudbanks we see a great dammed-up flood which makes it possible to form some slight idea of the reality – it is easy enough to talk about it, but how to conceive or imagine it, if our sense of this reality is beyond words and sensations, yet can be conveyed in no other language? The ceiling could crack under the pressure of that light, and the sun grow dim in its rays.

*

I drink an amazing *kvass*[1] here – cold water in which cherry leaves have been soaked. It produces almost the same taste in the mouth as the actual cherries. Pleasant to think that the self-same juices are present everywhere – in leaves, in grass. And all this in the cleanest of vats still pining for the country.

Sometimes I treat myself to mushrooms – there are people in the compound who love picking them. "People outside would very soon have been poisoned by this kind!", one of these mushroom enthusiasts said recently. He's a real expert – before frying toadstools he first boils them, changing the water

[1] A beverage usually made of malt, water and bread, but sometimes the name is applied to fruit juices.

many times over. This makes them edible.

*

"*And what sort of habits has garlic got? In the winter it crawls into the earth. In the spring, you come out into the garden – and you see a whole sea of it in front of you!*"

*

I have been given some honey. What an ornate taste it has and how much skill and talent comes out of all those little striped bees' bellies, out of flowers and air into this granular substance, into this dense and sparkling viscosity! Honey tastes of summer in all its fragrance, of forests ablaze with colour, of the singing of birds. Everything is crammed into it and condensed into an elixir of life.

*

In an ancient Egyptian tale of two brothers there is the following nice phrase about a tower the hero had built with his own hands:

"It was full of sundry good things which he had made so that the house be filled."

*

Looking at forests one realizes that good is spread throughout the world, like a vast kingdom. It is not in the other world or the afterlife, but right here. Like the City of Kitezh.[1] Except that it cannot be seen, or rather, only its peaks can be seen – the domes peeping out from the depths in which they are submerged. When a wife says to her husband about a prisoner on the run: "If you turn him in, I'll leave you!", we realize that the good is great and rules over us invisibly, dressed in a mantle of evil in order to preserve its secret.

"*I would send people like that to a resort hotel for the rest of their lives: so they could do nothing but eat and enjoy themselves.*"

*

[1] see note on page 79.

The pleasant thing about the theory of evolution is that at the sight of a frog you think: "I too am descended from a frog, and this one is like a sister to me."

I am falling in love with Russian fairy-tales. But I appreciate them not so much for the stories they tell as for their affinity to painting and music – for their sparkling colours and winged phrases. Take a clean piece of paper and draw a cottage on chicken's legs,[1] and you have a whole fairy-tale spread out in front of you. Or even better, imagine a landscape and try to describe snow. Yes, "snow" I said – snow. Haven't you ever seen *snow*? Everything is dinned into you. In language that brooks no contradiction you are told about a talking dog, a holy old man, a centaur (Polkan[2]) in a field of oats or an aspen wood, and other miracles – hey, presto, there you are! On and on it goes like this! . . . Without end. What joy! And Ivanushka[3] will never extricate himself from the adventure that begins at the crossroads.

27th August, 1969.

*

A metaphor is a memory of that Golden Age when all was everything. A fragment of metamorphosis.

*

Do you know what it means when there is rain and the sun shines through it? "The water-nymphs are praying to God." This is a Latvian saying they told me about. Let us hope the Russians, too, may turn out to have something similar.

*

"*He had a common language with his cat.*"

(I also had a common language with his cat – it served as

[1] Generally the home of a witch in Russian fairy-tales.
[2] Mythical half-man half-dog derived from the Italian *Pulicane*.
[3] Ivanushka (Johnny): generally the "anti-hero" of Russian fairy-tales, the simpleton who gets away with the prize and marries the King's daughter.

go-between and interpreter, bridging the gap between us in culture, nationality and age.)

*

. . . At long last I have grasped why Lorelei combs her hair: because hair is identified with waves. Woman – yarn – water: these form an entity of which the unifying element, apart from anything else, is hair. As witness the Armenian spell to make a girl's hair grow: it is pronounced by a stout woman who pats the hair and says: "May this hair be as broad as I am, and as long as flowing water."

It is this flowing water that Lorelei is combing.

Oh, if only I could tie all cats together by their tails! This would introduce a certain symmetry into life: a combination of visual fantasy with the magic of fairy-tales and the metaphysics of the Middle Ages. That would be realism with a vengeance.

By the way, a magician likes *everything* to have a spell on it – even his *kasha* and butter, and the plate he eats them out of. And when two magicians fight, since their magical powers are roughly equal, they gradually come down to earth and fight on with anything they can – saucepan, fists – like humans.

But when a *bogatyr* engages in battle he must keep in constant communication with his own limbs – which to use to strike where. And with his eyes and ears, too – to make sure of his aim. Not to mention his heart and liver. A *bogatyr* is wholly engaged in the business on hand, with every bit of his body. He must occasionally dismember himself and then put himself together again in one piece.

The difference between a fairy-tale and a *bylina* is that magic is converted into physical force. They are like two different circus acts. A fairy-tale is an exhibition of conjuring, but a *bylina* is a heavy-weight act, a strongman showing off his extraordinary biceps. By and large this is a decline, the degeneration of sleight of hand into muscular display or the use of bare fists.

In general, almost all that is left of the fairy-tale is now to be found in the circus. Magician – conjurer – thief: the evolution of an image. I started with the circus.[1] And with the circus I must end.

*

The Black Sea. A better name for the sea cannot be invented. Not the reproduction of a single attribute, as in "blue sea", but the expression of its essence – black: sea and darkness and death. At first, any sea was Black. Only later did we have the Red Sea and the White Sea . . .

*

Strange: you can live a long time before suddenly seeing something you always knew (together with everybody else) but which for some reason you had paid no attention to, until the very moment when you see it – much to your surprise.

Yesterday I was being marched off to load timber and all of a sudden I saw: the forest was – dark. Really dark, darker than anything around, as if it had assimilated all the darkness, and absorbed it into its blotter-like greenery. This has been known for a very long time – not for nothing was the forest always called "dark", never "green".

The same thing, if one thinks of it, is true of the "damp earth".[2] It is always damp, even in the driest season, infinitely damp. Which is why springs and rivers originate in it and never dry up.

This is what is meant by a "standard epithet". God, how right and how profound!

*

From the discourse between Pepin, the youthful son of Charlemagne, with his tutor, the writer Alcuin (or Albinus the Scholiast), one may draw a number of conclusions concerning the nature of poetry. Their dialogue is built on finding the answers to a series of riddles. For example:

[1] One of the author's first stories was "At the Circus".

[2] "Damp" is the traditional epithet of the earth in Russian folklore: "mother damp-earth".

Pepin: What is faith?

Alcuin: Being sure of something you do not understand and consider miraculous.

Pepin: What is miraculous?

Alcuin: I have, for instance, seen a man walking on his two legs – a lifeless man who has never existed.

Pepin: How is this possible? Explain it!

Alcuin: It was a reflection in the water.

Pepin: Why, then, have I not myself understood that which I have so often seen?

Alcuin: As you are of good conduct and endowed with natural intelligence I shall submit to you several examples of the miraculous; try and guess their meaning yourself.

Pepin: Very well; but if I say not as I should, correct me.

Alcuin: Indeed I will!

A stranger spoke to me without tongue or voice, he has never been and never will be; I have never heard and never known him.

Pepin: Perhaps, master, this was an unhappy dream?

Alcuin: It was indeed, my son. Listen again: I saw something dead give birth to something live and the breath of the live thing destroyed the dead.

Pepin: From rubbing wood fire is born which consumes the wood.

Alcuin: This is so.

I have heard the dead talking a lot.

Pepin: This happens when they are hung high.

(Answer: bells)

Alcuin: That is so.

I have seen a dead creature sitting on a live one, and the laughter of the dead one made the live one die.

Pepin: Our cooks know this. (A pot full of broth, which has boiled over and put out the fire)

Alcuin: Yes; but press a finger to your lips, lest children hear what this is . . .

Who is and is not, has a name and answers a voice?

Pepin: Ask the forest thickets. (Echo)

Alcuin: What rises higher if the head is taken from it?

Pepin: Go to your bed, there will you find it. (Most probably – a pillow)

Alcuin: There were three men: the first was never born and died once, the second was born once and never once died, the third was born once and died twice.

Pepin: The first is consonant with the earth, the second with my God, the third with a pauper. (Adam, Elijah and Lazarus)

Alcuin: I have seen a woman flying, with an iron nose, a wooden body and a feathered tail, bearing death behind it.

Pepin: It is the warrior's companion. (Arrow)

And so forth.

Thus we see that the origin of riddles is here directly connected with miracles: a riddle is presented as the derivative of a miracle and more than that – as the manifestation of the miraculous in life. This is why theological disputations regarding faith (going back to St Paul) develop directly into the asking of riddles. But strictly speaking such riddles, being drawn from everyday experience, cannot serve as examples of a miracle in the full and precise sense. Otherwise Alcuin would have had to go on to make the preposterous and quite incongruous deduction that belief in God and His miracles may be equated with sure knowledge of the existence of echoes, fire, pots with boiling broth in them, bells and everything else that exists in ordinary life and can be presented entertainingly in the form of riddles.

Yet even so there *is* a hidden connection, unconfirmed logically, but naïvely proclaimed, between miracles and riddles, and it pervades the whole of the Discourse between Pepin and Alcuin – thus enabling us, in explaining the nature of riddles, to suggest that they derive from miracles in roughly the same way as the conjuring trick or circus stunt, making up for lack of magic by deception and sleight of hand, also derive from miracles. A riddle makes up for lack of the miraculous by glibness of tongue and mental agility. Language, which was once able to conjure up and exorcize fire, now resorts to the round-about stratagem of describing a flame figuratively, and instead of a literal ignition of brushwood by the action of magical language, something "clicks" in one's head as the result of a purely mental effort – and up jumps the flame of the riddle's answer. But the remote affinity between riddles and miracles is not only a matter of language and its capacity, in the case of both, to astound us with an unexpected experience. The actual subject of the Discourse – the world as depicted in it through a series of interesting riddles – is also in a certain sense miraculous.

It is noteworthy that a large proportion of Alcuin's riddles turn on the notion of persons or things being both living and dead, of being killed and resurrected, of existing and not existing at the same time – that is, on phenomena which may be universally known, but are of mysterious origin, not entirely explicable, miraculous in their source (an echo, a reflection in the water, a dream, fire), suggesting a world both enigmatic and bewitched. All these walking dead, invisible presences, gods dying and rising from the dead, beings living in a pot or in the fire, people the universe of fairy-tales and myths – and were still the stuff of riddles in the far-off, happy days of the 8th century when Alcuin lived and wrote. Thus, a pillow that swells up towards the ceiling when the head is raised from it co-exists comfortably with Elijah taken up alive to heaven. The Valkyries still meant something to Alcuin and his pupil and they compare the arrow to one. The world was then sufficiently metamorphic to keep turning on its side, changing one thing into another and prodding language to bring forth allegorical riddles. We are here present, as it were, at the act of the birth of art, when metaphors sprouted profusely in the still hot and steaming soil of folklore and when language, mindful of the miracle of its origin, still showed off the tricks – as well as the riddles, knavishness, deceit, invention and cunning which fill our fairy-tales and make them so effervescent. Here it becomes clear that a poet even in the new, modern sense of the word, is a failed magician or miracle-worker who has substituted metaphor for metamorphosis, word-play for deeds.

*

I cannot tear myself away from the combat between two heroes of the Irish sagas, Cuchulainn and Fer Diad. Neither yields to the other in strength and agility and they have been fighting for several days, choosing new weapons all the time until Cuchulainn has resort to the Gae-Bulg, the forked spear.[1]

". . . Then was Cuchulainn miraculously distorted: he puffed himself out and increased the breadth of his body like a swollen bubble; he became like the dread, the terrible bow, and the valiant warrior was now as tall as the wild men of the sea, quite overtopping Fer Diad.[2]

So closely were they locked in combat that their heads met above them, their feet below them and in their middles their arms met over the rims and the bosses of their shields. So closely were they locked in combat that their shields split and cracked from centre to rim. So closely were they locked in combat that their spears were bent, twisted and shivered. So closely were they locked in combat that the pale, goat-headed demons, the Bocanacks and the Bananacks, the spirits of the glens and of the air, let out a shriek from the rims of their shields, from the hilts of their swords, from the points of their spears. So closely were they locked in combat that they forced the river out of its bed and enough space was formed in it for a king and a queen to lie in and there was not a drop of water left except such as the two warrior-heroes pressed out of the soil as they trampled and hewed at each other. So closely were they locked in combat that the steeds of the Gaels pranced and rushed off panic-stricken, breaking their tethers, chains and traces, and fled south-westwards, trampling women and children, the ailing and the feeble-minded in the camp of the men of Ireland.

Now the champions fought with the edges of their swords. And there was a moment when Fer Diad found Cuchulainn off his guard and with his fish-bone-hilted sword he struck him

[1] The secret of the Gae-Bulg has not reached us, though the weapon has apparently a perfectly genuine ancestor. In the combat here described only Cuchulainn knew how to use the Gae-Bulg. (*Author's note*)

[2] Normally, however, he was not very tall. (*Author's note*)

a blow which wounded him and pierced his breast, and Cuchulainn's blood spurted out over his girdle and the ford was crimson with the blood from the hero's body.

And Cuchulainn could no longer endure Fer Diad's mighty and crushing blows, slanting and direct. He ordered Loeg, son of Riangabair,[1] to deliver him the forked spear, the Gae-Bulg. Now the manner of using it was this: it was immersed in water and was cast with two toes of the foot. Though it was one, it pierced the body with thirty barbs and it could not be drawn out without cutting the body all round.

Fer Diad heard the Gae-Bulg mentioned and he lowered his shield to guard the lower part of his body. Then Cuchulainn thrust his spear off the centre of his palm into that part of Fer Diad's body which appeared over the rim of the shield just above the neck of his horn-plated armour. To guard the upper part of his body Fer Diad raised his shield. But too late came that protection. For Loeg had made ready the Gae-Bulg under the water, and Cuchulainn seized it with two toes of his foot and thrust it with a distant flying cast at Fer Diad. The spear went through the firm deep apron of wrought iron and shattered the goodly stone, as large as a millstone,[2] into three parts and pierced the clothes and stuck in the body, filling with its barbs every muscle and every joint of Fer Diad's body.

'Enough now', cried Fer Diad. 'Thou has struck me to the death. But, behold, thou hast delivered a mighty blow against me with the toes of thy foot and thou canst not say that I have fallen by thy hand.' "

The remarkable thing here is the compact quality, conveyed by the closeness of the combat, of the descriptive texture – a mass of heads and feet so dense that the feet sticking out below and the heads above astonish the narrator, while the demon spirits usually hovering round the hero are physically squeezed out in this locking together of bodies, and it all

[1] His charioteer. (*Author's note*)

[2] Which Fer Diad had put on himself as additional protection against the Gae-Bulg. (*Author's note*)

needs to be tailored to an intricate pattern bringing out essential detail. The compactness is such that the overall image could easily be stamped on a buckle or a ginger biscuit[1] and brings to mind the interlacing patterns of Viking ornaments, a type of design in which the letters of the Russian alphabet[2] were later to become enmeshed. However, in spite of its density the pattern is extraordinarily elaborate – it thus belies the notion that the saga or *bylina* is a severely schematized form by bringing to our attention a mass of details, sharp and bristling, yet tightly disciplined, like the forked spear which Cuchulainn drives into Fer Diad with one upward thrust of his foot. This forked spear is the very symbol of the Vikings' art, an image both ornate and lacerating which acts on all our nerves and sensations at once. And then there are other extraordinary details worked in with all the rest – such as the special mention given to the ailing and the feeble-minded trampled by the heroes' horses and not forgotten among the women and children; or the king and queen who could have lain down in the bed of the ousted stream which, for all the story's compactness, insists on being measured by nothing less than the width of the Royal couch, thus cramming the narrative full to bursting and at the same time lending it a sharpness of vision and truth to life almost morbidly rapacious in its refinement and concern for minutiae.

But the most interesting and rewarding thing about all this from the point of view of poetry in general is the clearly miraculous distortion of the hero in his frenzy. This, in fact, is Cuchulainn's special gift: he swells like a bubble, rather in the manner of a toy balloon, and becomes all transfigured at the peak of the battle, exciting the admiration of the demons whom he now outdoes by this change in appearance, and thereby presenting an image of the beautiful at the culminating point where it borders on the monstrous. Similar models of beauty can be seen in the dragons with which the Scandinavians

[1] Traditional Russian ginger biscuits (*pryaniki*) with designs stamped on them.

[2] i.e. the Old Russian (Church Slavonic) letters.

adorned their ships. To show the role of the fantastic in Irish art, I quote here a more detailed account of the change that came over Cuchulainn in the heat of battle:

"All his joints, chords and articulations would start to tremble . . . His feet and knees would turn inside out . . . All his bones would be displaced and muscles would swell and become as big as a warrior's fist. Tendons would be pulled back from his forehead to the back of his head, swell and become as big as the head of a month-old baby . . . One eye would sink in so deep that a crane could not have reached it; and the other rolled out on the cheek[1] . . . His mouth would stretch to his ears . . . The gnashing of his teeth exuded flame. His heart-beats were like a lion's roar. Lightning sent forth by his frantic rage flashed in the clouds above his head. The hair of his head would become as tangled as the branches of a blackthorn. His forehead put forth a 'hero's frenzy' which exceeded a whetstone in length. Broader, denser, harder, and higher than the mast of a great ship did a stream of blood spurt out of his head and scatter to the four corners of the earth, causing thereby a magic mist like a column of smoke above the King's house."

This fragment is for me tantamount to a revelation. Firstly, it reveals why a clash of arms becomes the centrepiece of a work of art, requiring separate treatment and the creation of its own special context. Since it shows man in a miraculously distorted, picturesquely distended guise and brings out all his qualities and capabilities to the full, combat is the ideal subject for artistic representation. Not only because of its dramatic potential, but also by reason of the sharply defined sense it gives of the beautiful merging into the grotesque, the description of combat and war (including theatrical spectacles such as gladiatorial contests and knightly tournaments) has always held the centre of the stage in world art, never failing to thrill the multitudes. In this respect a fairy-tale is no different from the Iliad, and the theme of military parades is just the same as

[1] Hence, it is said, the women of Ireland who all fell in love with him, lost the sight of one eye in order to resemble Cuchulainn. (*Author's note*)

in Red Indian war dances: not only incitement to deeds of strength and prowess, but also the display of bright plumage and a prefiguration of the whirl and tumult of battle. The basic element of combat is an explosion of physical and magic powers – something that engages the graphic capability of art in the highest degree.

In the second place, as already mentioned, this passage shows how the grotesque is entirely compatible with the beautiful. Pushkin expresses the same idea in his portrait of Peter the Great at the battle of Poltava: "His eyes are ablaze. Awesome is his face, his movements rapid, beautiful his aspect . . ." – here too we have beauty's capacity to horrify and its tendency to verge on the monstrous. The beauty of various idols, barbaric masks etc. is due to the face appearing in them in a miraculously distorted, ecstatic state, close to that of artistic inspiration. Hence, too, we realize why at all times, and especially at the stage of creating their folklore, men liked monsters and fervently devoted themselves to the art of depicting serpents, dragons etc. – for the sake not of offending against beauty, but of fulfilling its highest potential. Except in the ancient Greco-Roman world which fell for the anthropomorphic fallacy (though by no means invariably), all pagan religions were attracted by the representation of the deity as a monster, perceiving in this a sign of the magic of the super-beautiful – the gods' way of killing by merely showing their dazzling countenances. The god made his appearance, so to speak, in the fury of his splendour, as an erupting volcano of the miraculous.

Finally, the Irish saga demonstrates that the much later art of Christian Europe arose not *in vacuo* and not on Greco-Latin foundations alone, but on the basis of ancient pagan forms of its own, which proved entirely consonant with the aesthetics of the new era for the very reason that they already combined the extremes of the beautiful and the grotesque. Magic cults and images showed themselves more easily adaptable to the higher religion than the conventionalized forms of classical antiquity. In this respect, the miraculous distortion of Cuchulainn is rich soil indeed for the gargoyles of Notre-Dame, and on a wider scale – for the whole system of twisted limbs, disproportionately foreshortened or lengthened figures and contorted physiognomies in the art of the Middle Ages – an art which passed naturally from depicting the frenzy of battle to the recreation of spiritual rapture and divine transfiguration. The face of the deity had already appeared in miraculously contorted form in the paganism of Celtic, Germanic, Slav and other heathen temples and thus easily assumed the features of Christian sacrament which, though ennobled and purified in comparison with the monsters of the past, was expressed no less trenchantly by the forked spear of the grotesque.

*

In the autumn the orange colour blends with the violet and they both have something in common – over and above their yellow and blue foundation, and that common quality rushes about and darts in and out of the two colours like lightning and suddenly strikes – red!

9th October, 1969.

*

Density of style appears in my writing when I have nothing but a sheet of paper – a tiny raft on which I must clamber, trying to settle there while all the time my thoughts are palpitating and thrashing around. It is then that I have to keep myself afloat on my little ark by binding it together with a superfluity of metaphor.

*

For my birthday I was given a present. A prisoner, almost a complete stranger to me, handed me a little paper bag and in it there was a single refill for a ball-point pen. Oh, that onion! How many times it has saved me! I would allow all who ever gave me one to climb up to heaven on it, as on a ladder.[1] In

[1] Reference to the legend (told by Grushenka in Dostoyevsky's *Brothers Karamazov*) about an evil woman whose only good deed in life had been to give an onion to a pauper. She tries (but fails) to clamber out of the pit of Hell by holding on to this onion proffered to her by her guardian angel.

poverty kindness is more keenly felt. Just as rags give more warmth: their very raggedness makes them cosier and better suited to us. The mere fact of being rags does not make them unpleasant to wear, unless they are someone else's – the sensation of their having been "someone else's" is very acute because a soul which has once made its home in them always clings to them ever afterwards. For someone they were "his own" and they remember this. But our own rags – what, of all the things we possess, can be nearer and dearer to us? . . .

I have sewn new laces[1] on my winter cap – the old ones had rotted away. Funny and touching – these strings, this helplessness and meekness of man. It is what keeps us all going – and why we are still alive.

13th October, 1969.

*

The days are drawing in: it gets dark early these days, and the electric light looks romantic when it is switched on. It is worth reflecting a little on the mystical qualities of electricity. The entire 19th century put its trust in it and never ceased prating about it. Going back in my mind to my childhood, I remember electric light as my first contact with the more raffish kind of magic. Electricity combines the glitter of brilliantine with the pertness of a Bengal light. Something other-worldly, and also something of the mountebank and clown . . .

*

We are more than accustomed to fire leaping out of a match, but for children it is something of a novelty – as are dogs barking and cocks crowing . . . In their early days some scientific discoveries also make a fantastic impression on the mind. I can just imagine my father, with all the ardour of a neophyte, giving a magic lantern show in the provinces to demonstrate what a supernatural place the earth was in the distant past and the comic way in which man is descended from the ape. It would look like a conjuring trick, like showing off a miracle to a

[1] i.e. to tie the earflaps under the chin.

crowd, with the part of the Demiurge being temporarily played by vulcanoes. The vulcanoes must have been made of iron – and taken a long time to build – to work so well . . . What a divine game there is behind all this!

*

How much richer and more rewarding than realism romanticism proved to be in the history of our culture, even stimulating the development of scholarship in a number of fields – history, philology, ethnography, aesthetics etc. Even realism's discovery that simple peasants also have feelings was only possible because of the Romantic search for the outlandish in the ordinary folk around us – Platon Karatayev[1] had his forerunner in Quasimodo.[2] Edgar Allan Poe's interest in science spoke of a similar hankering for the exotic and mysterious, an attempt to harness reason – now found to be rearing its head close at hand – for romantic excursions into the miraculous. A learned man's study still smacked of the magician's den (Faust), holding out the promise of things to astonish minds that were consumed by curiosity and had already sallied beyond the confines of everyday reality, but were so far concerned rather to marvel than to study or digest. Men of science – more like sorcerers or anchorites in those days – were idolized by the Romantics. Science was still a matter of esoteric knowledge, while technology, with its balloons and electromagnetic waves – which went hand in hand with hypnosis and spiritualism! – constantly lapsed into pure lyricism, into art for art's sake.

*

On the subject of violins again. Was not the violin a companion to the homunculus – and later to the steam engine which set technology on the path of metamorphoses? Before people learned how to convert energy there could be no progress. Musical instruments, twanging and whistling, were intended as

[1] Platon Karatayev: character in Tolstoy's *War and Peace* representing the humility and wisdom of simple peasants.
[2] Quasimodo: character in Victor Hugo's *Notre Dame de Paris*.

an accompaniment to dancing and singing and not as an imitation of the human voice, as a way of converting resonant vibrations into a vocalization of the soul. The appearance of a singing box emitting a melody as sinuous as a snake was thus originally felt to be something unnatural, and the first virtuoso violinists were suspected of intercourse with the Dark One. One can indeed detect something demoniac in the squealing of violins. Not for nothing is the violin particularly adept at producing such diabolical arpeggios! What is more, the violin has outdone the flute – once considered the most depraved of instruments – in the matter of sensuality. It was through the violin that the souls of Faust, Schwarz and the other numerous magician-alchemists of the 16th century found expression. Sorcery then almost came out into the open as a manifestation of the Renaissance, and alchemists sought to unlock the secret of transmuting substances and energy, discovering by mistake gunpowder instead of gold. Flights to the Brocken were in fashion and the violin took them up . . . There is something peculiar even about the handling of this retort for distilling music into voice. All bent and hunched, a man shoulders the violin like a rifle and presses it to his body in such a manner that it seems to sprout from his gullet, or perhaps from his chest, harrowing the souls of listeners with its life-like and piteous miaowing. Scriabin came clawing his way – with the claws of ecstasy – out of the violin. To the accompaniment of its sounds electricity crackles in the audience's hair and light magnetic storms shake the hall.

*

"*And various philharmonicas visited our town . . .*"

*

"*We aren't musical folk – we don't need any of them symphonies.*"

*

"*When they start playing a symphony I want to throw up.*"

*

"I don't like this Schulbert, somehow. If only he could sing. But he sounds like a power-saw."

*

Listening to a radio broadcast of Mozart's violin concerto, a peasant said:

"It's like a mosquito flying."

*

A comment on Lensky's aria "Oh, whither, whither have you gone . . .":[1]

"Will he be singing long, this Maupassant?! . . ."

*

Art is not the representation, but the transfiguration of life. An image arises in response to the need for impelling it towards change in another, transfiguring, direction. We notice an "image" only in so far as it displaces what it is supposed to depict. "Table" or "forest" is not an image. "Golden table" is. "Green forest" is not an image: we need "green murmur".[2]

*

The Indian "Tale of the Knaves" (according to the Mahabharata and the Puranas) tells the story of Brahma's temptation by the beautiful maiden Tilottama, who was created by the artist Vishvakarman and whose beauty eclipsed that of goddesses. Tilottama dances before Brahma. Her gestures and movements and the way in which Brahma contemplates her beauty are depicted in the style characteristic of India, where sculpture seems to have grown out of the dance – into a forest of many-armed and many-faced gods. Reading on a little further about Tilottama and Brahma we suddenly realize why elephants live in India: their trunks are in the style of the country. We also see the birth of the image as the *eyes* of an object. In actual fact, it is the beholder who grows new eyes, but

[1] From *Eugene Onegin*.
[2] Famous image for the forest with its rustling leaves in a poem by Nekrasov.

they are transplanted to the picture or – as the case may be – to the language of the narrative, or to a temple. These new eyes open more and more the closer we look at them.

". . . Sensing this, like a river full of nectar and delights, she passed to the right of him in her dance. And he, spellbound by her beauty and filled with the passion of love, in order continuously to admire her charms created for himself another face looking southwards, a third gazing westwards, and a fourth turned to the north. And when she swept over his head as she leapt, he created a fifth face for himself directed upwards."

It is just like a tree growing and bearing fruit in the form of eyes. At the sight of it you understand that art or poetry consist above all in the opening of eyes in the raw material and thereby endowing it with their own vision, and that an image, a true image, is akin to Transfiguration.

*

In the Javanese shadow theatre ("Wayang"), the dolls are said to have their features shown in detail, and to be elaborately decorated and gilded, though nothing of all this is reflected on the screen. Is not this because the world is a shadow and hence the substance (in this case – a puppet) must be brighter, more vivid, more real than its shadow? The artist is concerned not with appearance, but with reality. It does not matter if the spectator does not see the actual doll: after all it *is*, it exists independently on its own! . . .

*

Cannot a sentence, with all its subordinate phrases, be likened to a box which contains a duck, a hare, an egg, the death of Koshchey the Deathless[1] (or the love of Helen of Troy)? Can it, in short, be turned into a labyrinth, or, better, into a *matrioshka*,[2] rolling itself into a ball and running into the depths of itself by

[1] An evil genius and miser of Russian fairy-tales.
[2] Russian wooden doll containing replicas of itself of progressively diminishing size.

means of various "that's" and "which's", filling its intricately composite body with a soft light coming from inside, from its very core, like the soul – whence, which, where, because, which once more, and unless, then this that or the other? . . .

*

Why does "Princess" sound so much more attractive than "Queen"? Is it only because she has a royal future in front of her? Or because it is simply a beautiful attribute without the heavy weight of power, not an office, but merely a title, not a throne, but an individual – the very crown on her head only a proud ornament? In "Princess" there is always that extra little flourish.

*

Knowing nothing about someone or something we often form a notion of it according to a verbal image, the colour and fragrance of the name. Thus the Grimm brothers are twins in thick woollen stockings and identical broad-brimmed hats – or, if you wish, embroidered waistcoats, wigs and cocked hats. There is a touch of showmanship about the name – not that of the operatic performer but rather that of the conjurer, a mixture of benevolence and sorcery. And to think they were brothers! Just fancy that – the Brothers Grimm! . . .

But what a lottery everything is! Wrubel[1] would have lost half his attraction if he had lived not in Russia, but in Poland. In Polish he is "Sparrow". What price then all his polygons and beautiful crystals?

*

. . . I like dashes too. But colons are more significant: they indicate the direction of a sentence as it leads into the depths of the text: they introduce an idea perhaps as yet insufficiently clarified, too verbose or diffuse: but roaming in search of its final, definitive expression.

And then parentheses I love too – or rather, I constantly

[1] M. A. Wrubel (1856–1911): Russian painter.

feel the need to take refuge in them, going to earth in them at intervals between phrases. Sometimes, apart from parentheses, I am also tempted to enclose things in square brackets and oblique strokes – not to lose the way as I retreat into my labyrinthine burrow.

*

. . . Prose has so far taken little account of the possibilities of brackets. By and large, brackets have always played an ancillary role and have never presumed to claim special attention. Yet a verbal construct moving on parallel and intersecting ways or levels, which can be shown graphically by means of brackets, brings writing close to certain forms of geometric art, where the eye jumps from object to object, from one point to another, setting off the verbal field in a kind of relief, bringing to it unevenness, a layered depth – something in which brackets can, in principle, play a major part by forming the dams, caves and canyons whence the main, all-pervading sense flows and percolates throughout the text as a whole.

*

Suppose one created one's own language and lived in it like an ape in a forest?

*

In English literature the damp climate of London plays a by no means unimportant part. Fog, rain, evening mist, and, by way of pleasant contrast and the starting point for a story, a cosy fire-place and a glass of punch – of which we mentally take a sip, and then tuck our feet under us, making ourselves comfortable and preparing to listen.

In Russian literature the climate is not as clearly defined, or at least has not been elevated into a leading component of style. Pushkin was the first to regale us with winter – in *The Snowstorm*, *The Devils*, and "Tatyana's Dream",[1] and we should hold fast to it. What do we want with "spring waters"[2]

[1] In *Eugene Onegin*.
[2] Reference to Turgenev's novel *Spring Waters*.

when we have such a winter up our sleeve! . . .

In Russian fairy-tales, for all their summery stock-in-trade of flowers and berries, the inevitable piece of furniture is the stove. Fairy-tales are told sitting or lying on stoves, the fool or the *bogatyr* sits on a stove for thirty-three years at a stretch and some poor fellow has to ride all over Russia on a stove at a magician's behest. In other words, fairy-tales quite literally "dance from the stove".[1] The fairy-tale has harnessed the stove to its sleigh and driven away on it like a wedding party.

*

Snugness and warmth give birth to new ideas.

*

I know why the crows have been cawing so much of late: they were feeling too black on this white snow.

*

Oh to snuggle behind a stove and listen to it roaring.

19th November, 1969.

*

He hid in a cellar for sixteen years until a son-in-law gave him away. The family secret was kept – until the girls (he had five daughters) married. At the age of five or twelve they knew how to hold their tongues. When they married every single one of them told her husband.

*

When photographs of nuns were hung round his neck and a Special Correspondent was just about to take a picture of "the dissolute priest" for the newspapers, the old man could bear it no longer and said ominously that the prosecutor's daughter, a young girl, would henceforth be hanging round men's necks

[1] Russian idiom for embarking on something from a familiar point of departure.

like the photographs now being hung on him. At this the prosecutor cancelled the photographing session . . .

*

"Because you never know what's in store for you either."

*

"And, lo, he became invisible". (About the Devil) It is amazing how much a well-worn turn of phrase can suit the event or action to which it refers. Slipped into the context of modern Russian speech, these Church Slavonic words (*nevidim byst*) crackle like a flash of lightning – the effect of disappearance is precisely captured in their sound.

*

. . . It is amusing to discover that all these extraordinarily earnest scholarly arguments tacitly start from one initial premiss – the simple and unshakeable assumption that in olden days people were fools. To feel the power of fairy-tales you have to *believe* in them, if only a little. Children are helped by their natural trustfulness. But for scholars, well, – it's just hard.

Then there is a second difficulty for them: they insist on understanding everything figuratively rather than literally. (A cottage on chicken legs[1] is not a cottage and does not stand on chicken legs, but represents something far more recondite!) All the same, the good thing about Propp's[2] theory is that he has at least found another pivot to replace the wearisomely omnipresent sun worship: namely, that the concept of the other world is the same as the far-away land of the fairy-tales. Reading Propp you realize the immensity of people's yearning for immortality – this is what moves mankind. Although the author is not likely to have had this in mind.

*

[1] see note on page 195.
[2] Vladimir Propp (1895–1970): eminent Russian folklorist. Author of "*The Morphology of the Fairy Tale*".

In the mythology of the Altai peoples, the first men, still ignorant of sin, were born of flowers and had wings which radiated light. The heavenly bodies did not yet exist. Then men ate of some root and knew sin – whereupon they lost their luminescent wings, and the Sun and Moon were created at their request. (*The Legends and Fables of Central Asia*, collected by Count A. P. Bennigsen, St Petersburg, 1912.) To think there are books like this somewhere in this world!

*

The dragon of the fairy-tales resembles a sort of insect: it flies in the sky and when its wings get tired it alights in a field and darts around like a cockroach.

*

At a certain moment the Dragon and Ivan[1] change places, not noticing they have done so: lust and chivalry, pursued and pursuer, cats and mice thus prove to be entirely interchangeable.

It is the established convention that the plot of any good story revolves round some catch or deception. The story of the world starts with the Fall, and ever after we have been able to think only of how to cover up for our failings. This is doubtless why there are so many fables about the fox: the devil-deceiver stalks the earth in the guise of a fox.

*

In Ancient Egypt, besides the astral double, "Ka", there was the soul, "Ba", which was portrayed in the form of a bird with a human head: she certainly gets around, our little Sirin![2]

*

. . . A new mode of discourse might be born from loss of memory. As you struggled to regain it, floundering in the quicksands of oblivion, dragons and the Baba-Yaga[3] might come to mind again.

[1] Ivan: see note on page 195.
[2] Sirin: see note on page 161.
[3] Witch in Russian fairy-tales.

A bird which a half-wit first saw in a dream later turned up in the zoo. "I know you, Nastasya!"

I loved that pheasant so much I would gladly have turned into it myself.

They fed the bird with nothing but the brains of animals.

Every sentence, like an emerald, must sparkle with wild fancy. (And it must contain a concealed refrain in invisible parentheses: I love you.)

There is always a part for birds in any score – the flutes. Bartok and Breughel could help us out here.

*

Just suppose that in his battle with Polkan, Bova the King's son[1] had lunged out with his sword and missed – so it went deep into the ground, and he was unable to pull it out, and jumped around tugging at it and crying bitterly.

The question is what did the Dragon do with girls like Lucy? Lucy can turn at will into Nastasya or into Helen of Troy – depending on the class of person concerned.

Names get lost or forgotten. A man comes in as Antony and leaves as Andrew: the same thing that is liable to happen to numbers in a flood of words.

It was the 10th century AD in Russia – the dawn of our history was trying to get up and walk. Knights rode on steeds which were as straight and foursquare as tables.

Let us take an exercise book, light a candle-end, dip our pen deeper into the ink-well and set out on our travels. Where the spirit moves us. Wherever the pen leads us. An ancient city – for all the world like the forbidden zone inside the camp, the watch towers, the fence. It is bitterly cold and the sun resembles the planet Jupiter. Snowdrifts, sledges. A horse, flat on its back, thrashes about with its long extremities resembling the tiny legs of a cricket. By now the 15th century is already under way in Russia. (We've made it – the 15th century!)

A fairy-tale is composed of broken, loose bricks. They are

[1] Russian fairy-tale derived from an episode (battle of Buovo d'Antona with the monster Pulicane) in the Italian 14th-century poem *Reali di Francia*.

ready beforehand. The order in which they must be placed is also more or less known. The one thing not known is what they are for and what they are all about. What the Dragon did with Lucy is also unknown. One brick may be a little sturdier, another a little more awkward, but the job gets done. The knights now gallop on steeds as lean as greyhounds.

*

The Dragon must have looked like a big black tree. One of its heads was sleeping, snoring rhythmically; another, with a leering expression on its face, watched the comings and goings of Ivan the King's son, and two others whispered something into each other's ears, breaking into peals of forced and exaggerated laughter, like actors on the radio; a fifth licked its own neck like a cat; a sixth stretched out towards its dozing partner and lit the cigarette between its teeth from the bluish flame breathed by the other's nostril . . . All these branching heads made Ivan imagine that he too was numbered among them in that black forest. Who *is* the Dragon? Ivan himself, perhaps? At any rate, from what we are told in the fairy-tales, the Dragon has no clear-cut image and variously rides a steed, walks about a room in galoshes, drinks water with his trunk (like an elephant's), or drags a princess behind, like a dog on a lead. These transformations are in no way explained and the wretched spectator feels his head spinning.

*

As a historian Suetonius, it is said, was interested mainly in various entertaining oddities and hence gathered together a good many facts that throw some light on very ancient, prehistoric matters otherwise reflected only in myths. A modern scholar will remark with a hint of disdain that Suetonius often misses out important things and pays undue attention to the merely entertaining ones. But, personally, I find that in working this anecdotal vein he produces nuggets from a way of life which would otherwise be quite beyond our grasp.

"For him the interesting fact about the decisive battle of the

Sicilian War is that Octavian was fast asleep just before the actual encounter," sniffs the scholar derisively. Mock him, if you will, but look at that part about the Sicilian War when Augustus has defeated Pompey between Mylae and Naulochus: "Just before the battle he suddenly fell into such a deep sleep that his friends had to wake him to give the signal for action to begin".

Now, I recall that in fairy-tales the hero has the habit of falling into a deep sleep before a battle or any other important undertaking, and that the poor princess finally succeeds in awaking him only by shedding a bitter tear, a tear like a star. This kind of sleep is perhaps an appeal for help to a region beyond one's ken – a region from which the soul of the elect draws sustenance. Such sleep was more crucial than any battle plan.

Whatever the scholars may say – and however right they may be – I simply cannot overcome my inclination to regard fairy-tales as information about something real. Further on I read about the same divine Augustus:

"His chest and stomach are said to have been covered with birthmarks resembling in appearance, number and disposition the constellation of the Great Bear . . ."

Here I am reminded of a fairy-tale in which someone's son has the bright moon on his back and a great host of stars on his sides – his whole horoscope is imprinted on him, in fact. According to the Koreans, the Chinese and other peoples, the Great Bear ensures peace in the home, wealth and long life.

That's what a perfectly useless birthmark may bring you . . .

*

For the fairy-tale's roots one should pay more attention to the iconography of dreams. Then much would be clearer and the ontology behind the metaphors would come to life. Here I have often listened to people telling their dreams and many of them contain undoubted echoes of myths – about snakes, for instance.

An elderly Ukrainian, a former partisan, told me of a dream

he had had in his youth and which he felt was of prophetic significance. He dreamt he was sitting on the stove (on which he was in fact sleeping[1]), when a serpent crawled in through the door. Not an ordinary serpent, but one with paws: a huge lizard. With one gulp it swallowed his elder sister – there was nothing left of her except a few drops of blood. Then it raised its head and their eyes met – at which he woke up out of sheer fright. His mother said: "You didn't say the Lord's Prayer before you went to sleep!" Twelve years later this dream came true.[2]

Many years later – by which time he was in the camp – that same serpent hung down from the ceiling over him and they struggled for a long time until he strangled it. But it still managed to sting him in the leg and his elder sister, by then no longer alive, sucked the poison out of the wound. None of this has come true yet, but he believes it will in good time.

Then I was told a dream about a kingdom underground – exactly as described in the fairy-tales (though I ascertained through round-about questioning that the narrator had never heard a fairy-tale in his life):

"I fell into a well and went on falling for a long time until I landed in another world" – this is exactly how the fairy-tales put it – "and it was just like the world here, with flowing rivers and everything the same." (This in a bemused tone)

In contrast to these dreams, where there is a hint of something authentic, I was also told a story about a drug addict in the camp who while "high" saw extraordinary visions which vanished into thin air the moment he came to again, but contained the secret and meaning of creation. Once, summoning up all his strength, he wrote it down – the whole secret in one phrase – and when he came to, he found that it read: "*There is a smell of petroleum everywhere*".

14th December, 1969.

*

[1] It is the custom in peasant houses to sleep on the broad-topped stove for warmth in the winter.

[2] The man's sister was arrested by the NKVD (secret police) and vanished without trace. (*Author's explanation*)

After seeing a miracle a man desperately wants to smoke and looks for matches, running about the compound with an empty matchbox in his hand, and going into the smoking room where he hears a hum of voices, but he finds there isn't a soul in the place, though it is thick with smoke, and suddenly sees at his feet on the floor a clean, unused match whose supernatural appearance astounds him more than the miracle he has just seen, and when telling people about it he constantly comes back to the match – now the stumbling block in his life.

*

The temperature has gone up a little and this is bad – there is a heaviness in the air, and I feel a physical lassitude, but the worst thing is the sheer waste: the amount of warmth expended to no purpose in the winter! If only it could be saved to warm up all those *cold* days in the summer to come. Who needs it now?!

*

How do I start my day? If snow has fallen during the night I quickly change into all my dirty clothes as soon as I get to work and, broom in hand, like Leo Tolstoy, clear it away from the gantry. Mice and birds have left their tracks on the white expanse – which means they must have come to hop around here at dawn. It's a pity to sweep all this away.

In the meantime the stove has been lit in the hut and I can warm myself a little until there is unloading to be done. Suetonius. Caesar's wolfish face. And then the prison train by which we tell the time: ten o'clock.[1] Smoke, Shakespeare's characters billowing out of the chimney. Sometimes it's Macbeth, sometimes Richard III. In the human figure drawn by Yegor the hair is particularly good – it looks like a little house on the crown of the head.

"What are you sending a living man to the devil for?," asks a wretched old man, sentenced for the fifth time.

*

[1] The train always arrived at the local station, situated not far from the compound, at exactly the same time. (*Author's explanation*)

The forest is quite violet. This is due to the birches. Their white trunks are in fact all inky, and from afar the impression is that of a whole sea of ink.

*

What is a forest?
A forest is a sea, where, which, to which . . .
What is a forest?
A forest is a city, from which, which, in which . . .
What is a forest?
A forest is a sky, thanks to which, because of which, in the absence of which, as if . . .
What is a forest?
A forest is a forest.

*

Part Five

A man just about to be released says thoughtfully:

"*I'll have a beer . . .*" (long pause). "*And a sausage to eat with it*" (pause) . . .

*

". . . *And the streets are so long that you walk along them for ever. And every window has a light shining in it.*"

*

I was lucky that we lived near the Museum of Decorative Arts, and that it was thus a part of my childhood – as a boy I used to run off there simply to sit in the company of the statues, and dream, all by myself, in some little Italian courtyard, always so deserted and plunged in semi-darkness; that courtyard and the antique portico, particularly in the winter when everything outside was covered in glittering hoarfrost, have remained with me ever since, all my life. Works of art, unlike books, provide an environment in which you can live – they surround you like the trees in a forest and gradually permeate your being in the same way as any other habitat. Forests and museums – these are what I should like to go to; they are somehow intertwined in my memory, and are what I miss most.

*

When we recall our childhood the members of our families seem to have been giants – in keeping with our own smallness at the time. But no doubt they were then even bigger in our eyes, coextensive with the universe and embracing the whole of visible reality, which was divided into two halves: into Mummy's and Daddy's, as it were, with "Hazelnut Hill" being a further projection of my father's body, while "Pinewood" was a part of my mother.[1]

[1] "Hazelnut Hill" and "Pinewood": names of localities in the Volga region which the author remembers from his childhood. (*Author's explanation*)

An individual dear to one takes on substance not against a background of objects bearing no relation to him or her, but as an extension of them – they coalesce in a visible unity with the face that is so familiar. Not "mummy is coming down the street", but the street takes on the shape of mummy – she materializes out of her inchoate state, summoned forth at a moment's notice from a world as much part of her as her dress or coat. A child calls for his mother, however far away she may be, in the certainty that this universal maternal principle animating the world of things will shine out on him, manifesting their inner essence as her presence: he only has to call. He is not, therefore, unduly surprised when his room turns into his mother or she peeps out, like the sun, from behind a cloud. In the same way, memories of a beloved person imperceptibly take on the character of a tale, diffuse and spreading out in all directions without end. They amount not so much to a portrait as to a landscape – the geography of a cherished name, dotted about everywhere and waiting for a summons.

*

Today we had a lovely winter's day – quite pink, as in childhood, in a beautiful harmony of snow, frost and air.

10th January, 1970.

*

According to a learned article on the subject the custom of singing at sea existed up till quite recently among our coast-dwellers – as witness the White Sea *skazitel* (minstrel) M. M. Korguyev and another one from Pudozh – F. A. Konashkov. The reciting of *bylinas* is said to have calmed the elements – hence the story of Sadko playing his *gusli*[1] to the Sea King. The same magic purpose is served by the very frequent formula at the end of a *bylina*: "for the calming of the blue sea and the amusement of good people".

But if this line of thought is pursued, it could be noted that there is in general a close connection between water and

[1] A kind of psaltery.

singing. This must surely be the reason for so many songs about boats or ships, such as "On a little boat we sailed . . .", "Lone White Sail", or "Stenka Razin" – which go so naturally with the rolling waves. Whatever the words, the music of these songs is always slow and soothing. It occurs to me indeed that songs are just as bound up with water as fairy-tales are with forests. The Russian word for "boat" (*lodka*, or in an older form *ladya*) is similar to "harmony" (*lad*), and when Väinemäinen or Haiawatha sang as they built their boats they were hence establishing concord – for which "boat" is an objectivized image – on the waters. A song is a boat which we launch on the waves in order to calm them. I also believe that we have in general a natural urge to sing when we are on the water (just as in a forest we are moved to speak in whispers) – and as we do so it never even crosses our minds that we are actually praying to the Sea King. I certainly never suspected as much when I sang "And the stormy sea roared and moaned" on my way to Kiy Island. In fact, however, the unconscious burden of my song was a prayer that it should *not* roar. But all I felt at the time was a kind of exaltation. It is this sense of exaltation – the expression of a wish, deep down inside, that harmony should regulate the waves – which impels people to sing on the water.

Many of the ancient traditions preserved in folklore still live secretly inside us and manifest themselves because they are sustained from within by our nature – whose working principle is a mystery to us (though the ancients knew all about it). If it were not so, the persistence of these traditions which have existed, scholars tell us, since primordial times, would be incomprehensible. They would simply not have survived. Unless they were fostered by the modern psyche – which, it is true, no longer finds support for them in any logic or ritual, but nevertheless knows their meaning and quietly suggests to us what we can or cannot do – we would not remember either fairy-tales or songs. Nature is more powerful than rational arguments and even at official funerals we put black slippers on the feet of the dead and take flowers to their graves, though we have long ceased trying to bring them back to life with our gifts. Similarly, we sing on the sea, and about it.

*

"The night of the Prophet's birth was not as others:
The sun had not yet arisen, but the world glowed with light.
When as a child the Prophet once felt wronged and wept,
Word came from the Lord that he was never to weep.
'Wherever one tear will fall from thy eyes,
The grass will no longer grow, and the earth will dry up.'
In fulfilment of the Lord's will he ceased weeping,
And merely whispered with his lips:
'La ilah illa-l-lah'."

I have started collecting Chechen[1] songs which, apparently, have never been recorded in writing. They are rather in the style of Russian "spiritual verse",[2] and represent a blend of Arabic tradition with local legends and customs. They are extraordinary for the complexity and suppleness of their psychological portraiture – something usually lacking in songs. Everything is built on half-tones and nuances, and the song is borne along on an eddying current that produces constant shifts of meaning while conserving the monotony of the general melody – this is mainly choral, though with strong lyrical overtones.

It should be borne in mind that this vast and complex body of religious songs which epitomize the soul of the people and are alive to the present day, was composed in Daghestan no earlier than the last century when the ideas of Islam came to new life in the conflagration of Shamil's[3] uprising. This means that the genesis of an epic cycle which with other peoples happened in time immemorial has in this instance taken place almost before our very eyes.

While carefully checking names and other details so as not to

[1] A Muslim people in the Caucasus.
[2] Religious songs recited by wandering pilgrims.
[3] Shamil (1797–1871): religious head (Imam) and military leader of some Caucasian tribes during their insurrection against Russia, 1824–29.

distort the sense of the events described, I have kept almost word for word, apart from a few minor improvements, to the literal rendering of the songs as given to me: I hope that the poetry of the original will come through better in this unpolished state.

"When the great Prophet's time had drawn nigh,
He summoned to him, they say, his askhab Bilal,
And said to him: 'The time of my death has come,
Call to the mosque all my trusty askhabs.'

And Bilal called together, as bidden, all that glorious brotherhood,
Declaring that the Prophet was inviting them to his mosque.
The askhabs, weeping and crying, gathered, as bidden in the mosque,
Reciting prayers and appealing to the Lord.

And standing at the place where he always recited his prayers,
The Prophet said to them, as he appealed to God,
'I have cared for you as a man cares for his father and mother,
And as a sister suffers for her brother, so have I suffered for you.[1]
Soon I shall pass away, my good askhabs,
Loving you, to-day I must bid you farewell.
Let him whom I have wronged in my life
Rise and take what I owe him – before the Day of Judgment has come.'

Then, so they say, his faithful askhab Ukashat rose up,
Saying to the Prophet: 'We were on the Gazawat
When thou didst strike me. If thou hadst not twice and thrice,
Declared thy wish, I would not have claimed my due.'

[1] Had he been speaking in terms familiar to us, the Prophet would have compared his love for his disciples to parental love, but among the Chechens love for one's father and mother has a higher value than love for one's children. And a sister's love for her brother is considered specially strong and exalted. (*Author's note*)

And the Prophet sent his askhab Bilal,
Bidding him go to Fatima and bring him a rod.
Fatima, on hearing this, pitied the Prophet and wept:
'Who will dare gratify his own whim by demanding his due from my father?!'

And Bilal, so they say, handed the rod to the Prophet,
The Prophet handed the rod to the askhab Ukashat,
And Ukashat said: 'Thou didst strike me on my naked body!'
And the Prophet then pulled up the shirt on his back.

Then up rose Abu-Bakr, and Omar and Osman,
And by them it was said: 'If thou shouldst strike the Prophet,
Who would then appease our indignant hearts?
For that old wrong settle accounts with us.'

Then up rose Hassan and Hussein, and by them it was said:
'We are the sons of Ali, borne by Fatima.
If thou strikest us thy vengeance will be accomplished.
Thy debt shall be paid by us – what more dost thou want?'

Then up rose Murtazal-Ali himself, and by him it was said:
'If thou shouldst strike the Prophet, who would appease our hearts?
If thou shouldst strike the Prophet, where wouldst thou go thyself?
Behold our bodies, have them instead of the Prophet's!'

Then up rose Ukashat, and by him it was said:
'Who could think of striking thee, Prophet?!
That shame I took on myself for fear of hell,
So that the sight of thy holy body should save me in the life to come.' "

*

I am amazed how much my father and mother have given me and how their quiet life goes on in me, albeit indirectly. How vivid in my memory are all those places like Zhiguli and Ozerki where they lived before I was born – I have never been there, and it makes no sense, but I can't get them out of my mind. I recall my father's snoring as something protective. Hearing it I felt safe. And his smell was a protection too.

*

Fingers preternaturally stubby, like carrots. How massive they are to look at! And what if they are also white and carefully tended – with a thick skin? And belong to a puny wizened little man – the picture of a clerk with a taste for philosophy? What did he do with these fingers, each of them as fat as an elephant's trunk? Yet the palms of his hands are really quite small . . .

*

Predictions are misleading when people fail to take account of the possibility of some new force appearing in the configuration of future events and limit themselves to names familiar in their own time. Suetonius, noting that the reign of Vespasian (whose road to Imperial power began with Judea) was foretold in advance, comments as follows:

"According to an ancient and firm conviction current in the East fate had decreed that at about this time rulers of the world would come out of Judea. Events proved that this referred to the Roman emperor; but the Jews, who took the prediction as referring to themselves, rose in rebellion, murdered the Procurator, put to flight even the Consular Legate who had come from Syria with reinforcements, and captured his Eagle."

It is amusing to see how both sides interpreted the omens in their own favour, when they in fact more likely referred to the still scarcely noticed progress of a new kingdom – that of Christ. We find the same thing in Tacitus – in connection with Titus's siege of Jerusalem:

"Portents began to appear over the city, and that people, steeped in prejudice, but ignorant of religion, was unable to ward them off either by sacrifices or by propitiatory vows. Warring hosts fought in the sky, swords blazed with a crimson flame, fire coming from the clouds encircled the temple. Suddenly the doors of the sanctuary were flung wide open and a voice of superhuman power, like a clap of thunder, proclaimed: 'The gods are departing', and steps were heard leaving the temple. But these portents struck terror in only a few. The majority put their faith in a prophecy written down, as they believed, in ancient times by their priests in sacred books: just about this time the East was allegedly destined to achieve supremacy, and men ordained to rule the world were to come out of Judea. This vague prediction referred to Vespasian and Titus, but the inhabitants, as is people's wont generally, interpreted the prophecy in their own favour, maintaining that it was the Jews who were destined to be raised to the pinnacle of power and glory, and no misfortunes could force them to see the truth."

There's self-confident, enlightened Rome for you! And then that voice saying: "The gods are departing" – to announce a change in values, culture and the course of history – something which always begins from the temple!

*

. . . What a dream I saw last night! Even the sensations of colour and smell were so distinct that I am sure we must have a depository within our souls where images of long ago are preserved as in a museum, and are liable at any moment to come back to life, return whence they came, and continue to exist outside time and space. How terrifying to think we carry round within ourselves such a vast store of images! The colour was green, a translucent green, as of a precious stone or a crystal – a piece of congealed colour, gleaming out of your eyes, but now having a significance all its own – that of colour pure and simple. And directly afterwards, in no way connected with it, but also as an absolute quality, I dreamed of my father's smell: it was so distinctly present that I recognized it at once and was surprised in the dream at the exactness of the sensation – which I would not be able to evoke now in my waking state. The extraordinary thing is not the theme of my dream – it was no doubt suggested by my day-time thoughts and letters to you – but its matter-of-fact quality, the amazing faithfulness of these phantasmal images to reality. If the soul is more enduring than things and clings so hard to them, then things too, perhaps, will never die? . . .

*

What does a child need? – to be near his father and mother. Isn't this just what our soul yearns for – but when and where?

*

In the icon of the Assumption of the Holy Virgin, as I remember it, the Son receives the Mother's soul and holds it in His hands. The tiny white figure looks like a swaddled babe, prompting us to imagine that the soul does in fact have the appearance of a child.

Formally, however, it can be argued that what we see here depicts not the soul as such, but the Virgin's body wrapped in its shroud and about to be taken up to Heaven. Its smallness is possibly explained by the distinction in scale traditionally observed in icons between the earthly and the heavenly – and, as usual, the icon is composed in such a way as to give unity to the different stages of what was indeed one single Event.

Yet, even so that little figure like a candle in His hands makes one long to say: the soul is a child.

*

. . . Snow is good, too, because it falls to no purpose and is useful only in distant and indirect ways. Snow has no intentions. Unlike rain. Or even the sun. It is disinterested and aimless.

"A horse so white that it can't even be seen when it gallops in the snow."

*

In order to write something worthwhile one needs to be absolutely empty.

*

I never cease wondering at the fact that a writer knows nothing, remembers nothing, can do nothing, does not know how to do anything, and that this impotence of his – his utter inability to say anything of note – makes him turn to the whole world and only then can he do and know something.

*

I like Matisse's drawings more than his paintings. In contrast to other artists whose drawings have an ancillary function and serve as preliminary sketches, Matisse's paintings come back to mind rather as sketches for his drawings, which, strange to say, take things a stage further in regard to pure colour.

*

. . . I measure life by the number of times my head is shaven.

*

I like the slow tempo of our existence here compared with the usual rhythm of life which people outside willy-nilly adopt in order to be in time for the bus, the office or the cinema. The mind, therefore, works somehow more naturally in camp – it doesn't have to calculate all the time how to get ahead of somebody else. Apart from certain exceptional cases, one practically ceases to hurry (where to?). And existence opens its blue eyes all the wider.

*

The one thing that life teaches you is to be grateful. To the stereotype question: how are you?, a young man answers "All right" (with a hint of "not too good"); in later life it is: "Can't complain", and in old age: "Very well, thank God".

*

Let the soul be peaceful and pure.

*

It *is* His mother's soul that the Son holds in His hands – this is made quite clear by the text of the service for the Feast of the Assumption. The same text throws light on another question: why so much importance was attached to the Assumption in Ancient Russia. It has always been the most popular name for churches, and over half of our cathedrals alone are dedicated to it.[1] The reason may well be that the Assumption, apart from its significance in the worship of Christ's Mother, has about it something of the Easter miracle – to which the Orthodox religion assigns first place (as distinct from the West where the Nativity is the principal feast). The clue can be found in the collect for the Feast of the Assumption which says (in the Old Believers' version of the service, the only one available to me here): "The laws of nature are overcome by Thee, Virgin undefiled, for birth cometh from a virgin, and life vanquisheth death. Thou givest birth and art a Virgin, and Thou livest after death."

The greatest miracle in the world is precisely this: "the laws of nature are overcome", death is defeated both in the grave and in the seed. Almost as at Easter, "life vanquisheth death" – which is made manifest in the Resurrection and Assumption of the Holy Virgin. How can we fail to celebrate this double miracle, this double victory over the laws of nature! . . .

*

"Thou art our holy defender,
Thou art our own mother,
Will it not be for Thy sake
That we shall have to suffer?

[1] There are also many dedicated to the Transfiguration, but relatively few to the Nativity (on the other hand, many to the Birth of the Virgin), according to early lists of churches. (*Author's note*)

Thou hast comforted all of us, sinners,
And hast brought us up like children.
But a strange time has come to pass –
We forgot about Thee.

Thou didst toll bells
And daily call us to church.
Why, then, Beloved,
Dost Thou stand like an orphan?
Where is it gone, where has it hidden itself –
All the beauty of the earth?

Open Thou the doors of the temple,
Uplift our hearts,
We never see, we never hear
The word of God."

(Spiritual verses[1])

*

In a recent article entitled "On the Unity of pre-Mongol Russian Architecture" M. A. Ilyin tries to base the distinction between Byzantine and Russian churches on a fundamental difference of outlook rather than on formal details, as is usually done. Comparing the St Sophia of Kiev – a structure in the Byzantine tradition – with the Novgorod St Sophia and later churches, he shows how the emphasis in Russian architecture shifts from inner space to outside appearance – a trend towards "ornamentalism" that culminated in the church of St Basil in Moscow.

This is true enough. The Kiev St Sophia is unique of its kind in this country: compared with purely Russian churches, it is remarkable both for the ampleness of its inner proportions and for its unprepossessing exterior. The only question is: what was the reason? Ilyin believes it must have been a throwback to pre-Christian times. Although we know nothing of the appearance and nature of Slav pagan temples, Ilyin assumes

[1] see note on page 228.

that the external form was of paramount importance, since they served as objects of worship in themselves and must, hence, have been designed to produce an effect from the outside:

"One may assume that the introduction of Christianity into Russia did not change the basic attitude to places of worship. For this reason, the Byzantine model, with its inner spaciousness, underwent a radical change and much greater stress was laid on the external appearance of the church. In other words, our 12th century ancestors went back, as it were, to an earlier conception of religious architecture. Even though the Christian temple was intended for the celebration of divine service within its walls and was thus more accessible to ordinary worshippers, its architecture was still dominated by the time-honoured idea of the temple as an object of devotion, as the dwelling place of the deity. This explains the indifference of the Russian builders to inner space and their close attention, on the other hand, to the outside appearance of the church. The latter, as something tangible and material, was more readily appreciated by the practical mentality of the mediaeval Russians than the rather notional idea of inner space, which could be sensed rather than seen and derived from an abstract concept of the deity on the part of Byzantine scholastics and mystics."

Our learned writers are very fond of reminding us of the Russian people's pagan roots. For atheists paganism is, after all, more acceptable than Christianity. This, by the way, explains the unparalleled success, in the 19th century, of *The Lay of Igor's Host* – in preference to all the Christian literature of Ancient Russia. The Chronicle of the Church Fathers from the Kievan Pechora Monastery, a no less striking and original work than *The Lay*, is forgotten. But even if we admit the pagan antecedents of the Orthodox Russian people, we find them reflected in early church architecture in a way that suggested abhorrence of dangerous temptations rather than a return to the old and still influential idols (just as people preferred not to represent the Devil in Holy Russia because they imagined him all too vividly and were afraid of him).

Apart from this, however, there is no reason to suppose that the pagan temple as an object of worship and the dwelling place of the deity was necessarily distinguished by external magnificence. This would be altogether too simple and crude an assumption. On the contrary, there was just as likely to have been a deliberate tendency to make the deity's abode a rather modest or inconspicuous affair. Thus, the Hebrew tabernacle was obviously not a thing of splendour in its external form. God's presence on earth was marked primarily by mystery, by the seclusion of the place. "The Lord said that he would dwell in the thick darkness." (1 Kings VIII, 12) . . . There are many reasons to think that our pagan sanctuaries and temples, as objects of worship or abodes of the deity, were likewise not particularly striking or ornate to look at. The Slav idols most likely lived secretly and unassumingly in forests, caves, or holes in the ground.

The Christian temple in Ancient Russia was something quite different again, and if the external form dominated over inner space, this may well have been thanks to the special place accorded in our national religious outlook to the Virgin's Cloak of Protection – not a pagan, but a thoroughly Orthodox, even if predominantly Russian, concept. The Russian church *is* the Virgin's Cloak. Inside it we find not infinity of space, not the Cosmos, not the harmony of the spheres, but above all – warmth, protection, cosiness. It was the custom of our ancestors to go to the church for warmth, to keep their treasure there, to seek refuge in it from enemies. To enter a Russian church is rather like creeping under a blanket, or throwing a fur coat over one's head. But this fur coat is God's own, and it is only right and proper that it should be truly magnificent. The heavens are studded with stars and when we build a cathedral we wrap ourselves in the starry sky, dress in the snowy raiment of winter, in the green superabundance of summer: we spread a cloak, a tapestry over the Universe (for every temple is a Universe). The predominance of ornament in Russian architecture (sometimes at the expense of structural elements) is due to the fact that the church is less a building than a cloak of protection.

The Russian idea of the Cloak, as reflected in the cosiness and intimacy of our church architecture, is well brought out by the following passage in Leskov's short story "On the Edge of the World", where the narrator is describing the sense of God's protection he felt as a small boy hiding under a shelf in a bath-house to escape some punishment or other:

"And how I felt Him, Lord! He so surprised and gladdened me when He came. Just fancy; the whole Universe cannot contain Him, and yet, seeing a child's distress, He steals into a bath-house . . . to that little mite under the shelf and bides a while in his breast-pocket . . . I must admit that, more than any other notion of what the deity is like, I love this *Russian God* of ours who can take up His abode in somebody's breast-pocket. In fact, whatever the Greeks may say and however much they may tell us that our knowledge of God comes from them, they did not reveal Him to us. Not in their pompous Byzantinism and the smoke of their incense did we find Him – no, He is our very own, familiar and homely, walking about everywhere, creeping under a shelf in a bath-house and snuggling like a dove in a warm breast-pocket."

The author could not of course refrain, in his Russian humility, from proclaiming our superiority over "pompous Byzantinism". We have not been free of pomposity ourselves. But if we take this "breast-pocket" and, mindful of Him who protects us in it, richly embroider the outside, we shall have our favoured architectural form: the church that covers us like the Cloak of the Virgin.[1]

*

Let us heave a gentle sigh, gather our thoughts together and write a little more . . . The *Nunc dimittis* – "Lord, now lettest thou thy servant depart in peace", is read daily as the concluding part of the evening service. The question is: why this choice of words? Simeon died after uttering them, while we live on. The reason, they say, is that the service refers to our

[1] Many churches in Russia are called *Pokrov*, literally "covering", or "protection". The word is commonly translated "Intercession" in English.

departure to sleep, the ending of the day's journey. The symbolism of night and sleep resembles the symbolism of death. The *Nunc dimittis* is an expression of this.

*

Why does death occur so frequently in the spring and also at dawn? You would think that winter and night would be more appropriate. But dawn and spring are the beginning of a cycle, and when he enters it, a man whose hour actually came in the winter and at night is at once revealed as a supernumerary, a cypher. He does not survive at the beginning of the new cycle because his life has been completed earlier, at the end of the preceding one, and his time has now run out. The new day dawns and, no longer needed, he departs.

*

We speak of the fullness of the day, and of the depth of the night, but the evening is somehow nothing much at all.

4th March, 1970.

*

Ungainly and dogged, as if paid to do so, Blucher's[1] killer walks back and forth over the melting snow, working away with his arms and legs – physical jerks to enable him to go on living.

*

From Chechen songs:

> Turning a quern with her hands, reading the Koran with her lips,
> Pondering in her mind on what she had read,
> Fatima, daughter of a great father, sat one day, it is said.
> "Peace unto thee, oh daughter of a great father, Fatima!",
> Bending over her, said the Angel of Death, Mulkulmot.

[1] V. Blucher (1890–1938): Soviet Marshal arrested on Stalin's orders during the Great Terror and executed.

"Peace unto thee, too, oh Angel of Death, Mulkulmot!
Is thy coming occasioned by chance or hast thou come on an errand?"
"Not by chance is my coming occasioned, I have come to thee on an errand:
Now, by Allah's will thy time is at hand."

"I have not yet cut the nails on my fingers and toes,
I have not put Hassan and Hussein to bed after feeding them,
And my husband Murtazal-Ali is not at home."

"Let me on my return find thou hast cut thy finger- and toe-nails,
Put Hassan and Hussein to bed after feeding them,
While I myself shall fetch thy husband Murtazal-Ali."

In a mountain cave, sitting in council with the Saints,
He found Fatima's husband Murtazal-Ali.

"Peace unto thee, oh Murtazal-Ali!"
"Peace unto thee, too, oh Angel of Death, Mulkulmot!
Is thy coming occasioned by chance or hast thou come on an errand?"

"My coming has not been occasioned by chance, I have come on an errand:
By Allah's will have I come for the soul of Fatima."

"Oh, Lord God, daughter of a great father, Fatima,
Who shall wash thy body?"

"Oh, Lord God, Murtazal-Ali,
The maidens of Paradise will wash my body."

"Oh, Lord God, daughter of a great father, Fatima,
Where shall I take a cloth to make thee a shroud?"

"Oh, Lord God, Murtazal-Ali,
The Angel Jabrail will make me a shroud."

"Oh, Lord God, daughter of a great father, Fatima,
Whom shall I command to carry thy bier?"

"Oh, Lord God, Murtazal-Ali,
The maidens of Paradise will carry my bier."

"Oh, Lord God, daughter of a great father, Fatima,
Whom shall I command to dig a grave for thee?"

"Oh, Lord God, Murtazal-Ali,
The Angel Jabrail will dig a grave for me."

In this song, where such a decorous balance is maintained between holiness and humanity, Fatima's sons Hassan and Hussein are represented as small children. In the preceding song on the death of Mahomet, i.e. on an event earlier in time, the very same Hassan and Hussein appear as men. There is something delightful about the spontaneous way in which art, while strictly pursuing the truth, adapts the facts to the exigencies of a given time and place. On the day of Fatima's death it is fitting that her sons – even though they have long been grown men – should be treated as children. We are reminded of Goethe's remark about how right Shakespeare was when he sometimes endowed Lady Macbeth with children and sometimes – depending on the character of the monologue – represented her as childless. Rubens did the same kind of thing in a landscape painting where there is only one source of light, but shadows are cast in two contrary directions.

*

How an old man will try to ingratiate himself with a young and healthy one – just to have someone to talk with for a while! He'll take his cap off and say how-do-you-do, and ask how much the young man earns, what he spends on food and how much is left over. As if this could be of the slightest interest to him. He simply needs to exchange a few words, to boost his morale by showing that, crutches or no crutches, he still has a little life in him and knows a thing or two – like a real person, like a grown-up.

*

"*Nowadays you have to buy a dress for your girl – and trousers too!* . . ." (On fashions)

*

"*That shirt he wears is a centre job.*"[1]

*

"*The cigarette case is plastic: put a cigarette on it and it'll burn a hole right through.*"

*

"*A real cultured fellow he was too – you could tell by the way he talked. He had a gold ring with a big stone in it. And he was a first-class driver.*"

*

"*Tom is squealing.*" (About a cat)

*

"*I take a pretty dim view of cats.*"

*

"*In '38, I went into a shop, took half a litre – no, I didn't, I took two quarter-litres, I remember* . . ."

*

"*Shut your great porridge-eating gob.*"

*

"*I still can't put myself in the picture of how it all happened.*"

*

[1] i.e. good quality because coming from the central stores, or perhaps from "the Centre", Moscow. (*Author's explanation*)

"But by some means or other he managed to stay alive."

*

"In such cases it doesn't depend on the head."

*

"Instinct plays its own little game."

*

"Well, of course, inside of me I'm all worked up, but it doesn't show on my face. And I says to my legs: 'Legs, get my arse out of here!' "

*

"Till our children's dying day!"

*

A woman laughing on the radio – like a nightingale singing, for no particular reason. Women simply love to laugh. There is even a special breed of them who giggle all the time. There is something incomprehensible – a kind of coldness – about laughing for no reason. It must be physiological in some way – like being ticklish. Laughter without humour, in response to an external irritant.

*

On the other hand, how marvellous children are in their sprawling helplessness! We are often the same in our sleep – spread-eagled, with legs apart, and knees up.

*

During these years I have grown so tired of always being with other people that sometimes, when I go into our part of the barracks, my body feels bliss surging through it physically, in waves: the place is empty!

*

But what really drives me mad is people's feet. A man may be silent, but his feet carry on just the same, tapping away in time to radio music, or without any reason at all. Even a deaf-mute holds forth with his feet. There is never a moment's respite: the body sleeps, but the feet still continue their frenzy. Someone is lying on a bench when suddenly one foot slips down on the floor, looks around, takes in the situation, and is now doing a furious tap-dance. I recognize people by their feet: here a familiar shoe, and over there – a boot. Each one of them goes tramp-tramp-tramp. Just like soldiers. The noise here is not enough – they need drums as well. To read and write I would like to be deaf.

*

The cosmography of the Middle Ages is excellently represented in the edifying tale *Of a Certain Brother* by Nicodemus, a monk in the Solovki Monastery. In this tale the Archangel Michael conducts the soul of a sinful monk all through heaven and hell, and the latter afterwards relates in all sincerity to the other brethren what he has seen. At first they rise past the clouds and up to the icy firmament, and then higher still, to the waters lying above the firmament and the clouds, until they reach heaven which opens to reveal to them the spectacle of the ineffable light. Then they descend back to earth and go down under it, past the nether waters which lie there, until they reach a dark region near the flames of hell. Here the hapless monk implores St Michael to let him go and repent in peace, and at a sign from the Archangel all the storeys of the Universe are immediately flung open:

"And he raised his eyes and looked up and straight away the waters and the earth opened overhead, the clouds and the firmament and the waters above also opened, and the sky was as a trumpet stretching upwards. And as the Archangel looked up so did I look, and I saw as through a trumpet even up to the ineffable light which I had previously seen in the sky, but did not hear any sound from it."

Space opening like a trumpet is exactly the same as the

inverted perspective of an icon. In fact, this whole description closely resembles an iconographic composition of the Last Judgment.

Even in our own reality, any wide expanse – such as the sky, or a field – opens up in inverted rather than in ordinary perspective. We are tiny, but space is enormous and the further away or higher it is, the larger and broader it appears to be. The mouth of the trumpet opens upwards and outwards, and in order to convey its music we must apply its perspective to what we see all around us – looking up from the bowels of the earth to the ineffable light.

*

. . . If Catholicism lives and breathes through and by the Father, if Protestantism accords its preference to the Son, Orthodoxy, whether by design or not, puts the stress on the third person of the Trinity – on the Holy Spirit. The image of the Holy Trinity (for which the Third Person is indispensable) has hence acquired special authority for us – as has also the Feast of the Holy Trinity, timed to coincide with Whitsun, the day of the Descent of the Holy Spirit. This is why the addition of the *Filioque* clause in the Western version of the Creed provoked such violent disagreement that it led to the separation of the Eastern and Western churches. Orthodoxy thought of it as belittling the Holy Spirit, which was relegated, as it were, to a position below the second Hypostasis – the Son.

However insignificant it may appear in modern eyes, much in Russia's religious and historical life is bound up with this emphasis in favour of the Holy Spirit: the fact that Muscovite Russia began with the monastery of the Holy Trinity founded by St Sergius, that the most famous Russian icon is Rublev's *Trinity*, that we have the institution of *starchestvo*,[1] and that we had Serafim of Sarov . . .[2]

[1] A man – sometimes, but not necessarily, a monk – popularly revered for his wisdom and holy life is known in Russia as a *starets* (literally, an elder, plural: *startsy*) from which the abstract noun *starchestvo* is derived.

[2] Serafim of Sarov (1760–1833): monk and *starets*. Like other *startsy* he was much influenced by Byzantine Hesychasm and practised spiritual exercises, such as the "Jesus Prayer".

Our Russian feeling for miracles, icons, relics and ritual is fed by a sensitivity to the life-giving Holy Spirit so intense that it approaches the reception of magical impulses. The Holy Spirit permeates the world, and – particularly during such sacramental feasts as Epiphany, Whitsun and Easter – invites the whole of creation and all earthly flesh to partake in the bounties of the spirit. The supposed "pagan" or "pantheistic" aberrations in Russian Christianity are in fact basically Orthodox: we tend to comprehend the spirit in terms just as real as we do the flesh.

This religion of the Holy Spirit somehow accords with our national characteristics – a natural inclination to anarchy (which, seen from outside, is commonly mistaken for barbarous or immature behaviour), fluidity, amorphousness, readiness to adopt any mould ("come and rule over us"[1]), our gift – or vice – of thinking and living artistically, combined with an inability to manage the very serious practical side of daily life: "Why bother? Who cares?", we ask. In this sense Russia offers a most favourable soil for the experiments and fantasies of the artist, though his lot as a human being is sometimes very terrible indeed.

Because of the Spirit we are sensitive to the influence of all kinds of ideas – so much so that at certain moments we lose our own language and personality and become Germans, Frenchmen, or Jews and, then, recovering our senses, rush from our spiritual servitude to the opposite extreme, freezing in a posture of narrow-minded suspicion and hostility towards everything foreign.

A word, says the Russian proverb, is not a sparrow: once it leaves its cage you will never catch it again. The Word for us is such a substantial entity (spiritually) that it comes to resemble a physical force which must needs be hedged around by safeguards – by censorship. We are conservatives because we are nihilists – the one turns into the other and they are inter-

[1] The words used, according to tradition, by certain Western Russian tribes in their so-called "invitation" to the Vikings in A.D. 862 which laid the foundation of the Russian State.

changeable in our history. But all this is because the Spirit bloweth where it listeth, and in order not to be blown away by it we turn to stone, protect ourselves with the crust of ritual, the ice of formalism, the letter of the decree or the standard formula. We cling to form because we have not enough of it; probably it is the only thing we have not enough of; we have never had and never can have either hierarchy or structure (we are too spiritual for this), and move freely from nihilism to conservatism and back again.

Hence, too, the striking lack of Russian sculpture (which more, perhaps, than any other art implies an awareness of form), and this in spite of our feeling for the bodily, our "idolatry", and the Hellenic heritage (which failed, incidentally, to revive sculpture in Orthodox Byzantium as well). We made up for this by a spate of song and painting (something that *flows*). In the same order of things, there is our violation of the hierarchy of *genres* (though the nomenclature is duly preserved), our craving to write gospels instead of novels, our constant disagreements with strictly literary frames of reference, our failure to produce stories with a strong plot, the amorphousness of our prose and drama, the spiritual overcharging of our speech . . . To a ludicrous extent we want to say everything at once.

To some degree these characteristics were already manifest in Byzantium. The Eastern world, where an absolute sovereign ruled over slaves, stood in sharp contrast to the West with its feudal lords and vassals. The absolute ruler does not give guarantees under law, but only grants amnesties and pardons. The Tsar, as God's regent, never needed to argue his case: being slaves, all men were as equal in his sight as they are in God's. In practice this meant arbitrary rule; in theory (in the spirit) – the Kingdom of God on earth. There was no scale of values, only an absolute top and an absolute bottom (on occasion they could change places); everything depended on the one deified person of the Basileus. He distributed favours and punishments according to his whim, himself scarcely able to move under the weight of vestments and regalia (the crust of splendour rather than of form), as he stood the prescribed number of hours – a majestic dummy representing the Deity. There was no one higher than he, no one more frightening – and no one more helpless; prod him with a finger and you would find no one there, only a Symbol. In the vast formless plains men jumped about like fleas – upstart slaves moved from rags to riches and became Emperors; pretenders, zealots and mutineers jostled round a pinnacle of power constantly threatened by catastrophe.

Is this bad? Perhaps from a practical point of view it is; but for the Spirit it is perfectly acceptable (more so than the West's cosy attachment to form and law).

In contrast to Europe's mediaeval gardens, the East has its endless plain where people huddle together in the wind – equal, accessible, sociable, *zemlyaki* (fellow-countrymen)[1] and neighbours. Who isn't a *zemlyak*? (Even our slit-eyed Kazakh and Kirgiz guards are *zemlyaki*!) What a comprehensive word! Kinship based not on blood, but on domicile, on the place where you live – a "place" that spreads right through the Eurasian plain. No, my home is not my castle (only the Spirit is my castle). *Zemlya* (the earth) is the material made animate: more than the family, it means good-neighbourly dirt and squalor, the warmth of another man's side, overfamiliarity alternating with treachery, the all-embracing word "*zemlyak*", a round temple with a world-embracing dome.

"The ideal of family relations in Byzantium," writes a modern scholar, "was not unlimited and absolute paternal authority as in Rome, but the indissoluble spiritual intimacy of husband and wife: 'as if possessing not two souls, but one'."

When I read this it was as if I had again felt the presence of the spirit: a distant, earthly echo of the spiritual exercises of the *startsy*. This is Peter and Fevronia,[2] whose story can be

[1] *Zemlyaki*, (sing. *zemlyak*) derived from *zemlya* (earth), usually refers to men of the same village, district or province rather than the same country. It thus has a more local significance than "compatriot" or "fellow-countryman", though here the author extends it to cover the whole of Russia.

[2] A 16th-century Russian tale, probably composed by a monk in the time of Ivan the Terrible.

numbered among the most outstanding half-dozen literary works of Ancient Russia: what a contrast to the courtly lyrics of the West and the knight's longing for his lady, to Tristan and Isolde with their Gothic yearning and quest for the loved one, their eternal desire to attain the unattainable (Faust). Peter and Fevronia are almost like the couple in Gogol's "Old-World Landowners", an Adam and Eve whose domestic bliss is sanctified and ennobled by the fact that their frail little nest is built in a wilderness, at a tempestuous time when spirits are unleashed – it floats on the sea of life like an ark, a last refuge. And what a rare synthesis of icon and fairy-tale – usually so remote from each other, yet here brought together to tell the story of a wise woman's love. I know of no more powerful work of literature dedicated to the bonds of matrimony than the *Tale of Peter and Fevronia.* The thread of the couple's destiny, from their first meeting to their last sigh, is intertwined with Fevronia's yarn, right up to the full-stop put by her needle, which just before death she sticks into an unfinished paten cloth,[1] after carefully winding the thread around it. How clever of the author not to have overlooked this needle and thread in the text of their life and death together . . .

*

What a pell-mell rush of things: sunny days, cigarettes in bright packets, your pale little face in the train window, narrow paths dried out by the sun in the snow of the "forbidden zone".

10th April, 1970.

*

"*And a clap of thunder was heard over the bare forest.*" (As an omen of drought)

*

"*All of a sudden he was mortal.*"

*

[1] A cloth that covers the plate with the Eucharist bread.

"Vouch for him in triplicate."

*

"My pal who was had up and given the high jump."

*

"He conked out on the way to a labour camp."

*

"He fancied he saw a 25-year term coming to him."

*

"It's clear to everybody – like 12 o'clock at night."

*

". . . rather than be a burden I'd sooner disappear like an apparition."

*

"A desert where even stones don't grow."

*

"Twenty years old, but his blood is cold! . . ."

*

"My mother is an old lady now, but she still feels pretty nifty."

*

"I was just a tiny tot then, no bigger than a bedbug."

*

"How I loved it! Just like a baby! Never missed at 500 metres." (Revolver)

*

"I used to have a girl. But there was no happiness for her and none for me either. And she was no smarty-boots or show-off,

mind you. A bit of a red-head. No higher than this, she was. But strong-minded! . . ."

*

"*His wife is the sort who won't ever let him have a drink. So I used to arrange things for him . . .*"

*

"*I don't really like beating people up. For one thing, it's immoral. For another. you can find yourself in court, and then – they're human beings after all. I feel sorry for them in a way . . .*"

*

"*Now don't you get all high and mighty!*"

*

A pleasant remark about a horse: we ought to feed it, someone says, because it brings us our meal but is half-starved itself; mustn't *we*, of all people, be fair and just whenever we can?! . . .

*

Horses always seem utterly inscrutable. Even when they laugh or weep, they look quite imperturbable. All the horse's powers of expression have gone into its ears: these are never still for a minute, twitching, twirling and signalling in various directions. It is a real pleasure to look at them: such mobility against the background of a dolefully-despondent, somewhat disapproving muzzle. The horse's soul – sensitive and finely-tuned – is wholly in its ears.

*

Since Easter Saturday the warm weather has definitely come to stay. It was the bees that brought us this welcome news more reliably than anything else. "The bees are here, so winter won't return!" – I heard someone say three days ago, and was struck at the resemblance to the phrase "the rooks are here".[1] But bees are a surer sign.

*

[1] Traditional sign of the arrival of spring in Russia and the title of a famous painting by Alexei Savrasov.

I hear on the radio that Thor Heyerdahl will be sailing in a papyrus boat "Ra-2". "*Et tu, Brute*?" Suppose he had decided on some Arab route or other, would he then have called his contraption "Allah-4"?!

*

Tolik, the cess-pool cleaner, came up and told me how many barrels of sewage he carted away in the course of last month. We all need to talk about our work.

*

"*Chirp like Chekhov!*" (Used in the sense of "gabble away", "talk nonsense")

*

But birds talk as they always have done, and listening to them one feels convinced that there really is such a thing as bird language, the study of which must once have been the greatest of sciences. A friend of mine here had a splendid dream (in general, he is lucky with his dreams): he saw a bird with a long beak sitting on the window-sill and spoke to it, as we often do to hens and other domestic fowl: "Don't be afraid of me!" And the bird suddenly replied: "But I'm not afraid of you!" This set off a conversation between them which was remarkably significant in some way, but he had unfortunately forgotten the sense of it.

*

. . . On the locker by my bunk (I almost said – on my balcony) I have a bunch of wild flowers. Today we ate a salad made of dandelions. And soon summer will have driven by on its *troika* of bay horses: June, July, August.

7th May, 1970.

*

It is cold. Clouds, looking like the smoke and soot of fires, are floating past. The sky seems to offer a panoramic view of an ancient field of battle. Is this the reason for the belief in Perun[1] in those times when men more commonly looked skywards, seeing there signs and portents as distinctly as we see news on the cinema screen in the dark? Perun was obviously not associated only with thunder and lightning, but with the sky in general: with the sinister hosts of clouds besieging fortified cities high above them, and with the movement of the sun, the moon and the planets – which were more striking at a time when the earth lay in humid immobility, while the heavens, shot through with comets and lightning flashes, seemed to have more to do with the dynamic workings of history than with the inertness of nature.

*

In Avraam Palitsyn's *Tale of the Siege of the Monastery of the Holy Trinity and St Sergius*[2] the account of the bombardment by the Poles is accompanied by a precise description of every hit. In such a manner cannon balls thus serve as guides round the sacred precincts. "During the singing of the psalms a cannon ball suddenly struck the great bell and rebounded through the chancel window and made a hole in the right-hand leaf of the Triptych of the Archangel Michael. And that same cannon ball struck a pillar near the left-hand choir and bounded against the wall and glanced off, hitting the candlestick in front of the icon of the Holy Life-Giving Trinity (Andrey Rublev's perhaps?!),

[1] Principal god, and in particular god of thunder, of the Eastern Slavs before their conversion to Christianity.

[2] This account, by the manciple of the Monastery, relates to the so-called *Time of Troubles* (1608–10), when the Poles invaded Russia in support of the Pretender, the "False Dmitri", who claimed to be the son of Ivan the Terrible, and was commonly supposed to have once been a monk in the Monastery of the Miracle. He reigned from 1605 to 1606, having killed Theodore, son and successor of Boris Godunov. The Civil War ended with the election in 1613 of Tsar Michael Romanov, the first of the dynasty that ended in 1917.

The Monastery of the Holy Trinity was founded near Moscow in the 14th century by St Sergius of Radonezh and gradually became one of the most important centres of the Russian Orthodox Church. To protect its great wealth it was surrounded by heavily fortified walls and towers. There are several churches within the precincts.

and it damaged the candlestick and bounced off into the left-hand choir and broke into pieces. At the same time another cannon ball smashed through the iron doors at the south side of the Holy Trinity Church and pierced the wooden board of the icon of the great Miracle Worker Nicholas above the left shoulder and next to the halo; but the cannon ball could not be found behind the icon."

This unhurried and carefully structured bill of particulars concerning the cannon balls' trajectory sets the tone of the whole narrative, providing a kind of chart in which war and icons, history and the Holy Trinity are linked with each other diagramatically. A police report made on the scene of a murder is written in this way – with a detailed list of all the injuries caused to the body. The event was all the more dramatic in that the bombardment took place not on any ordinary day, but on the 8th November,[1] the Feast-day of the Archangel Michael, at the moment of the solemn service, while the congregation was at prayer, beseeching the protection of the very icons which were being hit by cannon balls. As we read we do not know where these will strike next on their wavering course, nor do we know what is more terrifying – the fact that the Archangel Michael silently endures the onslaught (is he unable, or unwilling to reply?!), or the feeling that the enemy's reckless sacrilege must surely bring down a fearful visitation. So we too waver between hope and the general lamentation which has interrupted the service.

That same day a cannon ball tore off the leg of the precentor Cornelius on his way to mass in the same church, and as he lay dying on the square in front he prophesied that the Archangel would not leave unavenged the blood of the Orthodox. A nun, too, had an arm torn off: people suffered as well as icons, and they bore it all in hopeful expectation as the beleaguering forces surged around them.

But the cannon salvoes of 8th November 1608 are also aimed at a more oblique target in Palitsyn's description, which is the

[1] i.e. in the Eastern Church calendar. In the West this Feast-day ("Michaelmas Day") falls on September 29th.

centrepiece of a whole narrative hinging on the dynamic interplay of icons and history. Those responsible for persuading Boris[1] to accept the Crown had presumed to take the miracle-working icon of the Blessed Virgin of Smolensk out of the Monastery of the Virgin – for the sake of the usurper. "Unrightfully was that image disturbed, and so unrightfully was Russia also disturbed."

The Time of Troubles is thus held to have begun with the "disturbance" of an icon.

*

The Monastery of the Miracle where the Pretender came from was dedicated to the miracle in Chonae or, as it is also called, the miracle of the Archangel Michael who had once diverted a stream underground in that place. But later the stream had somehow gushed forth again from under the earth and flooded the country, and the Archangel was compelled to intervene once more to allay this calamity coming from the Monastery of the Miracle. How interconnected everything is, how full of significance! . . .[2]

*

In a chapter about getting firewood, which could only be obtained outside the monastery walls with great loss of life, Palitsyn suddenly introduces rhyme into his prose: "Cutting young branches in a copse, we left behind us many a corpse . . . Those who joined this cruel quest oft did earn eternal rest", and so on and so forth.

[1] Boris Godunov was crowned Tsar in 1598 after a show of being persuaded to accept the Crown against his will.

[2] i.e. the calamity in Chonae (as related in a Greek tradition of the 5th century A.D.) appears to prefigure a calamity, in the shape of the Pretender, which was to issue centuries later from a Russian monastery dedicated (like the original Greek one) to the miracle of Chonae. As mentioned in the preceding passage, the cannon balls of the Pretender's Polish allies struck the Monastery of the Holy Trinity on the Feast-day of the Archangel Michael. Since the Pretender was eventually defeated it could thus be said that the Archangel had once again allayed a calamity from a Monastery of the Miracle.

It is interesting that rhyme comes in here and nowhere else. Doubtless thanks to the incongruity of the situation – firewood costing lives – the narrator's thoughts here took a turn which, though not exactly playful, was at least more ornate or convoluted, as he creates an association of ideas between winter fuel and sudden death. This would suggest that rhyme in general is more apt to link widely different rather than related things, and is conditional on the subject matter having a certain piquancy or paradoxical quality which invites the mind to play games; not for nothing did Pushkin think of rhyme as a means of displaying wit.

*

It may be noted, if one compares the two, that although secular art feels freer to be itself and may indulge in all kinds of frolics, religious art, even while forswearing the conscious pursuit of artistic aims in the proper sense, actually proves to be art of a higher order, with a double aesthetic charge in it. This is because it tends to view the world as an icon and therefore interprets it in a distinctly figurative manner. As illuminated by religious art every fact receives a two-fold, if not a three-fold significance, the figurative sense thus becoming denser, the interaction of idea and subject-matter giving rise to more supple and intricate shapes; if all art in effect consists of "playing" with life, then wherever life shimmers continually with the bright reflection of heavenly "play", art will be doubly animated, imparting enormous vigour even to the most inert forms. There can be nothing flat here, in this movement of light from above (and back again), where every trifle is significant and all abstractions take on concrete shape, and where everything touched by the artist's vision is quickened by an awareness of its place under the sun – to which it reaches up, throwing a deep shadow.

Could this be why some great works which are otherwise quite divorced from the religious tradition, such as Goethe's *Faust* or Tolstoy's *War and Peace*, also resort to the light coming from above? Take away the ghost of his father and

Hamlet will at once be sadly diminished.

*

. . . Again this loss of a sense of time, never being sure of where we are in it. Even my age – if someone asks me how old I am, I have to do sums in my head before I can give the answer: I know it's somewhere between 40 and 45, but what exactly I find very hard to say at a moment's notice. And as for putting the date on a letter – suddenly I realize with a start: 11th of June?!

11th June, 1970.

*

All the time I have been hoping I might draw a deep breath and wake up – to some higher life.

*

From the start, from the very first paragraphs you must write in such a manner as to cut off every way of retreat and thereafter live only by the law of the train of words now set in motion as being the only course available to you, not giving way to any hopes for some world other than this self-sufficient text which is henceforth wholly in command of both theme and language, and you must cast aside all mental reservations and burn all your boats in order to act with uncharacteristic self-assurance. Artistic creation is a desperate posing of the question: to live or not to live?

*

"The train sped swiftly on,
Cleaving the frosty mist . . ."

This has a splendidly weighty ring to it – like some of the expressions used by the criminals in their argot.

Words should have a certain gravity or solemnity – particularly those used in literary language. Gregory of Tours' *History of the Franks* relates an episode about some fugitives sheltering at night in a forest. They have not eaten for three days while evading their pursuers. "But here, by God's will, they found a tree, commonly known as a plum tree, with fruit in abundance. Having eaten and somewhat restored their strength, they continued on their way, heading for Champagne. As they were proceeding they heard the clatter of galloping horses' hoofs and cried: 'Let us throw ourselves upon the ground so we should not be seen by the men approaching us!' Fortunately for them a large blackberry bush happened to be growing just there and they lay down behind it with their swords drawn in order, should they be noticed, to defend themselves against evil men. But when those riders, too, came to the place and stopped at the blackberry bush, one of them, while the horses were making water, said: 'Woe is us! These rascals have escaped and there is no finding them! . . .' "

Three knock-out effects: a plum tree so marvellous that the use of its common name requires apologetic mention; a blackberry bush brought irresistibly to life by the fugitives giving the reader, as they go to hide behind it, a circumstantial explanation of the need for such thorough concealment; and thirdly – the whole cliffhanger episode carries absolute conviction when the horses make water.

I have a real passion for such sterling, grainy-textured pieces of prose. They could be made into a collection, rather like the minerals and stones my father kept in the cellar in those yellowish boxes. Oh, God, I can remember them to this day – by their smell. Stones – by their smell! They had such a sharp and heady smell, those stones . . .

*

In principle only miracles are worth writing about – as the fairy-tales knew. And if we ever do decide to tell about ordinary things, we should show them in a supernatural light. The art of narrative is to see things like this.

*

Two bosom pals on the run meet a beautiful girl on a railway station and she invites them home to supper. (At this point we are given a description of a sumptuous meal with herring from the bountiful Atlantic and a large choice of wines.) Then the hostess produces a pack of cards and invites her guests to take one. If it's red she'll give herself to the lucky man. But black means death. A latter-day Cleopatra. The two friends exchange glances (both are infatuated by now), and then the gallant hero of the tale, after a second's hesitation, takes the plunge . . . A black card! An ace! But suddenly, at this moment of climax when all his listeners are leaning out of their bunks, staring wide-eyed at the black card in his hand, the story-teller stops to ask: "Anybody got something to smoke?", and this pause at the edge of the abyss forces the least generous of those present to start reaching for his tobacco-pouch – everyone urges him on impatiently and that black card leaves him no choice: he digs down into his pocket with a sigh, and with casual, unhurried movements the narrator rolls himself a cigarette, lights up and inhales somewhat theatrically as he urgently tries to think of a way to save his hero, whose fate now hangs on a card . . .

*

What precious objects originally stood for and the higher meaning with which they were once invested may be gauged from Paulus Diaconus's *History of the Langobards*. The following passage refers to Gunthram, King of the Franks, who lived in the 6th century and was famous for his good administration and love of peace.

"He chanced once to be hunting in a wood and, as is wont to happen, his companions scattered far and wide and he was left with only the most faithful one; and now he felt oppressed with heavy slumber and laying his head in his companion's lap he fell sound asleep. And, behold, a small creature, in the shape of a lizard, crawled out of his mouth and tried to cross a narrow brook that flowed near-by. Then he in whose lap the king was resting drew his sword from its scabbard and laid it over the brook, and along it the lizard of which I speak made its way to the other side. Then it crept into a small crevice in the rock and some time later came out again, crossed the aforesaid brook along the sword and once more slipped into Gunthram's mouth out of which it had come. On awakening Gunthram said he had seen a wondrous vision. He related how it had seemed to him in his sleep that he had crossed a river by an iron bridge, climbed a certain mountain and found there a vast pile of gold. And the man in whose lap the sleeping king had rested his head told him one by one the things he had seen himself. To cut a long tale short, that place was dug up and countless treasures were discovered which had been put there in days of old. Later, the king ordered a goblet of surpassing size and great weight to be made out of this gold, and after adorning it with many precious stones, had in mind to send it to Jerusalem to the Sepulchre of our Lord. But, having failed to do so, he ordered it to be placed over the tomb of St Marcellus the Martyr who was buried in the city of Cabillonum[1] (where the king's residence was); it is there down to this present day. Nowhere is there any work made of gold that may match it."

If we reduce it to its bare outline, the story of the creation of this precious and unique object is that, gliding on its way like a lizard, it goes through various intricate but precisely defined motions and eventually returns whence it came. It is a miracle told rather in the form of a weird and wonderful tale owing something to an ancient, perhaps pagan archetype of the soul leaving the sleeping body in the guise of a lizard – a miracle consummated by the making of a wonderful goblet which, like a flower on a stalk, crowns and immortalizes the event, and itself then returns to where it belongs – to God, to the other world, via the Holy Sepulchre or the near-by tomb of St Marcellus. We have here a kind of miraculous manifestation of a masterpiece which is then found and returned. (And how striking that it reveals itself in a dream – here serving with the same infallibility as in a fairy-tale to link the hero with some well-spring, with a magic realm or force, or with the unconscious life of the soul which, as in this instance, is liable to turn into a lizard – possibly in remembrance of an earlier animal stage of existence, of the king's primordial ancestry, or even of the

[1] Now Chalon-sur-Saône.

magic, long-lost ability of kings to transform themselves into the beasts and reptiles whose likenesses figure in the coats of arms of so many great families!) In earlier times the goblet would have been laid in King Gunthram's grave or barrow at his death – with the same purpose of returning it to the source from which it originally came. There was thus a powerful supernatural motive for such objects: they were created not simply in passing, for their own sake, but as things journeying between two buried hoards of gold – exactly in the way that a man's life spans the brief interval between his sojourns in the two infinite treasure chambers of pre-existence and the hereafter.

Another striking and very agreeable aspect of this story is its extremely crisp, neatly chiselled quality – a concise narrative line in the West-European manner, with everything sharply delineated and falling into its proper place: a lizard crosses a brook by crawling along a sword. In Russia the same basic elements would become blurred and imprecise in the telling. In this sense the West has a better gift for fantasy even than the East: its chimeras are presented more clearly, with greater particularity. Not just some nondescript serpent, but a lizard. And instead of slithering along any old how, it crosses to the other side over a sword. On an iron bridge. It knows where it's going. A subject fit for a coat of arms or the engraver's needle. Albrecht Dürer stands here ready – like the knight so prompt to assist King Gunthram's soul with his sword, or like the lizard so durably implanted in the King's very core. Like the whole tale, with its parts so rigorously interlocked – talon hooked to talon.

•

The Middle Ages in Europe are bonier and more structured than in Russia. Even the squat Romanesque style has a certain trim shapeliness about it. In Europe they have more of what can be compared to the veins of leaves or the spreading branches of trees. Our Middle Ages are boneless; there is more pulp in them – but this, by its very nature, has rotted away.

Also striking in European art is its graphic quality, its geometric starkness, its trenchant way of depicting things: over there, ornament stands out in harsher relief, in all the gauntness of its structural lines (ours is more flowery). This firmness of outline already contains a hint of classicism and cubism. The elongation of figures seems to bring out not so much their height as the sharpness of their lines. Sharp elbows, sharp knees, sharp-toed shoes peeping from under dresses. Everything is here – Europe's self-assertiveness, the sharpness of her imagination, her spiky engines of war, her ironclads. Her space is criss-crossed by cutting edges, like broken glass.

To shatter space and put it together again as a mosaic, to reassemble it, so to speak, out of innumerable sharp-edged splinters, you needed all those folds in clothing – a veritable riot of folds of every kind splaying out in clusters like quiverfuls of arrows (their lines taking little account of the body's proportions or the cut of the dress) and going on to form the bared skeleton of counterforts and flying buttresses, the entire network of blood-vessels and sinews of a cathedral that openly displays its graceful anatomy, the complex articulation of its organlike structure. This superabundance of folds is sometimes seen as a clumsy imitation of the Greeks and Romans, but in fact it was a passion for folds as such, pursued quite without reference either to classical antiquity or the human body. The human figure is indeed treated in the same way: as an articulated structure assembled out of a multitude of pieces and sections, each one, down to the last finger, being neatly joined to the whole in which – again without any interest for anatomy as such – the body's architecture is meticulously displayed: first divided in two by the impassable barrier of the diaphragm, it is then laid out for inspection in full with all its jointed limbs and segments. Here art seems to take its cue from the structure of insects. The skeleton is external to the body and the inner nature, the overall design – whether of men or cathedrals – is exposed to view, like a horny carapace formed of chitin – or the suit of armour worn by a mediaeval knight.

No wonder stained glass windows caught on so in the West.

Just as important as the pattern of glowing colours is the dark tracery of lines formed by the leaden strips of the design – the effect of these and the glass between them is to provide something like an X-ray of the window's skeleton. To look at a stained glass window is to pick out the dark crystallogram of its armature. Stylistically, Europe's mediaeval art is pre-eminently a hymenopterous structure.

The Byzantine-Russian tradition is dominated by the rotund and the circular, but in the mediaeval West any such element in the basic composition will be broken up and fragmented by divisions, by the naked structure thrusting out to the surface; the pattern is pointed and aggressive like Gothic script. The plans of cathedrals remind one of blueprints for aircraft or the designs of submarines. What bombers are these – something from the future or a flight of Valkyries out of the past?

*

Here we are, like it or not: the tenth anniversary. There was the truck carrying the coffin, and the store with slippers where he was fitted out.[1] It was like the crumbling of an epoch: the monument in the dusty little square and the dust behind the truck – his gun carriage – and the sun. And not a soul by my side. And a monologue, a monologue instead of a salute.

People talk about "personality". I don't really know what they mean. What I mostly feel in myself is my father and mother, you, Yegor, Pushkin, Gogol. A whole crowd. They all colour my perception of reality, share my destiny and go with me wherever I am taken, constantly making themselves felt. If a man is to be described realistically the result will be a landscape, or an ocean rather than a personality.

It was then, as I followed the coffin, that I realized how much of my father I have in me.

16th July, 1970.

*

[1] The author speaks of his father's funeral. In some parts of Russia it is the custom to put special slippers on the dead man's feet. See reference to this on page 173.

The loss of a sense of time also happens because letters travel so slowly that I live simultaneously both a month behind and a month in advance: behind until your letters reach me. and in advance until mine reach you. "Today" is perceived only in a very general sense, vaguely in relation to the seasons – as being somewhere in the middle of summer or nearer winter, as the case may be.

*

"*You don't have to feed me, but give me my letter!*" (Plea to the camp authorities)

*

"*I know that name 'Margarita' – I used to write letters to a girl called Rita.*"

*

A prisoner who used to write letters to a "pen-pal" was so unsure of his grammar and had so little to say in any case that, as he told us himself, he simply put down a great many entirely meaningless words and crossed them out again as thoroughly as possible so that the whole letter consisted of almost nothing else. The girl would try to read these blacked-out passages by holding them up to the light or by dabbing them with milk, imagining that they must be the most important of all, and she kept on asking him to repeat in his next letter the words he had crossed out. To her they were the sweetest of all. This illustrates the importance of the poetic law of always leaving something to the imagination.

*

An expression of female solicitude in a letter to a prisoner:

"*Take care of yourself and don't go about with your coat not properly buttoned up.*"

*

The things people write to each other:

"Do you want to be frank? I do. The fact of the matter is

that I have taken a proper fancy to you."

You don't know whether to laugh or cry at the way women express themselves. There is always something touching, and at the same time horrifying in their desperate self-exposure. The radio is at the moment playing Tatiana's aria[1] and I am amazed how true to life it is . . .

"I give you my word that I shall write to you. I shall not promise you anything definite because I am not a nun. But I shall write all about myself in detail. And it will be the truth, too. All right? And then we will see how things work out."

All rather hackneyed. She has already served her sentence – a pretty stiff one for taking part in an armed robbery. There is just one human, heart-rending note: "I don't know why, but I immediately felt I could trust you." Like Manon Lescaut.

*

Yet another philosophy of local origin. A mixture of Russian marxism and matriarchy. Contact with horses ennobles man. Coarse rye bread massages the bowels and therefore peasants are healthier and better than the upper classes. Woman is man's support in life because she is closer to nature. Woman is the basis.

*

In the 18th century Russia was ruled mainly by women. It was not, of course, mere chance or the whim of fate that placed almost only representatives of the weaker sex on the autocrat's throne in such a cruel and, on the whole, virile century. A certain design is discernible here – something which allowed the century's profile to assume a softer, blander outline. Not that life was easier under a tsarina than under a tsar. But Peter's edifice had to be made habitable and needed all those finishing touches that could best be added by women with their understanding of service at table, cuisine, fashions and other such domestic matters. Thanks to the rule of these barbarian women with a weakness for entertainments, dresses, masquer-

[1] From *Eugene Onegin.*

ades and courtly manners, Russian civilization assimilated Western tastes and ways with such natural ease that a hundred years after Peter it was able to rear a Pushkin in its lively and fragrantly hot-house atmosphere. Even the fact that our empresses were indifferent mothers and wives, resembling hetaerae in their constant pursuit of love, pleasure and social glitter, gave our civilization a ballroom lustre which it retained for a long time and which allowed it to compete in such trifling matters as literature and art with glamorous Europe. An ode dedicated to a woman was apt to sound something like a madrigal. Elizabeth's[1] accession to the throne, to which she was carried in the arms of her Guards' officers, forced the latter to absorb a spirit of chivalry in the style of the Three Musketeers and turned yesterday's loutish dunderheads into gallants and scribblers. Without women on the throne the Russian eighteenth century, which began with problems of etiquette and dress, would have been unthinkable. Neither Russian classicism nor Russian baroque could have brought forth their golden fruit on the swamp turned by Peter into a building site. It needed the critical interaction of soil, fertilizer and air – and all this was accomplished by the ladies.

*

"*Why are you sometimes pleasanter and at other times less pleasanter?*" (Conversation with a lady)

*

"*Minocle*" (Monocle)

*

"*Mindalion*" (Medallion)

*

"*Radicule*" (Reticule, handbag)

*

[1] Daughter of Peter the Great and Empress of Russia from 1741–1761.

"*She goes into such estasy* . . ." (Ecstasy)

*

. . . And women sitting like condors on their bunks, displaying themselves frankly, with an air of total abstraction.

*

The other day we both saw Gogol in a dream when we visited the village where he was living in retirement – though whether it was in heaven or on earth I am not sure, since Gogol was not quite flesh-coloured, but had a bluish tinge and was about twice the size of ordinary men. But he was alive, a little sad, sunk in his usual state of prostration, so we did not venture to worry him and just admired him from a distance. He sat sideways to us, looking very pleasant and kind, but I was surprised at the smallness of his chin. Nadezhda Vassilyevna, who was accompanying us on our tour, said that Leo Tolstoy considered Alexis Tolstoy[1] to be the best Russian poet, to which I angrily replied that this was because he wanted Tolstoy to be the first name in Russian poetry as well. In Gogol's village the favourite icons were those he had himself designed – the original, drawn on a piece of paper for icon painters to copy, was pinned to a wooden wall so everyone could see it: a somewhat schematic, childishly simple representation of two saints, John the Warrior and another I can't remember, and I was vaguely tempted to beg the villagers to let me have that piece of paper with the sketch by Gogol – of whom they were none too sure whether he was their master, or whether he was a bit on the saintly side himself and not quite right in the head.

*

From a letter:

". . . Yegor has now been put to bed, and I read him some Kipling again. This time about the baby elephant. And suddenly, when I got to the part where all that trouble with the crocodile begins and the poor baby elephant has such a

[1] See note on page 14.

terrible time, Yegor pressed his little fists to his nose, and his eyes, round and full of tears, blinked so hard that I could stand it no longer and tried to console him:

'Don't take it to heart, Yegor, you know everything will be all right and the crocodile won't eat the baby elephant. We've read this story many times before . . .'

'But suppose he won't be strong enough this time to keep on his feet and falls in the river . . . and that's the end of him?!' "

In my day I also found this story hard to bear because of the somehow senseless torments inflicted by the crocodile – they are described at such great length and in such horrible detail that even now it leaves an unpleasant taste in my mouth, as though the author were deliberately keeping his young readers on tenterhooks and putting their trust to the test. But how wonderful of Yegor to worry that in this new reading the baby elephant might suddenly topple into the river! What better example of the capacity of a literary theme for perpetual self-renewal: every time one must agonize over the outcome, if one wants things to end as they should. Hence the unfailing dramatic tension of mystery plays which might turn out goodness knows how if the actors did not play their parts correctly and the audience, with its tearful pleas or cries of encouragement, failed to urge the familiar personages and events along the desired path. This is why a fairy-tale should never be interrupted while it is being told. And also why the Great Drama was not merely a single occurrence in history, but continues to be performed through the perennial round of its Feast-days. Here we have the manifestation of a myth based on an Event which was not only real, but which through its continual re-enactment exists eternally and universally.

28th August, 1970.

*

. . . I wonder what Tverskoi-Yamskoi Street[1] used to be like? In the old days the pavement in front of our house in Khlebny Street[1] was made of large square flagstones with grass growing

[1] Old streets in Moscow.

between them in the summer; the roadway was cobbled, there was a bollard at every corner, and we had lampposts with open-work gas lanterns – I vaguely remember the lamplighter who every night did his rounds with a ladder on his shoulder and lit them one by one, making Andersen's fairy-tales seem not quite beyond the bounds of possibility.

But I must admit I do not remember a chimney-sweep.

Why do chimney-sweeps and lamplighters belong to a fairy-tale profession? As do dustmen, though to a lesser extent. Is it because they are on the periphery of our existence, skirting our day-time lives and our dwelling places? Almost in the sky? . . .

*

The prisons are the generators. The camps are the accumulators. All the blazing light produced there ("Oh, nights so full of light!"[1]) here goes to earth, to be preserved for a long time. Thus, the prison always remains the centre, however distant it may be. For its functioning, so vital to our existence as a whole, it needs a counterpoise, a store of reserve energy. The sweetness of that void, of that atmosphere as rarefied as mountain air, and the longing for it in advance – a longing for the source! That's where everything is produced.

*

Northwards we go, vast convoys of wretches,
Ask any man – the *ukaz* is the reason why,
Look in my eyes, my stern, my sullen eyes,
And kiss me once more before I die.

Friends with my prison coat my corpse will cover
And take me up for burial on a hill,
And in the frozen soil they'll lay me
And sing a dirge to shew they love me still.

[1] Line from a prisoner's song sung in the Taganka prison, Moscow. In the prisons (as opposed to the camps), bright lights are kept on all the time.

But at the coffin's foot you'll not be standing;
With cambric fine you'll wipe your tearful eyes.
Oh please don't cry, don't cry, beloved, darling,
You'll find your life mate yet, 'neath other skies.

Northwards we go, vast convoys of wretches.
Ask any man – the *ukaz*[1] is the reason why.
Look in my eyes, my stern, my sullen eyes,
And kiss me once more before I die.

*

To begin at the end: a plain deal coffin rather resembles a boat, and is hence more appropriate to death than the confections of a Moscow undertaker who fixes frills to his coffins, making them look like wedding cakes. In the camp it is all more spare, simple and explicit. More serious, in fact. The horse, quite unconcerned, pulls the cart, and the placid escort guard trudging after the coffin drops a little behind – whether for decency's sake or because he really doesn't care it is hard to say. I have never seen a more dignified and honest burial ceremony. And how good to come out of the iron gates, from behind the wire – into the fir wood, to freedom . . .

*

"*A medical block of the sanatorium type.*"

*

"*The doctor comes in, puts his muzzle on, and starts slitting your belly open.*"

*

"*All kinds of doctors and surgeons had a look at him and every one of them said 'Not in my line'.*"

*

With some distaste:
"*Don't take your underpants off. I can feel the hernia without that.*"

*

[1] *Ukaz* (Decree) – popular name for Khrushchev's anti-parasite law of 1961 under which many criminals were cleared out of the cities.

Nurses ("female medical personnel") are "free employees". Ours is a washstand on high heels, a surrealist chiffonier. She preens herself like a bride-to-be, mincing about in her doll's shoes. A small nose, and tits like spouts. A fashion-crazed, saucy little wench. Glazed looks from shrunken men in dressing-gowns: not lust, but curiosity at the spectacle, as in a cinema or the circus: "Look – a miniskirt!"

Yet she can let herself be roused even by these walking skeletons. As she boasted to one patient (with a kind of sadism): "After you've walked up and down with them staring at you all day long, you go home and hop straight into bed with your husband! . . ."

*

I'm writing to you from hospital where I've been for the past few days. It's a quiet place, rather like being on vacation in miniature, with the result that even my writing, I see, is getting smaller – as befits a microclimate.

I did not write to you at once because of the effect being moved here has had on me. Either I have become so sensitive over the last five years that trifling changes assume the proportions of a mental cataclysm, or perhaps it really is an immense and stunning thing, this transfer to a neighbouring zone where, only 200 metres away, everything is utterly different? . . . What is so disconcerting is not so much this other reality in itself as the mere possibility of its being so near that you only have to make one step to cross over into a new existence just as self-contained and valid as the previous one, and thus find the thought of a plurality of worlds confirmed with terrifying suddenness . . . All the more comforting it was to receive a card from you this morning (yes, not in the evening as usual: here we get our letters in the morning, almost as though the sun were rising in the West instead of the East). It was comforting, I dare say, because one feels so bewildered by this abrupt transition to a new dimension – life, which seemed so incredibly stable in its repetitiveness, suddenly reveals itself as unpredictable and liable to dissolve in a myriad chance events of the smallest kind . . .

8th September, 1970.

*

It could well be that we perceive different epochs and countries as distinct areas with their own particular coloration ("The Eighteenth Century" or "Renaissance Italy") by virtue of sharply drawn lines of chronological-cum-territorial demarcation which are in fact only a matter of accepted convention. But thanks to their existence, there it is: "Italy", or "The Renaissance", in other words – a zone. Its boundaries are determined by interlinking mountains and rivers, centuries and decades which shade off naturally into other ones, but the dividing lines are by now indelibly fixed in the human mind and cannot be wiped out, though what difference does it really make whether Derzhavin[1] died twenty years earlier or later than he did, and how important is the border between the Italian and the French Alps? But the lines are drawn: the such-and-such Alps. or the Eighteenth Century, immovable locations enclosing whole precisely delineated expanses of time, with no room for overlapping, tracts of civilization lifelessly marked off into geographical and historical zones, from here to here and no further!

*

A person in prison corresponds most closely of all to the concept of man. He is, so to speak, the most natural man – man in his pristine state. For the simple reason that in prison he is marked off, separated. But out there, beyond the bars, living in freedom . . .

*

"*If only I could break free and get away – to drink some koumys!*"[2]

*

[1] G. Derzhavin (1743–1816): Russian poet generally regarded as transitional between the 18th century and the age of Pushkin.

[2] Fermented mare's milk, once popular as a cure for tuberculosis.

Three people come through carrying a stretcher with a corpse clearly visible under the sheet. A girl has committed suicide by taking poison. The stretcher is held by the supervisor at the rear and by two women prisoners (non-politicals) in front. One, in a hospital mini-dressing-gown, terribly thin and drawn, with a peasant woman's kerchief on her head, crosses herself with the left hand. The second, plump, dolled up and painted, bawls drunkenly for all the zone to hear: "Oh, for even the smell of a man!"

Both roar with laughter. The most normal thing in the whole procession is the corpse showing through the sheet.

*

A dying man a week before his death stole another dying man's glasses.

*

A psychopath from among the chronically ill patients: every evening he must have a look, however fleeting, at the corpses in the morgue, particularly if a new one has been brought in.

"If I don't go and look at them they come to me in my dreams!"

*

Perhaps corpses frighten us because they seem to keep a sharp eye on us from under their lowered eyelids. This is why the specialists – gravediggers, hospital orderlies, crematorium and morgue attendants – refer to them disrespectfully as "squinters".

*

The morgue attendant and also dissector, a prisoner serving a long-term sentence, is called Koralis. A spruce, sombre old man from Lithuania, he has no friends and occupies a bunk somewhat apart from the others. No one wants to sleep next to Koralis. He has the air of a mediaeval executioner: awesome and deferential at the same time, and somehow satanically repulsive. A ghoul rather than a human being. He has sold himself for food. After taking a swig of the spirits issued to him as a precaution against ptomaine, he sings an incomprehensible ditty in his workshop. In his free hours he sometimes pores over a book, always the same one – it's really too good to be true: Koralis reads Dante's *Inferno.*

He is also disliked because he sews up the brains of his fellow-prisoners together with their guts – in the stomach. And once he nearly got beaten up for stealing a shirt from a corpse.

Koralis's shoes – infernally black – have a bright orange lining of a kind never before known to exist.

*

The weather is lovely and I spend my days outside, on a bench, feasting my eyes on a clump of trees through which the horizon is faintly visible – it is like a Japanese flower arrangement of two or three sprigs, at first enveloped in a haze of sunlight and then forming a lattice over an improbably large and pink moon, and life from morning till night is the length of a single sigh.

*

. . . How long ago it was! Not even dawn, but the dawn of the dawn, a presage. There had been no Nativity yet, no Annunciation. Nothing. A Daughter was born to a barren old couple. The beginnings of the new age. A first glimmering in the depths of the ancient temple. The faint light of the miracle to come still played in the homely setting of an unsuspecting and artless childhood. What gentle colours would be needed to depict the scene!

Why were infants so important for the new era? Children had never been so much in evidence. Thoughts of the future became somehow interwoven with the idea of innocence – and never before had there been so much about the future. Now, for the first time, an infant became a symbolic figure – quite apart from the main symbol of the Crucifixion – and His mother together with Him: Mother and Child. And all fell prostrate before Him, remaining as innocent as babes themselves.

This was hardly the way of history, of future generations. Their attitude to infants has always been condescending, the patronizing one of those who know in advance what the outcome will be, and that the first blind steps made in ignorance never seem to get you very far. The future laughs at the past, as it surveys in retrospect the course of a destiny neither seen nor understood by the present – which is always left to its own devices, and gropes its way in the dark, learning to live from the beginning, like a new born babe.

But here we have a Child who seems to be not in the past, but still ahead of us, in future prospect – the germ not of history but of eternity, and through the Birth of His Mother a constant reminder that in God the Child is never extinct.

21st September, 1970.[1]

*

I live as on a desert island and read the myths and fables of Oceania. They suck me in like quicksands, full of wonderful possibilities. Here's the beginning of one of these fables – from New Caledonia. It is rather like the children's story about the busy dwarfs. It is also very reminiscent of *our* life!

"Chief Tuo was clearing the branches of fallen trees round his house, casting them now to one side, now to the other. He thought: 'What shall I do to eat some meat? Let me make a snare for birds.'

He lay down to sleep, and in the morning started weaving a rope. By the evening he had made the snare and went and put it in a large fig tree. Then he returned home, had a smoke and went to bed. He slept till day-break, and in the morning he got up and went off to look at the snare. There he saw two flying foxes. Tuo climbed the fig tree, untied them, cut off their paws and wings and threw the flying foxes on the ground below. Then he climbed down himself, took them and brought them to his mother. His mother took a mattock and dug out two yams and two taros, wrapped the flying foxes in some leaves and put all this in a pot. She cooked it on a stove and kept

[1] Nativity of the Virgin in the Julian calendar.

sniffing the steam to tell when the food was ready. Then she took the food: there was one flying fox for chief Tuo, and one for her – his mother; there was one yam and one taro for chief Tuo, and one yam and one taro for his mother. So they ate until they had eaten everything. They had a smoke and went to bed. In the morning chief Tuo rose and went to look at his snare.

And what did he see there? What will our story be about?

Our story will be about chief Tendo, about the spirit caught in the snare."

In a word, before launching on a story you must first eat. You expect the plot to start unfolding, but things are held up for the sake of this account of a mode of existence important and interesting in its own right to the story teller – who is also thinking how nice it would be to have something to eat, to smell it cooking, and then to have a smoke and a sleep. It is a brilliant beginning, which gives a very clear picture of the savage's mentality and way of life – and all by the way, in passing, without any conscious intention of doing so. "So they ate, until they had eaten everything." But what really matters, and the reason why books are written and tales are told, is that after first having eaten and slept, you catch the spirit in a snare!

*

. . . We are through with summer. On the nearby trees the leaves now sit like a few birds. It is time to start drawing in one's horns and getting used to a more cramped existence.

How old the news is! Your letters now take over a month from Moscow, and at this rate I shall catch up with today only at the end of October. It'll be snowing by the time I get to it.

24th September, 1970.

*

The cat has lost the fur on its chest and the flesh is hideously torn and lacerated: the poor old thing was caught in a trap for crows. And when it licks its pink chest you can hear the tongue making a scraping sound.

And it has started to snow. The very nerves can feel it snowing.

*

. . . This morning I got up at dawn to go and fetch hot water and suddenly saw that the forest, quite autumnal by now, was glowing with a special, self-generated light of its own. Remembering the gold in icons one may surmise that the forest is giving back the sunshine accumulated during the summer, and therefore turns yellow – like the light to which it owes so much.

*

I wonder why I devote so much space in my letters to nature – because I have too much, or too little of it in my present life? . . . Be that as it may, I have grown to trust it – for all its drenching rain, sweltering heat and icy cold. Everything it does must be seen as its way of caring for us, of giving direct help. The sky is now more reliable than the roof over our heads – not in some figurative or exalted sense, but in the most tangible and down-to-earth one: you can actually feel nature's supporting hand on your skin. How can it be indifferent, when everything depends on it? They now tell us in the magazines that with the slightest overheating through all our physics, chemistry and waste products everything will go to the devil – so what an accurate course nature must have been steering, leading us along a path as straight and narrow as a razor's edge between hot and cold, flood and drought, if we have lived so many centuries never deviating from it and always choosing among the myriad possibilities this one extraordinarily narrow and only right way! . . .

*

. . . And with the first snow we are always back in childhood again. This happens neither in the spring nor in the summer. Why would people be so pleased if it were not a sudden transfiguration, a miracle?

*

We should be more modest and not imagine ourselves to be all that superior to horses and cats. We are closer to them than appears at first sight, and this is not such a bad thing. Why should it be so wrong to beat me, but all right to beat a horse, rather than the other way round? My possession of a "developed consciousness" means that I can at least understand what it's all about and hence more easily bear it. If I am to be pitied it must be rather because I have less physical endurance than a horse – that is, not because I am superior to it, but because I am weaker: for the same reason that it is wrong to beat a woman.

Notions like "human dignity" or "the inviolability of the person" are to my mind a kind of gobbledegook, part of a generally accepted jargon or code serving the same sort of practical convenience as exclamatory phrases such as "you don't say!" or "goodness gracious!" – which are all very well in polite conversation, but make little real sense and cannot be taken very seriously. At bottom there is no such thing as "personal dignity".

In some book or other great indignation is expressed at the fact that Plato was sold into slavery: Plato – into slavery!? But why not? What more suited to Plato? . . .

*

When all is said and done, a camp gives the feeling of maximum freedom. (Perhaps only a closed prison[1] gives it even more.)

*

. . . But, someone asked him, suppose a priest were to abuse his position of father-confessor and become an informer?

"What a thing to say! That could never happen! He forgets everything at once! And then for such a thing the Lord would seal up his lips for ever!"

In my youth I had always imagined a confessor as a person overburdened with other men's sins. How much he must hear

[1] i.e. prisons like the one at Vladimir, where people are kept in solitary confinement.

and remember – enough to put him off people altogether! But in actual fact he hears and remembers nothing. In practice he is a sieve with no capacity to retain the secrets learned in confession, let alone to store them up for some purpose or other. He is a funnel rather than an ear – a funnel with a spout leading to the dark heavens above. Or perhaps better still – a duct that whirrs away like a vacuum cleaner, sucking in the accumulated dirt of years, prising loose and snatching up whole pieces of caked filth, as though a powerful jet of air were drawing them through an outlet into the wide, open spaces, through into yawning gates which swallow everything so greedily that you feel you could be whisked up there yourself in the wake of your sins. This lack of the human element in confession also removes the sense of shame which might restrain you from admitting certain of your sins: instead, you are anxious to remember everything, to make a clean breast of it, and the occasional words spoken by the self-effacing witness, his faint sighs and questions, only help you to shed the burden and leave it behind. His visible image in the darkness seems evanescent and wraith-like, present only as a mere voice, after the manner of the ancient chorus: a weak, murmuring accompaniment to what is being confessed and absolved. And now in your own self you no longer distinguish either name or personality, only a faceless chorus against whose background the soul swirls free of the skin it has sloughed in this wind, in this downpour of voices . . .

*

The month of October is now behind us – a month so hard that we must not turn round to look at it, but forge ahead without a backward glance; and then suddenly, with all the satisfaction of a man who has travelled further than he knows, we will see that the nights are drawing in early and that it gets light in the mornings as late as can possibly be – which means we have reached the depths.

Winter has been all around us for a long time now – it has never been known to set in so early. Though it is still a long way to the centre of winter (sounds like "to the centre of the earth"), the fact that it has started – in keys both major and minor – makes things much simpler.

By itself winter is definitely in a major key. It is wonderfully young and strong, and leads one back to life . . .

*

It is snowing. But the sky and the earth are still warm – which is why it is snowing. If they were not warm, there would be no snow and everything would bristle instead with sharp needles of ice.

*

After a visit to the bath-house I tossed my completely worn-out socks into the waste bin – with as much relish as I would tick off two remaining months of my sentence that had somehow slipped by unnoticed. Time and freedom are thus translated into material or concrete terms. A year or eighteen months before the end of their sentences people start giving or throwing things away with a feeling of huge and growing superiority: they are visibly preparing themselves to take wing. How much easier life is when you discard things!

15th December, 1970.

*

I had always thought of our existence as an island, but now realize that it has the dimensions of a whole continent, and that all the people who have ever been here, whether living or dead, for ever remain part of it, making it into a constantly expanding island which all the while stretches out to further horizons, yet never escapes beyond our ken, so that, sedentary and static as our lives are, one begins to understand how the epic came into being: it was always tied to some people or tribe which, though as self-contained as an island, was also the starting point of innumerable journeys, caravan routes and personal destinies that trickled out of it in all directions like rivulets, only to flow back eventually into what had become a zone of continental proportions. Widely scattered persons and ideas were thus held together by bonds of kinship based on a common lot or place of origin – thanks to which each individual, as a repository of the collective memory, could always become the centre of the whole far-flung continent and its story, as happened, for example, in the Odyssey.

*

Come December we have cut the winter in half: it has fallen behind us and lies there motionless while we trudge forward, knee-deep in snow – on to May, to June . . .

Perhaps our winter fears have also been left behind.

It is all slightly like a voyage: you look at the map to see what narrows or obstacles lie ahead. January and February are solid blocks. But March is a variable month. March is always variable.

•

Part Six

"Haji, oh Haji!
They say thou art God's own emissary,
They say thou art the Prophet's heir.
Were it so,
Would we two be locked up in prison?

Haji, oh Haji!
They say thou art God's own emissary,
They say thou art the Prophet's heir,
They say thou art the Imam of the Saints.
Were it so,
Would we have these steel manacles on our wrists?

Haji, oh Haji!
They say thou art God's own emissary,
They say thou art the Prophet's heir,
They say thou art the Imam of the Saints
And the teacher of *Murids*.[1]
Were it so,
Would we have these iron fetters upon our ankles?"

"Movsar, oh Movsar!
On the day we said farewell to Daghestan
Mount Gayrak came shuddering with grief to see us on our way.
Then the thought came to me
To shatter, destroy and raze the city of Vladikavkaz[2] with one blow of the sword.
But remembering what befell the prophet Yusup
When an earthly power had vanquished him –
I drew back.

[1] Moslem Sufi neophytes.
[2] A Russian garrison town in the North Caucasus and base of operation against Shamil's rebellion in 1824–29.

Movsar, oh Movsar!
On the day we said farewell to Daghestan
Mother earth came shuddering with grief to see us on our way,
Then the thought came to me
To shatter, destroy and raze the Capital city of the infidels.
But remembering what befell the prophet Yusup
When an earthly power had vanquished him –
I drew back.

Movsar, oh Movsar!
I shall pray, and thou shouldst say 'Amen',
And may God answer our prayer!"
He spoke and said his prayer,
And their chains turned to cinders and fell at their feet, and the doors were opened
And they saw the sky and a wide green plain.

"Now art thou free, Movsar!
The way to Daghestan is open and no one is there but God."
And Movsar wept and beseeched his brother:
"Do not make me unhappy, do not drive me away from thy presence!
For indeed we are brothers, borne by one mother, Heda,
And she bore thee and me to one father, Kishi!"

Because thou talkest to God,
We have grown to love thee.
La ilah-illa-l-lah. (3 times)

Because thou sayest thy prayers together with angels in chorus
We have grown to love thee.
La ilah-illa-l-lah. (3 times)

Because thou sayest thy prayers to God by the side of the Prophet
We have grown to love thee.
La ilah-illa-l-lah. (3 times)

This is one of the Chechen songs about Kunta-Haji. It is not customary to speak sacred names out loud and since he is the most exalted and venerated of the Chechen saints, he is generally called by his father's name – Kishi-Haji, or by the name of his native village – Haji of Ilaskhan-yurt. In the nation's spiritual life his authority is no less than Muhammad's, whose daughter Fatima is said to have been a friend of the saint's mother, Heda (before the birth of either, naturally: while they were still souls). His name is more famous and significant than that of Shamil, his contemporary and admirer.

For taking part in the religious and national movement Haji was evidently imprisoned by the Russian authorities and exiled from Daghestan together with his brother Movsar. In the song quoted above the saint is hinting that it would be a trifling matter for him to defeat the Russians by destroying Vladikavkaz and St Petersburg, and thus to bring everything to the best possible conclusion. But he is held back, so to speak, by his awareness of the necessity of all that has happened. The mention of the prophet Yusup – the Joseph of the Old Testament – obviously refers to the way Joseph forgave his brethren – that is, took no action himself, but relied on the will of God.

The prayer said "in chorus" (also known as the "speedy" prayer) needs some explanation: it was an innovation introduced by Kunta-Haji, and though it met with opposition from the local ulema and scribes it was considered one of the great achievements of Islam. It was essentially an appeal for immediate assistance, and Kishi-Haji has hence retained to this very day, in the eyes of his spiritual children, the right to intervene rapidly on their behalf, playing the same role in the life of the Chechens as St Nicholas does in Russia. The actual words of the prayer "in chorus", are scarcely decipherable, being a kind of sacred speech. According to indirect evidence I am unable to vouch for, it begins with what sounds like a garbled version of the traditional Arab formula "La ilah-illa-l-lah" – a distortion which can probably be put down to Kishi-Haji's illiteracy (but which does not, however, necessarily detract from its mysterious power).

The meaning of the words was apparently incomprehensible to those who themselves took part in this collective prayer.

Songs about Kunta-Haji usually have a predominantly choral ending which in various modified versions may be transferred from one song or legend to another, as a sort of invocation or incantation for general use.

*

"The ulema of thy day were thine enemies,
By not writing down thy knowledge they did evil,
That thy teacher was the Prophet himself they knew not,
May the Lord preserve thee, messenger of God."

The great Haji of Sayasan, seeing the ulema busily turning over the pages of their books in a fruitless search for the collective prayer which men were taught by Haji of Ilaskhan, spoke as follows:

"If all the waters of the earth turned into a sea of ink and all the trees and all the grasses of the world were used for writing, could much be garnered therefrom with the point of a needle? Thus much wisdom and no more has the Lord vouchsafed into the hands of the ulema, while all the rest of the ocean has become the property of the saints. Will you then really venture to assert that what you have found on the point of your needle will not be found in the whole sea?!

By denying the rightness of this prayer, do not make yourselves unhappy.
By denying the holiness of this prayer, do not become godless."

*

Plutarch tells us that Numa Pompilius, the ancient Roman king and sage, commanded that he be buried together with his writings, the sense of which he had previously explained to the priests. But he did not entrust them with the texts themselves, "considering it unbecoming to leave the preservation of secret knowledge to the lifeless letters of the alphabet. For the very same reasons, it is said, the Pythagoreans too did not write down their doctrine, but committed it unwritten to the memory of those worthy of it."

This passage reminds us that in the past the highest wisdom was never recorded in writing but transmitted only by word of mouth. What was the reason for this division between the truth and the written word – in ancient times, after all, books were always thought to embody not figments of the imagination but truth itself, even though it might lose something of its original import in such a form? Was it that the book was felt to be indifferent vis-à-vis the reader, to be too indiscriminate a vehicle for something that demanded a medium as profound as itself? Did men require the guarantee of absolute authenticity which can be ensured only by a living witness? Or was it legitimate distrust of the dead word which ossifies speech, destroys the living utterance by the very process of conserving it, and is hence quite unfitted to convey the voice of wisdom, a voice so vivid and inspired that any rigid form only distorts it? It was a rejection of the letter for the sake of the spirit which bloweth where it listeth, taking up its abode, whenever the need arises, in a disciple and by this means revealing itself anew to succeeding generations. (We might also mention here the inadequacy of all speech – of written speech in particular – when it comes to conveying what is left unsaid. Silence also has its importance. Doesn't one hear silence in poetry? A line of poetry is not only the alternation of sounds, but even more the organization of pauses, the arrangement of silence and stillness.) Truth takes no thought of the morrow, but only of the here and now, of just a handful of people brought together by it in a fleeting (and eternal) encounter. A father playing with his son and instructing him will likewise not think of writing down chapter and verse. A written record (except where it had the other more proper function of preserving codes of law, chronologies, names and various factual data) was usually made by those left without a teacher, without a father. What was the point of putting down in a fixed form things said by the living to the living? The living is recorded in such a manner only by the dead.

*

What form can a book take? Well, it can be like a heart, pumping out words in many directions at once. Or it can stretch out in a straight line like a road, for the author to advance along at the same pace as his narrative, receding into the distance with it until he disappears from view, physically swept into its rarefied far reaches where, now possessed of his soul and body, it breaks off in large letters which he makes with difficulty, grasping the pen in both hands like a child, already almost in the other world – in short, he writes himself to a standstill in pursuit of a material form which carries him away and eventually trails off into silence.

*

Let us fold a piece of paper in two, then fold it again to make it a quarter of its former size, and then carefully fold it once more and cut it, thus obtaining pages one-eighth of the original size, and on one of these fresh, small and neat little pages, or rather in this miniature book which we have so ingeniously contrived, let us inscribe four words: this will be enough, I assure you, this will be quite enough for us . . .

*

And so here it is, the gentle, stealthy month of February.

31st January, 1971.

*

Oddly enough, all this idle chatter in my letters is in large measure not so much self-expression on my part as a form of listening, of listening to you – turning things over this way and that and seeing what you think about them. It is important for me, when I write, to hear you. Language thus becomes a scanning or listening device, a means of silent communion – absolutely empty, a snare or net: a net of language cast into the sea of silence in the hope of pulling up some little golden fish caught in the pauses, in the momentary interstices of silence. Words have no part in this, except in so far as they serve to mark off the pauses. We use them only to jolly ourselves along as we make our way towards silence, perfect silence.

*

. . . In place of the exercise book confiscated from me during the "frisk" my neighbours have presented me with an entire roll of paper – lovely, thick, orange-coloured packing paper! – and I can now write without having to economize, in large bold handwriting. And I wanted at once to fill the whole of it with my writing, very rapidly covering over these blank expanses of yellow paper.

In fact, a blank sheet of paper acts as an inspiration in itself and I presume that Balzac and Dumas wrote such mountains of books because they were fortunate in being well provided with blank paper: it waited expectantly, asking to be used – much as a primed canvas yearns for the painter's brush in sweet anticipation; or as a restive steed paws the ground: when shall we go? *Terra incognita* athirst for the traveller . . . And how marvellous that this paper is not white, but coloured – as though endowed with its own ready-made background just waiting to bring out any configurations of lines in sharp relief. On orange paper black letters look so alert, so eloquent! . . . Even just to cut this roll into strips and pieces is an enormous pleasure; so what will it be like when I start, breathlessly, to write on it! . . .

*

. . . One day I would quite like to write about *Hamlet* as I see it from the distance, now that not only the details of the plot, but even the main characters have become dim and vague in my mind, and I am thus better placed to attempt to define the general idea and atmosphere – the only things that remain firmly in my memory since I last read it some fifteen or twenty years ago. If at that time I had ventured any opinion on such an enormous and unfamiliar subject, I should have begun by viewing it less as a work of literature than as a guide to life – which it has indeed proved to be for well-nigh the whole of the modern age, attracting hordes of devotees during the last several centuries, as no other work of the imagination has ever done. The reason, it seems, is that Hamlet is faced with the necessity of solving questions which had hitherto been answered by a strict and time-honoured order of things – until it suddenly collapsed and crumbled into dust, abandoning man to the mercy of fate, leaving him a suffering creature naked, free and called upon to restore justice in a situation of confusion and ruin, internal as well as external. In this sense Shakespeare was not a Renaissance writer at all, but a mediaeval one sent to re-affirm the old law in these new conditions when it had to grow again like a tree, to be discovered and tried out anew in the laboratory of one man's destiny, will and mind as he was compelled, on his own responsibility and at his own peril, to go through with actions which would previously have been undertaken simply as a matter of course, in accordance with custom and tradition, at the behest of a family and social environment now devoid of meaning unless its concepts of law and duty could be restated in terms of a personal approach to them. The behaviour which has often led people to regard Hamlet as a weak-willed neurasthenic incapable of anything but talk (though it should be noted that he displays enormous energy and resourcefulness, eventually showing himself able to choose the best and only right solution among all the many alternatives), was dictated by the very nature of the mission entrusted to him: namely, to rediscover for himself the path he was to follow and at the same time to give it new meaning by investing moral precepts with all the maturity of judgment gained in the course of his lone quest. After his mother had betrayed her husband by marrying the brother who murdered him, everything was thrown in doubt – disaster, sacrilege and treason were at large in the world, and nothing could any longer be taken on trust;

all things had to be carefully verified – which is just what Hamlet does, beginning with the command brought from his father by an unexpected and dubious apparition. Note the complicated interaction, in which they alternately diverge and coincide, between the law (applied in mechanical, literal-minded fashion – hence poorly – by Laertes, but orchestrated with musical virtuosity by Hamlet) and the hero's freedom to do as he sees fit – a freedom that turns into the duty to choose the best and most subtle course of action. Note also the interplay of feigned and genuine madness in Hamlet – the madness he so skilfully acts, the madness gnawing at him from within, and the madness of the life he lives, in which everything is sacrificed to the business of growing up a prince – a scion of the royal blood who learns, with an artist's flair, to bend destiny to his will. His various aspects, alternately coalescing or diverging, weave round the figure of Hamlet in a continual flurry and thus create the impression of a multiple image existing, as it were, in many different projections – a figure enveloped in its own emanations, never assuming a final shape and character, but only hazily sketching out the future contours of an identity that cannot be imposed all at once on a soul still growing and a law yet to be established. Hamlet is so devoid of predetermined qualities, so poor and yet so rich, so changeable and so receptive that we have no idea what he will do a couple of minutes hence, and are thus obliged – as he himself is – to decide for ourselves every time how he must act if he is to perform his allotted task with the artistic grace which can flow only from a unified personality, when reason, will, talent, taste, instinct, duty and destiny are all blended into one harmonious whole. Hamlet is open to all mankind. In theory anyone can become Hamlet. For the new age Hamlet was a mediaeval knight suddenly stripped of all his former resources and compelled to cross the sea of history by swimming it. What hero of the modern age casts such a spell over us – a spell based exclusively on the inner music of his image? Why does he exemplify in his person the first intellectual in the highest sense of the word, the true aristocrat of the spirit, and every prince who is born into an unsettled world, not to make himself king, but to come out on the stage and, having fulfilled his destiny unprompted, go to his death still a prince? The exploratory manner of Shakespeare's study, like a series of rapid sketches, is the way of the teacher who is never dogmatic, but proceeds by trial and error, always allowing life to have the last word.

*

. . . How raw it is in March – not just this year, but in general, always, any March. There is something genial and magnanimous about the cold in January. But March winds chill you to the marrow and take you aback with their quite senseless and inexplicable spite. March in camp is something I shan't forget in a hurry – by now I know its insidious nature: winter still stretches out ahead in an endless expanse of white snow, but I am already longing for the first signs of thaw, impatient to tear two tattered shirts into handkerchiefs.

2nd March, 1971.

*

The first spring day. It's hard to credit: the sun is quite hot and a few drops of melted snow fall pitapat from the roof. Still a poor and feeble thing perhaps, but spring all the same. And with its coming the sky has taken on a firm and solid shape once more: it is streaked with pink and mauve, providing a background against which the grey mass of trees stands out with a well-nigh ornamental precision. One can now see very clearly the way in which trees are intermediate between the sky and the earth, and how the separation of the two is the essential condition for the birth of the world, and for its continued existence. This is the theme of the Maori myths: while Sky and Earth remained fused in one there was darkness; light and life began only when they were separated, even though this was offensive to them. It is interesting that the Mother (Earth) could not be parted from the Father (Sky) by any of their children except a son who was god of the forests, the vegetable kingdom and all who dwelled in them. The medial role of trees becomes apparent. It is for this reason, perhaps, that we always think of them as being so normal, natural, and stable. There is nothing in the world more natural than trees. They are as run-of-the mill as our average selves. Trees are the world's measure and therefore its norm. Intervening between them, the tree is also *ipso facto* the road from earth to heaven (a sprouting coffin). And it can serve as an image or yardstick in our general conception of the universe: the world tree.[1] All three worlds (subterranean, terrestrial and heavenly) can thus be pictured with the help of a measuring rod growing here in the middle, in the midst of us. A tree is on our own level. As man is the measure of all things taken separately, so the tree is the measure of the universe in its overall range and compass.

6th March, 1971.

*

. . . No modern poet possessed such a lively, direct, and innate sense of history as Mandelstam. His was not the historicism of an archaeologist, collector, scholar, enemy of the modern world, or romantic, and least of all the interest of a contemporary who measures the great events of his time and his own personal worth against the illustrious deeds and time-honoured names of the past. Mandelstam lived in history as he breathed the air around him: it was a given quantity, a gift, part of the order of things, which can no more be left than it can be entered. He deals with it just as freely and unselfconsciously as Pasternak does with nature, and the effect is not to "bring back" distant eras, but to convey a sense of audacious intimacy with them, as though they were close at hand. He never made history into a thing apart, but lived with it on terms of natural kinship and was entirely free of those Futurist[2] affectations which merely emphasize our isolation and estrangement from the past.

[1] e.g. Yggdrasil in Scandinavian mythology

[2] Literary movement contemporaneous with Mandelstam, which was marked by linguistic innovation, and some of whose representatives (such as Khlebnikov) combined the use of experimental language and words of their own making with archaic or mythological themes.

In his free-and-easy way of dealing with historical figures, in the abrupt transitions and shifts of focus that show him to be quite unlike those awestruck devotees who turn the past into a sacred reliquary and life into the worship of things, there is the sense of measure we find in a son loving and respectful, yet natural and unconstrained in manner. He is on just as equal a footing with history as with the present age and it is only our own deformity as manifested either in our lack of roots and loss of bearings, or in our deification of antiquity – also a sure sign, by the law of opposites, of inability to be free and natural in one's attitude to history – that prevents us from unhesitatingly adopting Mandelstam's unitary approach to things which for the rest of us exist in different compartments, as it were, of our minds.

The painter V. Milashevsky's reminiscences of him are a good illustration of what I mean. So little is known about Mandelstam that every word is precious, and in this case we are also given a general summing-up of what the whole of the intellectual élite in the early '20s thought about his poetry:

"He seemed like a visitor from another planet.

His very mentality, the structure of his images were unusual.

Imagine a leaf in a herbarium and a leaf on a tree! A living, moist, maple leaf, a natural leaf, hardly attracts any attention at all. But the same leaf in a herbarium amazes one by the diabolical intricacy of its sharp, spiky form. It is freakish, almost terrifying! You can see the spires of Gothic cathedrals, the stifling ghettos of the Middle Ages, the apparel of Mephistopheles and Doctor Faustus. But a green leaf is as simple as a folk tune.

Mandelstam's art is also a kind of dried plant, and at the root of it there is a certain alienation from everything that others see as real life, the life of the world." (*Zvezda*, No 12, 1970)

I think the feeling people had in dealing with Mandelstam, that he was a "herbarium", a "dried leaf", a "Martian" arose not out of his alienation from the world, but, on the contrary, out of his extraordinary capacity for seeing history in the present and for living not just in the here and now, as everybody else does, but both in historical life and in the atmosphere of his own time. As a rule history appears to be of no concern to us, nor to have any direct bearing on us except, perhaps, for a few names dear to our hearts. ("But that is *history*!", our commandant protested on being reminded in some connection or other that the Roman Empire had eventually collapsed.) We usually think of history not as a living entity like ourselves, but as something fossilized and left behind, a matter for chronological tables and text-books. For Mandelstam history was real, and at once simple and complex like our own life – which was hence also historic in his eyes. We divide time into a living plant (our own era) and a herbarium (antiquity), but Mandelstam's herbarium grew in our own forest ("The ostrich feathers of the armature", "The Assyrian wings of dragonflies"), and his ancient history flowered into a living Salamis.[1]

In this sense I know of no other poet more loyal to the modern age, or one who has so immortalized his epoch in the hieroglyphs of "history". He contrived to isolate the quicklime in the blood[2] of our reality as it actually is, and used it to make a lifelike and clear-cut plaster cast of the epoch without impairing the tissues. This spoke not so much of poetic skill as of his ability to live as part of mankind in a completely concrete and integrated way, his feet planted firmly in the soil of those who lived before us; he fastened together again with a song the broken link between the ages, and suddenly embarked, without so much as a by-your-leave, on the ocean of space and time which is one and the same for all generations. This indeed was the reason why he was considered a kind of stranger – because he was closer than anyone to the un-ageing family of mankind.

*

[1] The three poems referred to here are: "Yesche daleko mne do patriarkha . . ." (1931) in which the poet compares the steel rods sticking up from the reinforced concrete of new buildings in Soviet Moscow to ostrich feathers; "Veter nam uteshenye prinyos . . ." (1922), where the massed aircraft of a future war are envisioned as having the "Assyrian wings of dragonflies"; and "1914" which draws a parallel between the battle of Salamis and the war in Europe.

[2] Allusion to a famous poem entitled "1 January, 1924" in which Mandelstam speaks of himself as a "sick son of the age" with quicklime in his blood.

Yegor writes in his letter:

"I want you to make me a picture of me and I shall make you a picture of a ball."

A sentence superb in the elegance of its composition. One expects: "and I shall make you a picture of you". But not a bit of it – not "you" but a "ball"! The way that ball bounces back and forth from one end of the sentence to the other . . .

11th March, 1971.

*

The other day, looking out at the forest which has always been so remote and inaccessible, I suddenly conceived of it as *my* forest and felt surprised at such freedom of thought. That's what spring does for you. During my last year here I imagine that I shall have other things on my mind than fine points such as this. And now spring itself – the last but one – is gradually becoming mine, as though I were being released tomorrow.

11th March, 1971.

*

March is proving harder than February and we must travel on to April before we get rid of this winter which began almost in September and still shows no signs of letting up. It must be admitted that these winters can be very gruelling. You get tired of feeling your neighbour's concentrated stare on your face – you want to brush it off like a fly, but it goes on crawling there just the same and makes writing very difficult. Even when I get Yegor's magnificent letters I never think of reading them at once: the flies would settle on these unusually large characters.

The month of April appears gentle and lilac-coloured in my imagination. By now it seems so near, but still just out of reach: March is in the way.

20th March, 1971.

*

When all God's creatures were reposed in sleep,
On a mat spread out for the night
He sat down, they say,
The one whose secret may God preserve.

Glancing sorrowfully at the house, taking a hoe in his hands,
Into the field cleared with his own hands
He came out, they say,
The one whose secret may God preserve.

Kishi-Haji again. His outward appearance is said to have been very strange. His dress consisted of two *cherkeskas*[1] worn one on top of the other, the one below serving as underwear. On his feet he had rawhide moccasins. His collar was fastened not with a clasp but with a small stick. He never walked along a road, but always by the side of it, aloof from other people. But the most peculiar thing of all was, of course, the collective or "speedy" prayer which he had instituted.

Reports about it began reaching Shamil from the ulema and he appointed a court to hear the evidence. If the reports proved false he swore he would behead those who had accused the Haji. But should the Haji himself fail to prove his innocence, then Shamil would be ready to make a public declaration to this effect.

Shamil and his men, the ulema with their books, the Haji with his *murids* – all duly took their places, and the executioners stood there for everyone to see. The ulema read passages out of their books and the Haji interpreted them until they had nothing more to say. Then the Haji turned to Shamil and said:

"Shamil," said the Haji, "have you heard that four Sentinels have been posted by God at the four ends of the earth?"

"I have," said Shamil.

"Have you heard that in the middle of the earth stands a fifth Sentinel to whom those four go when a miracle happens

[1] Circassian coat, long, narrow and taken in at the waist.

which is beyond their understanding?"

"I have," said Shamil.

"If you happened to meet him, would you recognize him, Shamil?", said the Haji and turned his back on the Imam.

And then Shamil rose to his feet.

"I have a request to make of you," said the Haji.

"I shall grant all your requests except one!"

"I have only one request – and it is the one I now wish to make."

"But at least three of them must pay for this!" said Shamil.

"People will say of me:

'Because of this crazed man from Ilaskhan-yurt three men of learning have lost their heads!' I ask you not to touch these heads either."

"I shall grant your request, oh blessed Kishi," said Shamil. "Now, if you consider us worthy of it, say before us this prayer of yours together with your *murids*."

And the *murids* rose to their feet and they said their speedy prayer and when it was ended, the Great Haji of Sayasan rose up and said:

"May God preserve your secret, oh blessed Kishi! You are always able, as now appears, to bring to your *murids* by your prayer the Prophet who but rarely comes with his disciples from Mecca to the help of my *murids*."

Then Gazy-Haji from Zandika rose up and said:

"May God preserve your secret, oh blessed Kishi! You are always able, as now appears, to bring to your *murids* by your prayer the angels who but rarely come to the help of my *murids*."

This blue sky, Movsar,
Appealed to God for thy brother.
May the Lord on High and His Prophet
Help them, Movsar.

The heavenly angels, too, Movsar,
Appealed to God for thy brother.
May the Lord on High and His Prophet
Help them, Movsar.

When through the slander of the impious and the scribes
The Haji was being taken away from Daghestan,
He stopped and said:
"No, I shall not leave here until I have told you how my
  teaching came to me!

Two thousand years before the creation of the world
The souls of men were created by God,
  Oh men of learning.

Two thousand years before the creation of the world
124 thousand souls of prophets were created by God,
  Oh men of learning.

Two thousand years before the creation of the world
124 thousand souls of saints were created by God,
  Oh men of learning.

Two thousand years before the creation of the world
124 thousand sacred doctrines were created by God,
  Oh men of learning.

Two thousand years before the creation of the world
The Lord spread out before us these sacred doctrines
And placed one at the head of all, encircled by a fiery dragon,
And said to us: 'Let each choose his share'.

We took them beginning from the lower edge,
And the one that was at the head remained last,
  Oh men of learning.

'Take up thy share, oh blessed Kishi, it has no other owner!'
Said the Lord to us, oh men of learning.

'No, I shall not take it!
The day on which the soul takes leave of the body
Will be grievous for my children.
The night on which man first remains alone in his grave
Will be hard for my children to bear.
The Day of the First Interrogation before the Lord
Will be terrible for my children.
If for all these occasions I shall not be given the right
Of prompt help to my children
I shall not take the remaining share!'
We said to God, oh men of learning.

'The day on which the soul takes leave of the body
I have left to thee.
The night on which man first remains alone in his grave
I have left to thee.
The right of help at the First Interrogation
I am giving to thee.'

He spoke and a paper with the signatures of the angels
Jabrail and Minkail, Israfil and Israil,
A fleecy paper, white as snow,
The Lord did hand to us, oh men of learning.

In the name of the Lord the merciful, the compassionate,
With this great name of God,
Stepping on the fiery dragon,
We took up our share, oh men of learning.

'Let this speedy prayer be spoken
On me and on me!' said
The high mountains and the low hills,
The wide plains and the narrow gorges.

And to resolve this argument
The angel Jabrail was sent from God.

Between the high mountains and the low hills
Lots were cast, and the lot fell to Mount Gayrak.
'Do not torment me, let me
(For I am not taking away from you your rights of village
mullahs)
Glorify my God and the Prophet!'

Between the wide plains and the narrow gorges
Lots were cast and the lot fell to Ilaskhan-yurt.
Do not torment me, let me
(For I am not taking away from you your right to the money
of orphans)
Glorify my God and the Prophet!

From the East let help come to us, oh Lord.
From the West let help come to us, oh Lord.
In a speedy prayer with a choir of angels
Send Kishi-Haji to our help!"

*

The water from the melting snow freezes over at night so there is very little mud and a light breeze blows over the soil, drying it out a little: spring is approaching in a businesslike way, at a rather slow but sure pace. And in the meantime I am just as delighted at the growing holes in my socks and shirts as I am at the spreading patches of earth where the snow has thawed away. "Hurry up and fall to bits!" I say to my miserable clothes. "Time is getting on, and we cannot wait!"

My attitude to spring this year reminds me how as a child I used to try to increase the speed of a train by looking out of the window and pressing my nose against the glass for hours on end. Perhaps it was the same last year? I don't remember.

"*Donatovich,*[1] *what is a stockbroker?*"

[1] Sinyavsky's patronymic.

"Donatovich, what is 'dualism'?"

"Donatovich, what is 'concupiscence'?"

Another reason why I am in such a hurry to reach summer is that my head must really be given a little respite; as it is, I've been driven almost out of my wits during these winter months. Just think – I'll be able to spend my day off sitting outside under the open sky!

28th March, 1971.

*

. . . How right you were, and how clever of you, when you said that time in the visitors' house,[1] looking at my woollen socks with holes in the heels, that it was better not to throw them away because they still had some warmth in them, worn out as they were. And they have indeed served me faithfully all through the winter. But the main point is the *way* in which you said it: seriously and with conviction, lowering your voice a little, as if carefully weighing your words in passing on this important piece of information; it was said very gravely, in true camp fashion, and I believed you at once. I never cease to marvel at this ability of yours to get to the core, not of socks, but of things in general, of life in all its painful essentials – just with a little shake of your head.

*

How tremendous to have reached March the 31st! The 31st is a supernumerary day in any month, but when it comes at the end of winter, right at its very furthest point, then arriving at it is – how can I put it? Well, it's just like getting to a kind of Land's End, or a Cape of Good Hope – though this was no doubt reached by sea, while we have been toiling our way across a continent and now we are there, you feel you only have to leap off from it to take wing . . .

31st March, 1971.

*

[1] Premises where some prisoners are allowed to meet their husbands or wives.

This evening – for the first time and quite timidly as yet – there was a smell of damp earth, and my heart jumped for joy at it. After so much winter – suddenly this heady, penetrating dampness. How very right: earth – water – serpent – woman. And also: "the damp earth".[1] Dampness is the basic element of life, its very foundation. And life, animality, love and freedom are more than anything associated with smell. So smell is also spirit,[2] though of a lower order. Which means that even the lowest forms of life are infused with the spirit.

How funny to apprehend myth through the senses, in the same personal way in which one becomes aware of one's body and one's own perceptions – just by peering into the bushes, into the night, into the air. But it is possible only on condition that a man be deprived of everything he has and completely isolated.

7th April, 1971.

*

The sun is hot and the air cold, and I feel I am getting quite a tan. I haven't looked at myself in a mirror for a long time, but I can judge by the other faces around me. The flies are coming back to life before one's eyes. Someone noticed that I too am perking up and asked: "How much time have you to go?"

When you want to say something nice to a man, that's what you ask:

"How much time have you to go?"

12th April, 1971.

*

"*In nineteen days' time I shall have exactly one year and seven months to go!*" (The art of reckoning)

*

[1] A standard phrase in Russian folklore; see note on page 197.
[2] The word *dukh* ("spirit") may also be used colloquially in the sense of "smell".

How odd that you sleep better when it rains. You have a heightened sensation of a roof over your head. Sleep actually starts with the semblance of a roof forming in the drowsy consciousness and this takes place more easily when it rains. It is rather like shutting yourself up in a cosy little house – to which a blanket adds its magic, for apart from warmth, it provides yet another roof. What it all amounts to is that we build ourselves a tunnel leading to other regions, or a covered station from which to set out on the journey of sleep. This is why we are so irritated by any noise that prevents us from falling asleep: it shatters the illusion of the safe refuge into which we have already crept. In this sense, sleep is a secluded abode for the soul, and like any other it must provide an increased sense of cosiness, of shelter, and we nestle down all the more blissfully in the knowledge that it is raining outside – but it doesn't affect us, we don't even hear it, we have a roof over our heads, we are asleep.

13th April, 1971.

*

But when we woke up, all was white. The windows are frosted over. It's winter again, for the fifth time. At this moment – it is getting towards evening – the snow is falling heavily. It almost looks as if winter (the next one!) is going to by-pass the summer and begin straightaway.

Yesterday was Maundy Thursday.[1] A marvellous name. I went to the bath-house: on Maundy Thursday it is customary to wash, as one man in the bath-house was explaining to everyone: "I washed yesterday," he said, "but today is Pure Thursday!"

16th April, 1971.

*

We had a remarkably windless and bright day today. With this cold spring it is simply a miracle: sunshine, starlings, and haze in the distance.

[1] The Russian name is Pure (or Clean) Thursday.

For some reason the first chapter of the Gospel according to St John is read, they say, in the course of the Easter service. This is, perhaps, the most spiritual of the four gospels and mentions the Spirit in the very first chapter – a chapter which is somewhat remote from Easter, one might think, in the events it describes. Yet the Spirit is indeed more keenly felt at Easter than on any other holy day, more so even than at Whitsun: there is something silvery, ethereal, slightly incandescent about it – a day spun from light, and light spun from the Spirit. The flint of life, ready to kindle and ignite. And how the little birds sing! . . .

The icons show only the Descent into Hell and the Holy Women who came to anoint His body with spices. But the Resurrection is somehow omitted. This is because there is no verbal picture either: all is darkness, mystery, forbidden. An icon needs words: "by His death He overcame death",[1] and in the Descent into Hell He literally overcomes it by trampling it underfoot. But what happens later on? All we are shown is the rather anticlimactic scene of the Holy Women finding the tomb empty. The supreme event remains undepicted. He rose from the dead and went out of the tomb, but it is not given to us to see, nor should we see, this crowning miracle – because it is the greatest, and hence quite simply beyond words or any pictorial representation. In the same way, the centre retreats to the forests, and the source of a culture lies outside it.[2] The Creator is outside creation.

The first chapter of the Gospel according to St John conveys the same feeling of something transcendent, beyond our ken. ". . . Verily, verily, I say unto you, Hereafter ye shall see heaven open, and the angels of God ascending and descending upon the Son of man." (I, 51). It is close to Easter not in theme, but in style and spirit, in its effulgence.

18th April, 1971.

*

[1] Words from the Russian Orthodox Easter Service.

[2] c.f. p. 96 – passage beginning: Take the North again . . .

Winter has come again for the seventh time – and is so much the real thing that this repeated descent of whiteness has begun to seem like a delirium, an obsessive hallucinatory vision of winter without end, and it makes you want to snigger behind your hand, like a madman who knows that everything is a put-up job. What a fast-moving life – and how long as well . . .

26th April, 1971.

*

I don't somehow seem to remember snow falling on May 1st ever before. But it happened this morning, and it came down so thick and fast that almost the whole earth was covered over in half an hour.

By the middle of the day the weather became just warm enough to make the snow disappear, and though it threatened to start again any minute, you could see through the window (now without its second frame)[1] how the willow branches, still supple and completely bare, have stretched out eagerly and responsively, ready to bud and blossom forth, now that their twigs have drunk freely, in generous draughts, of this bulging, white-dappled, blue-streaked sky, which has turned into a reservoir of bountiful summer air.

The birds are chirping as in an aviary.

*

In the natural world man serves as a model to be mimicked by the whole of the animal kingdom which makes grotesque faces, deliberately caricaturing its lord and master in all manner of ways – beginning with the frog, which certainly resembles us and was created on purpose to mock us. We live in the midst of these comical creations, with their improbable ears, noses and tails, as though surrounded by family portraits, representing, however, not our ancestors, but fantastic pro-

[1] Windows in Russia are double-glazed and sealed for winter.

jections of our potential selves as seen already in the animal fables – these successfully capture the humorous diversity of life taken by science as evidence for its theory of evolution, but understood by art in its true significance as a series of sketches for the design first conceived in the shape of the frog and later put on show in nature's *tableau vivant* as a finished model: man. Every cow and goat is a laughing, amiable skit on ourselves – something clearly and directly felt by young children who choose birds and beasts to be their friends for the simple reason that, being so funny, they are obviously fellow creatures and fit companions. If they were not a parody of us – a parody created earlier, perhaps, than the original, for its greater glory and easier recognition – there would not be such a bond between animals and children, who from the cradle on take this family likeness to be an invitation to play a jolly game of spotting the resemblances. Perhaps there is really only one face common to us all – a face assumed to have achieved its ideal form in man, but which still recognizes itself, winking and grimacing at its own image, in the innumerable mirrors of the animal kingdom – where man is simply a theme with variations.

1st May, 1971.

*

The most engaging thing about Yoshida Kenko's[1] *Essays in Idleness* is his ability to see things through the eyes of a long tradition in Japanese art and hence to convey in words what mediaeval Japanese impressionism was all about even more clearly than the painting itself, where figures taken from life are translated into the flowing hieroglyphs of the kind often seen by the author in ancient pictures – and which then, observing the reality round about, he unerringly recognizes for what they are: reflections of images frozen in complete immobility and animated only by the fact of being alive. His "Essays" are astonishing for their art of transferring to paper

[1] 14th century Japanese poet and essayist.

bits of life which might almost have been specially prefabricated by reality to take their place in Japanese painting or literature, and to be fixed there in the mind by the frequent reproduction of their every line and curve – invariably enhanced by the additional aesthetic touch that comes from the artist's eye having dwelt long and ecstatically on the object itself. Kenko is a kind of Japanese Van Gogh, but more serene:

"Say what you will, but a drunkard is an entertaining and harmless enough fellow. When his host appears in his room in the morning and finds him still asleep, tired out by his drinking, he is overcome by embarrassment and with his face still bearing the marks of sleep, his hair tied in a straggly knot on the top of his head, with no time to dress properly, he snatches up his clothes and, trailing them after him, takes to his heels. From behind, his figure with the skirt hitched up and his thin hairy legs is a funny sight that accords remarkably well with the whole state of affairs."

You feel you have seen that drunk many times in old Japanese prints, and in this very same posture – one which places him in timeless perspective. Here you realize that the true art of painting is in these infinitely perpetuated gestures that last for all eternity and invite you to brood on them without end, to let your gaze wander over them in unceasing contemplation of every brush stroke . . .

*

I recently discovered that in Gumilev's poem "The Tramcar that lost its Way" there is a fleeting allusion to a scene enacted a long time before and in a different incarnation in Pushkin's *The Captain's Daughter*:

"Oh, how you cried in your room and wept
While I, with powdered wig and pig-tail at my back,
Went off to pay the Empress my respects
And never again saw you in this life . . ."

Mashenka in "The Tramcar that lost its Way" can thus trace her origins not only to Anna Akhmatova (who much later took a line from the poem as an epigraph: "And in a lane a fence made of boards") or some other living wife or wife-to-be, but also back to Pushkin's Mashenka, the girl engaged to Grinev, – a metamorphosis perhaps suggested by Gumilev's resemblance to him and amply warranted later on by the manner of Gumilev's death.[1]

4th May, 1971.

*

The weather is just the same and is even fairly cool. But it has suddenly become twice as bright (in the way madder-red is twice as red). And this is because – what day is it today? Ah, you see? Summer, cold as it may be, starts today.

Perhaps the abiding, changeless, extra-historical character of Feast-days comes partly from being tied to a particular time of year, from having their fixed place in the eternal cycle of the seasons which, as they come round again, always bring back the event in its original clarity, never allowing it to grow cold and lifeless or fade into oblivion. Each time anew St George slays the dragon. Each time anew.

[1] Nikolai Gumilev (1885–1921): One of the leading Russian poets in the decade before the Revolution, who founded the Acmeist school of poetry, together with his first wife, Anna Akhmatova (1889–1966). "The Tramcar that lost its Way", one of his most celebrated poems, was written shortly after the Revolution and is a somewhat surrealist vision of the break-up of an ordered world and way of life, symbolized by a St Petersburg tramcar that leaves the rails and is displaced in time and space. In the lines quoted, the "Mashenka" of the poem (probably someone Gumilev was in love with at the time, or perhaps a composite figure based on Akhmatova and his second wife) is clearly "metamorphosed" into the Maria (Mashenka in the diminutive form) of Pushkin's short historical novel, *The Captain's Daughter*, about an episode in the Pugachev uprising in the reign of Catherine the Great. The "resemblance" between Grinev, the hero of Pushkin's story, and Gumilev is that both, as officers loyal to their respective sovereigns, suddenly found themselves in situations of revolutionary upheaval – a "Russian rebellion, senseless and merciless" (as Pushkin describes the Pugachev uprising in a famous phrase in his story) that destroyed the old order and threatened doom to all who resisted. In Grinev's case the disaster was local and temporary, since the Pugachev uprising was crushed. After the successful Bolshevik one of 1917, Gumilev, an ex-officer of the Tsarist Army, was accused of counter-revolutionary conspiracy and executed.

I have been loading all day. But how much easier it is in the summer. In the sun, in the open air – a floating sensation, like being on board ship. Clouds scud across the sky at midday. A clump of trees spins before one's eyes. An ocean of light given to us as a gift: live and reign!

6th May, 1971.[1]

*

Sure enough – it was indeed the turning point, and we dived in to come up again in mid-summer. May really is the brightest month of all. Either because the foliage does not yet hide the sky from us and nature has none of that *blackness* of summer, that worm-eaten and pestiferous aspect, or because the light has not yet been annealed by the heat and become harsh, but is still limpid and pure – a white, even rather cold light that scarcely brushes against us, burning only with the very tips of its rays, as though stinging slightly, like certain sea creatures, and stunning us with its inordinate brightness. I am not the only one to experience this – all the others can testify to the same sort of intoxication by light. You even feel quite overwhelmed and bewildered by this generosity; it is impossible to believe that so much is given to us all at once, in the manner of rivers flowing with milk and honey; and the sun not so much warms as prickles, playing on us from all sides, like the Charcot douche[2] and making our skin tingle.

I am trying to expose my sore elbow to the sun, hoping it will get better. This kind of sun bath is not only healing but also nutritive, I would say. Some element of the sap of plants and chlorophyll is absorbed by the body. You have the feeling that you could live on this mixture of sun and air alone. The days are short and bright like flashes of gunpowder. Nightfall takes you by surprise: already?

8th May, 1971.

*

[1] St George's Day in the Julian Calendar.

[2] Powerful douche used by the French neurologist Charcot in medical treatment.

Another pleasing aspect of spring is its resemblance to the preparatory coating of paint on a canvas: thinly applied to a white or black – by now completely unfrozen – background, it gives the first rough idea of a painting still to be born, leaving plenty of scope for conjecture and fantasy as to how it will finally turn out. Kept on the alert by this vagueness of the first sketch, the imagination plays an active role, running ahead in anticipation of the greater things to come and drawing its own castles in the air. The slight haze hanging over nature in spring compels us to guess at changes rather than passively observe them, thus inducing a sense of participation: it is this that makes a sketch so valuable in its own right, and even gives it certain advantages over the finished canvas.

By the very nature of his chosen theme of the Resurrection, which is quite beyond the bounds of the imagination, Chekrygin's[1] work inevitably had to remain on the level of studies, but these give a much better idea of it than any subsequent attempt at a more detailed depiction could possibly have done. Yet the thought of the fresco he eventually wanted to paint, an insistent craving to get on with it, must have been ever present in his mind – much as summer is present in spring, leading it forward by the hand, although it contains a promise of far more than anything the summer – like the fresco – can ever live up to. For Chekrygin his fresco was almost a mirage of immortality to be achieved, and in his drawings he was working towards it, demonstrating in the best way possible (and in something not intended for our eyes) his progress towards the rendering of a theme which by definition can find expression only in a remote approximation, in the unfulfillable yearning to come close to it.

Chekrygin's death was not so much untimely as providential: it preserved his work for ever in the form of preliminary sketches, before he had overstepped their limits, thus allowing him to show that this beginning, so abruptly brought to an end, was in fact the truest and closest possible approach to his subject. It was as though he understood that painting itself is

[1] V. N. Chekrygin (1897–1922): Russian painter.

nothing but a study in Resurrection, and this is precisely what he left us: a study.

19th May, 1971.

*

This is an odd summer. It might almost be rehearsing for next year, trying on May and June like costumes.

27th May, 1971.

*

"A certain hermit – I do not now remember his name – said one day:

'He who has no ties to this world is affected only by the change of seasons'.

And indeed, one can agree with this."

(Yoshida Kenko, *Essays in Idleness.*)

This is probably so because the change of seasons serves as an allegory of the human lot, yet is sufficiently remote from us in itself for the quite fortuitous similarity to strike us every time as an artistic parallel. We stay motionless as we observe the seasons running their course over and over again, repeatedly living out their lives, dying, and rising from the dead – while we are still preparing to do all these things just once. The basically unvarying character of the seasons and their fixed order of sequence only serve to strengthen the plot and give unity to the action, so that one enjoys it like an old play in an ever new performance. One new production after another – with the whole of mankind for an audience.

*

"Art thou sad because thou art parted from Daghestan?
Art thou sad because thou art parted from the *murids*?
Art thou sad because thou art parted from thy family?
Today I see thee sad, oh my brother, Haji."

"I am not sad because I am parted from Daghestan,
I am not sad because I am parted from the *murids*,
I am not sad because I am parted from my family,
Today the Lord on High said to me:
'When I took thee away from Daghestan
I felt no pity for thee.
When I took thee away from the *murids*
I felt no pity for thee.
When I took thee away from thy family
I felt no pity for thee.
Today I am taking thee away from thy beloved brother Movsar,
Today I feel pity for thee.' "

"Haji, oh Haji, why does the Lord part us?"
"Movsar, oh Movsar! I am going to the Great Sea
Which washes the earth. The peoples that live there have no faith.
To teach them faith in God does the Lord on High send me."

"But if, oh Haji, the Lord does send thee to them,
What does he say to me?" "From the calumnies of the impious and the scribes
Did our brother Viskhan flee and he hides now in Turkey,
With the name of the Lord on thy lips go to him, Movsar."

" 'Why didst thou return alone? What has happened to Haji?'
People will ask. What should I answer them?"
"Do not make them wait by promising my return.
Do not make them forget me by saying that I shall not return."

Half a day's journey did Movsar still have before him in order to reach his goal,
When Heda heard the voice of his first prayer:

"Viskhan, oh Viskhan! Dost thou not hear the prayer?
For it is the voice of thy living brother Movsar!"

And she came out to meet Movsar and asked as she embraced him:
"Why didst thou return alone? What has happened to Haji?"
– "May God give you patience!
May God give you patience!"

"Sayid Selam of Mecca, what have
Our Lord on High
And our glorious Prophet
And the Angel Jabrail
Done with our Haji?
La ilah illa-l-lah.
Ask for him to be returned to us.
La ilah illa-l-lah.
We have remained alone.
La ilah-illa-l-lah.

Angels of Heaven, what have
Our Lord on High
And our glorious Prophet
And the Angel Jabrail
Done with our Haji?
La ilah illa-l-lah.
Ask for him to be returned to us.
La ilah illa-l-lah.
We have remained alone.
La ilah-illa-l-lah."

This is the last thing we learn of Kishi-Haji. But there is a tradition that he is not dead yet and will come back again because he has been allotted a life-span equal to that of four men.

*

Part Seven

I walk about the house like a ghost. Not the ghost that lived here in the past. But the one that is yet to come.

9th June, 1971.

*

7th June. I sang in my sleep. At morning roll-call: "Stay behind and get ready to leave in half-an-hour." In the "cage"[1] I am an object of curiosity. Four suit-cases. A compartment with three bunks. Head of escort:

"Where are you being taken to?"

"Don't know."

It turned out I was on my way home.

*

The most interesting thing I have experienced during these first days and weeks after my release has been the feeling of a dead man appearing at life's feast.

*

A hunchback came up and looked at me closely, without blinking. What was he doing in this empty Stolypin coach? Was he there in line of duty? Or was he just curious about this animal in the cage? Beyond the face and the hump there was the hostility and aloofness of a well-dressed free man. Then he moved away a little and went along to a window out of my range, but I could see his hand with long, tapering fingers clutching the frame – a hand by which he was unmistakably recognizable as a hunchback although I could no longer see his hump. The hand betrayed the presence of a hump. A hand

[1] The compartments of railway coaches specially designed for transporting prisoners (and still popularly referred to as "Stolypin coaches" after a pre-Revolutionary prime minister) are divided from the corridor by a grille.

at the end of a hump is also something rather out of the ordinary.

7th June, 1971.

*

The impassive good nature, like an animal's, of the duty warder in a big transit prison: he's seen everything in his time.

*

The glass-like fragility of walls and their capacity to record sound. How great the will of the Lord that all this too He stores in His mind!

*

Deep down there is sadness. But it is slightly tinged by pity or even love – and finally there is laughter. Ripples of laughter breaking the mirror-like surface of sadness.

*

In the toilet of the Potma transit prison where men and women are taken by turns and use the walls to carry on a lively correspondence – constantly rubbed out and renewed – I am particularly struck by one message:

"Sergey, I love you, Marina,
Tarusa"

And suddenly I fancy that Marina Tsvetayeva must have been through here recently on her way elsewhere. The names do seem to coincide remarkably: Marina, Sergey, Tarusa[1] . . .

8th June, 1971.

*

A soldier at home, still holding on to his old uniform. Right

[1] Marina Tsvetayeva, the great Russian poetess, returned to the Soviet Union from emigration in 1939. Her husband, Sergey Efron, who had returned before her, was executed in the purges. For a time she lived in the small town of Tarusa. She committed suicide in 1941.

here in a tattered pocket he has his handkerchief and a bit of tobacco.

9th June, 1971.

*

What is the most precious, the most exciting smell waiting for you in the house when you return to it after half-a-dozen years or so? The smell of roses, you think? No, mouldering books.

*

Coming out of prison is like making a posthumous appearance in the world. It is not like being born again, because one is old and weak, but much water has flowed under the bridges and we find it odd to observe that time has continued to pass by quite unconcerned and indifferent to our absence; and the fact that reality has just gone on impassively turning the handle of its hurdy-gurdy, regardless of who leaves or rejoins its merry cavalcade, is the chief cause of irritation and gloom in those who come back. The sensation of a secondary, posthumous existence arises from our lack of involvement in life, from the fact that we still go on viewing it as distant observers even though it is now at close quarters again. Both mind and body are numbed. All you are aware of is your peculiar relationship to the world: your sense of existing in it as a spectre. Hence your inability and unwillingness (itself somewhat half-hearted) to fall in with any kind of fuss and bother, such as buying sandwiches, or drinking a bottle of beer – none of this is important or necessary, since all that really means anything to you is your function of being a spectral presence. Life is not to blame for this – only one's lack of interest in living it after having once been buried. Possibly for this reason, it frequently happens that those who come back die fairly soon after their "return to life". In theory they should live happily ever after (while they were in limbo it was the dream of doing so that gave them the strength to survive), but then they lose interest and no longer want to live. They simply lack the will or the desire to re-enter their former existence and wholly succumb to their view of themselves as ghosts.

9th June, 1971.

*

The main thing is not some kind of special inner "self-awareness", nor the intellect or the will. But, I would say, the sensation of your own limbs. The consciousness that you have a body, that you are you.

*

"Let me tell you how the earth was formed." (Yegor)

*

If they are to have a soul, things must be ancient. This is the beginning of all stylization. And the justification of anything new – which only dares to be new because centuries and centuries hence, if it still exists, it will be old.

*

What a likeness to the man is suddenly revealed in his coat left hanging on a rack. And in the shoes he has left behind. Things, I am convinced, assume the personality of their owners.

*

The young fellow going through my suit-case had curls down to his shoulders, as is the fashion nowadays. And suddenly I understood: jabots and Roman togas and, if you like, Egyptian wigs fascinate people by their millennial elegance, exoticism, and novelty – the delightful novelty of antiquity which makes no difference between Brutus and Caesar, Guelphs and Ghibellines, all so charming together, without distinction between killer and killed – mere form, of no significance and quite beside the point . . .

8th June, 1971.

*

And now you suddenly stand naked before men, and this nakedness sticks like a lump in your throat.

*

This must really be somewhere at the back of beyond – where people look over their shoulder before giving alms to a beggar.

*

The living should feel some indebtedness towards the dead: those who have got to Paradise go through agony on behalf of those still in hell – who don't really suffer all that much.

*

"*I lit two candles for you,*[1] *Andrey Donatovich – at 60 copecks apiece.*"

*

There is a strange air of desolation about all these lights and cars, these advertisements, restaurants, shops, suits: something of the provinces or the suburbs. The centre has disappeared (where has the centre got to?). One feels nothing but growing pity for this provincial benightedness. Poor children, poor dear children! Your amusements are not really much fun. How poverty-stricken they are, all these theatres and palaces of culture. And look at that good woman fussing over her mink coat – in the old days, madam, such things were far grander, I assure you, and yet they have vanished without trace. All those opulent furs and carriages have rotted away. And here are *you* with your car. What a joke.

*

"Time is ticking!" (Yegor)

*

Time goes more slowly here. Quite obviously so. Sitting here in my armchair while the hours drag on, I am conscious of how quickly, with what empty speed, they are racing along

[1] i.e. in church, according to Russian Orthodox custom.

back there – and I am still on *that* time, spinning out my hours here. This change of gear is perhaps the trickiest part of it all.

9th June, 1971.

*

What has changed? The sky and the "forbidden zone". The sky and the apple-tree. And the sparrows tapping on the roof with their little beaks.

*

My actual "self" really interests me very little – except just as something with which to conduct experiments, filtering stray ideas and formulas out of the mind or the blood.

*

Out there, after all, my own "self" counted for nothing. And now it is bewildering suddenly to be thrown back on it: where do *you* come from? And what are we to do with you?

*

On the whole, it's a pleasant room. Flies crawl over the ceiling, upside down. I don't care a rap what I do with my life. You understand – not a rap! I'm a spirit . . .

*

But if you're not dying, you have to . . .

*

When all is said and done, six years is not bad. It has weight.

*

There at least you understand that everything has an end – not for nothing is it the house of the dead. And I have been there. Only for a while, but even so . . . The fact is, however, that people are bored by the dead.

*

But how little, as it turns out, I need people! I am happy enough to sit quietly and unobtrusively by myself.

*

I am torn between a rose and a teapot, between listening and touching. I feel as though everything has been thrust upon me at once and I am standing there, clutching it all to myself, but not feeling in possession of it or knowing what to do with it. I am sure a pauper who has suddenly inherited a fortune must feel equally at a loss as he sits silent and bewildered in the banqueting hall of his palace.

*

When I was a child there was such a sweet-sounding word: cottage cheese. Father used to bring it sometimes.

*

Good Lord, this sausage looks so unreal to me that it arouses a feeling of indifference, of sadness.

*

When you've had something to eat, you realize the vanity of eating. And when you've had something to drink, you realize the vanity of drinking. What is food and drink after all? But first you must eat and drink. And when you've had your fill, you can say: the vanity of it all!

*

It's quite beyond their understanding that someone who has been in a camp can feel so eternally grateful – for white bread.

*

And for something else as well: that nobody is any longer breathing down his neck.

*

How much it means to have a table-lamp – not the kind of

bare-bellied bulb that hangs shameless and pitiless high above your head in the barracks, giving light to no one – but one like this, standing on the table, illuminating a corner of it, a cup, the table-cloth, a page of a book: a light coming down to shine in the darkness.

*

For some reason I always think of every printed volume as being quite unique. When I say: "The Works of Gogol" I see in my mind's eye the copy standing on my shelves in that particular binding and number of volumes. I find it impossible to believe that there can be thousands or millions of such "Works of Gogol" and that everybody has an identical set. I admit that in theory there could be a few (very rare) duplicates, but in practice you always find some little distinguishing mark, a different general condition, paper surface, or smell – all peculiar to your own copy. Hence books should be thought of not merely as printed matter, but as individual creations, rather like museum pieces. The fact that there may be many other specimens concerns me not at all. The one I have is unique – as is everybody else's.

*

A good word: "manufacture". Not "writing", not "creation", not "invention", not "a literary work", no – "manufacture" . . . Just so![1] (From the verdict)

*

Suppose I had been forbidden to write in an absolutely literal sense – not a word, not a single letter of the alphabet – I wonder what I would have done? . . .

*

I remind myself of the character who comes back from the war in Leonid Andreyev's "Red Laughter". He writes away furi-

[1] Reference to the trial in 1965 at which the author was found guilty of "manufacturing" anti-Soviet works.

ously with a pen that has no ink in it and leaves no trace on the paper: a madman. His book consists of a sheaf of blank pages.

*

I dreamed of the paper I am now writing on as of an open field or a forest: oh to be able to lose myself in it, to take off and run on breathlessly and, without reaching the end or even the middle, put down somewhere at the edge or in a corner just a few rapid lines . . .

*

You need paper to lose yourself in its whiteness. Writing means diving into a page and coming up with some idea or word. Blank paper invites you to dip down into its artless expanse. A writer is rather like a fisherman. He sits and waits for something to bite. Put a blank sheet of paper in front of me and, without even thinking, let alone understanding why, I am sure to be able to fish something out of it.

*

For this reason a pre-conceived theme or story is dangerous: it imposes its own rules, and instead of obeying the paper, you become captive to the plot. There is something false about this. What freedom and spontaneity, on the other hand, in an essay, in "notes" or "comments" from this or some other world! An essay just spreads out over the paper, like a pool of water or a splotch of ink, filling up the empty space.

*

Space is always suddenly bethinking itself: I am here, and here, and over there! It is forever cropping up somewhere at the back of your head. Not in front, but behind: sneaking up on you from the rear.

*

You toss it aside (in the air, almost) and say casually "I've finished" and listen to criticism – one man says you must change a sentence here, another says you must change a sentence there, or a chapter, or a page. But by then you don't care. It lives. Once born, it lives independently of you, asking no one's permission, with all its faults, left entirely on its own to fend for itself when you are dead and gone, and no one will help it, correct your bad grammar or pay the slightest attention to it; it will stand as you ordained, displaying all its infirmities (its own and yours), dwindling into total insignificance as the years go by, unwanted and forlorn, existing in three copies at the most – and then, goodness knows how, without you and utterly alone, it will gradually begin to gain strength, aided less by all the pains you took than by your mistakes and omissions, and will spread its wings in the grave and, forgetting and repudiating you (what use are *you*?) will set out, hundred-mouthed, to live its destined life as a book.

*

But they will still go on and on. And while I live here, while we all live – they will still go on and on . . .

9th June, 1971.

* * *